Psychoanalysis and Its Discontents

PSYCHOANALYSIS
and Its Discontents

JOHN E. GEDO, MD

THE GUILFORD PRESS
New York   London

© 1984 The Guilford Press
A Division of Guilford Publications, Inc.
200 Park Avenue South, New York, N.Y. 10003

Printed in the United States of America

Library of Congress Cataloging in Publication Data
Gedo, John E.
    Psychoanalysis and its discontents.

    Bibliography: p.
    Includes index.
    1. Psychoanalysis   I. Title.
RC504.G384   1984   150.19′5   84-4615
ISBN 0-89862-639-0

The clear voice of Reason first reached me when I was 15, in a chemical laboratory. It had the Italianate accent of Professor J. R., exhorting me to "t'eenk, t'eenk!"

A few years later, on the wards of a great hospital, it was leavened by the voice of Experience. My model was Professor L. E., who refused to intervene in puzzling crises until he had calmly reviewed the patient's records.

This book is dedicated to the twin gods of Reason and Empiricism.

ACKNOWLEDGMENTS

This book owes its genesis to the ingenuity and intellectual discernment of my editor, Paul E. Stepansky, who persuaded me that the statement of my psychoanalytic views in previous publications was by no means as complete or definitive as I had imagined. He has shepherded this project to completion faster than I thought possible, reviewing a mass of ill-coordinated drafts and lending them order and structural coherence. I owe him thanks as well for innumerable cogent queries about omissions and inconsistencies—not to mention matters of presentation, an area in which his skills are invaluable to an author impatient with the endless task of polishing.

To assemble these materials, I have had to rely on the cooperation of several organizations which have graciously agreed to arrangements for simultaneous publication or granted permission to reprint previously published articles. Specifically, Chapter 6 is scheduled to appear in a forthcoming issue of the journal *Psychoanalytic Inquiry* whereas Chapter 10 will be included in Volume 1 of *Psychoanalysis: The Vital Issues* (edited by myself and George Pollock). Chapter 11 was previously published in *The Annual of Psychoanalysis* and is reprinted here with the kind permission of The Chicago Institute for Psychoanalysis. Chapter 12 is also scheduled for publication in *The Search for the Future*, edited by Stefan de Schill.

Most of the other chapters in this volume have been presented in preliminary form to a variety of psychoanalytic audiences. Part of Chapter 1 served as my position statement at a "Meet the Author" session of the American Psychoanalytic Association devoted to two of my previous books. Portions of Chapters 1, 6, and 9 were likewise presented at different panels organized by the American Psychoanalytic Association. Chapter 3 was presented at the first Franco-American Psychoanalytic Encounter in Paris. The case material in

ACKNOWLEDGMENTS

Chapter 4 was discussed at a meeting of the Canadian Psychoanalytic Society in Montreal whereas that in Chapter 5 was similarly discussed at the 50th Anniversary Celebration of the Boston Psychoanalytic Society. Portions of Chapter 7 were prepared for a Symposium on "The Difficult Patient" organized by the Columbia University Psychoanalytic Center. Chapter 8 was presented to the Tufts University Symposium on "Language and Psychoanalysis" in honor of Paul Myerson. Finally, Chapter 10 was originally a Presidential Address delivered at the 50th Anniversary Celebration of the Chicago Psychoanalytic Society.

PREFACE

For the past 15 years, I have devoted myself to the development of a coherent body of psychoanalytic writings in which I have attempted to survey anew the major themes of psychoanalytic discourse. In the mid-1970s, in collaboration with others, I published two books intended to highlight the continuing value of basic aspects of Freud's legacy (Gedo & Goldberg, 1973; Gedo & Pollock, 1976). These works were followed by two volumes in which I proposed a comprehensive new clinical theory—based on a hierarchical model of mental functioning—and its corollary, an up-to-date theory of psychoanalytic technique based on therapeutic experience with the broadest range of psychopathology (Gedo, 1979b, 1981b). More recently, I have taken the foregoing hypotheses out of the realm of pathology proper and applied them to the study of creativity (Gedo, 1983). In this, the sixth volume of the series, I hope to complete this cycle of work by contrasting my views and their applications in the treatment setting with competing proposals available in the psychoanalytic marketplace.

I have organized the material of this book into four sections. To begin with, I offer an exposition of my theoretical proposals. In Chapter 1, they are placed within the context of the overall development of psychoanalytic ideas, and their applicability to clinical issues is illustrated by means of a set of concrete examples. Chapter 2 is a report on the actual therapeutic results I have obtained via the technical innovations necessitated by the developmental logic of my theoretical proposals—innovations that collectively point to a technique that extends "beyond interpretation." These therapeutic results are, of course, no more than the manifest distillation of a series of clinical judgments of an unconventional nature made in the course of a lifetime of analytic work. Chapter 3 elaborates one set of these judgments arrived at through trial and error within a particular analytic encounter. I trust that these examples will demonstrate the rationale of my major departures from the traditional technical precepts of psychoanalysis: They illustrate the range and complexity of transference configurations that require noninterpretive interventions. These clinical experiences betoken the omnipresence of archaic transferences, that is, of deficit states that invariably underlie the more manifest intrapsychic conflicts. It follows from my findings that analytic progress may in fact be incidental to the insight derived from interpretation—or, to put the issue more strongly, that one must often go "beyond insight" to account for the effects of interventions intended to be interpretive.

Section II presents two lengthy case reports (Chapters 4 and 5) of analyses conducted in accord with my current views. Although my selection of the data is inevitably skewed by my theoretical presuppositions, I have, to the best of my ability, tried to present narrative accounts of these therapeutic transactions with a minimum of "editorial" comment and theoretical discussion. I hope that such detailed narratives will permit my readers to form their own judgments about the consequences of my technical innovations.

In Section III, I examine neglected aspects of some of the principal features of analytic technique about which I hold innovative views. Chapters 6 and 7 demonstrate that the traditional injunction to conduct analyses from a vantage point of interpretive neutrality is impossible to achieve. In other words, *every* analytic encounter possesses features that go "beyond interpretation" in the sense that analyst and analysand alike bring specific values to the transaction. The effects of these clashing commitments are particularly apparent in cases characterized by delinquent enactments on the part of the patient, examples of which are described in Chapter 7. Moreover, as I proceed to show in Chapter 8, the technical need to make interpretations cannot exist *in vacuo*; it presupposes a shared language between the participants, the achievement of which usually requires lengthy preparation involving noninterpretive measures. In Chapter 9, I examine some of the consequences of the manner in which the analyst encodes his interventions, that is, the rhetorical dimension of psychoanalytic discourse that transcends the lexical content of its message.

Section IV shifts emphasis from the clinical arena to that of the psychoanalytic community. Chapter 10 deals with those intractable dissensions that forever seem to fracture the discipline; these disagreements are traced to the basic philosophical commitments that subtend different theoretical and clinical viewpoints. In Chapters 11

and 12, I discuss the crisis in psychoanalytic education and the catastrophic prospects for American psychoanalysis as a whole, respectively, as derivatives of the clash between the dominant pragmatism
of our culture and the basic values of the Freudian enterprise.

John E. Gedo
Chicago

CONTENTS

CONTENTS

Section IV. The Analytic Community

THE HIERARCHICAL VIEW

1

Reflections on the Concept of Self-Organization within the History of Psychoanalytic Ideas

I

Ideally, the clinical theory of psychoanalysis should be a coherent body of propositions that is capable of organizing the clinical findings —that is, data of observations and the interpretations and clinical generalizations based on them (see Waelder, 1962)—produced within the more or less standardized therapeutic setting designated the "psychoanalytic situation" (Stone, 1961). These propositions are inevitably encoded in one or another metatheoretical language—until fairly recently, generally in the "metapsychological" language Freud devised during his first decade of activity as a depth psychologist (see Freud, 1895, 1900).

Although the current fragmentation of the psychoanalytic community into a bewildering array of schools employing competing metatheoretical codes has led to considerable confusion and acrimony, it remains possible, through the exercise of steadfast good will, to translate psychoanalytic ideas from any one of these languages into the others. It follows that, in my judgment, the primary problems within contemporary psychoanalysis do not involve metapsychology, even though the abuse of metapsychology through anthropomorphism or reification may lead to severe difficulties in developing valid clinical theories, as a number of authors (Grossman & Simon, 1969; Schafer, 1976b) have recently pointed out. I believe, on the contrary, that the greatest challenge facing psychoanalysis at this time involves the construction of a maximally inclusive and relevant clinical theory (see Gedo, 1979b, 1981b).

Another way to articulate this challenge is to argue that psycho-analysis has yet to develop a consistent nosology based on its own depth-psychological premises. Although Freud's conception of psycho-pathology could be characterized via the metaphor of the past casting its shadow upon the present, this viewpoint has never won general acceptance as a guide for establishing diagnostic categories; these continue to be based on phenomenological criteria. Thus, clinical discourse is still anchored in categories such as hysteria, obsessional neurosis, narcissistic personality disturbance, perversion, and border-line state.

I believe the principal reason for this lag in applying psycho-analytic concepts to the nosological organization of clinical data is the sheer complexity of the task of delineating the sequential findings of any psychoanalytic treatment. In a stunning metaphor, Freud com-pared this process to the science of archaeology—that is, to the excavation, layer by layer, of a buried site occupied through numer-ous epochs (Breuer & Freud, 1895, p. 139). In terms of the successive phases of the human life cycle, derivatives of which confront the analyst in a confusing, achronological manner, the reconstruction of an individual analysand's relevant developmental history is a matter of daunting difficulty.

A hundred years ago, when Freud acquired the knowledge of the medicopsychological avant-garde from Breuer and Charcot (see Gedo & Pollock, 1976, Chapters 5 and 8), the task actually appeared to be much more manageable. The pioneering investigative work of Charcot, in particular, had focused on neuroses of traumatic origin, that is, on syndromes in which discrete events of pathogenic import had taken place in the recent past, generally in adulthood. In his historic therapeutic encounter with Anna O., Breuer in turn focused his attention on specific hysterical symptoms. He succeeded in tracing them to equally specific "traumatic" events of the proximate past—to traumata based on symbolic meanings, rather than physical injuries of the sort implicated in the cases studied by Charcot. In 1893, when Breuer and Freud reported on their various clinical experiments by announcing that "hysterics suffer mainly from reminiscences" (Breuer & Freud, 1893, p. 7), they had not investigated the influence of child-hood determinants on the patient's vulnerability to psychic trauma in a single illustrative case. It is true that, by this time, Freud had discovered that the prehistory of every neurotic illness could be traced back into the patient's earlier life; indeed, it was only the difficulties of joint authorship that kept this major research achieve-ment out of the *Studies on Hysteria* (1895).

As Freud revealed in his next major work, *The Interpretation of Dreams* (1900), it was the analysis of dreams, most notably his own, that consistently led back to the psychological world of childhood. The genetic point of view of psychoanalytic psychology was definitively promulgated for the first time by way of Freud's verdict that dreams invariably fulfill *infantile* wishes (p. 553). In parallel with the investigation of dreams, Freud's published clinical investigations during the period roughly bounded by 1899 and 1918—from his work on "screen memories" through the case study of the Wolf Man—revealed the rich variety of infantile wishes (sexual, aggressive, and narcissistic) implicated in neurosogenesis.

These unconscious infantile strivings were uncovered in psychoanalytic treatment in the form of transferences, that is, repetitions within the therapeutic relationship that usually involved the emergence of fantasies directed toward the analyst. On the basis of these findings, Freud arrived at a simple nosological schema centered upon the vicissitudes of transference developments in treatment. To wit, he distinguished "transference neuroses" (i.e., conditions in which maladaptive phenomena were transformed, in the course of psychoanalysis, into a relationship to the analyst reflecting infantile prototypes) from "narcissistic neuroses" (i.e., conditions in which such transferences did not develop, presumably because of the analysand's excessive self-involvement).

In *The Ego and the Id* (1923), Freud articulated a theory of mental functioning corresponding to the basic premise of the foregoing nosological schema. In accord with this hypothesis, known as the "structural theory," the analysand's endopsychic "resistance" to the emergence of infantile attributes in the psychoanalytic situation is conceptualized in an enduring functional entity, the ego. "Character" may be construed as the particular configuration of these resistances in every individual. Correspondingly, the analysand's self-centeredness in the narcissistic neuroses may be viewed as a specific, regressive method of avoiding the conflicts and anxieties that would be attendant to the potentiation of expectable infantile wishes in treatment.

The decade following Freud's revolutionary conceptual work of the mid-1920s might well be called the era of "character analysis." (cf. Reich, 1930). Parallel to the all-absorbing exploration of "the Unconscious" that marked the early years of psychoanalysis, the investigation of the various configurations of "the ego" (see A. Freud, 1936; Hartmann, 1939), implicated in elaborating a new characterology, was a complex enterprise that occupied analytic investigators for the better part of a generation. For my purposes here, perhaps the most important product of this body of research was the surprising finding that resistances generally derive from archaic fixations that antedate the oedipal stage of development. To put this insight into the framework of Freud's previously cited metaphor, the shadow of earlier childhood transactions seems to fall upon the events of the Oedipus complex, that is, on the "nuclear" conflicts that lead to adult neuroses. Alternatively, we may encapsulate this finding in the proposition that most of the ego defenses which serve to ward off oedipal strivings consist of behaviors that constitute, at the same time, adaptive solutions to the psychological vicissitudes of still earlier phases of development (see Gedo, 1981b, Chapter 14).

The most recent period in the history of psychoanalysis has been characterized by a gradual shift in focus from a view of these archaic phenomena as part of the background of nuclear oedipal transactions toward more complex conceptualizations that accord these phenomena various degrees of pathogenicity in their own right. In this country, at any rate, the most influential voice espousing the newer viewpoint was that of Kohut (1971, 1977, 1978), who attempted to delineate a whole schema of novel transference configurations situated within the very "narcissistic" sector that Freud had differentiated from the "transference neuroses." Because I am convinced that Kohut's clinical observations and classification of transferences by no means exhaust the possibilities for valid clinical generalizations in this realm, I prefer to construe the entire field of preoedipal derivatives as "archaic transferences" (see Gedo, 1977)—in parallel with the classification of Hellenic sculpture into "classical" and "archaic" phases.

Because of the novelty of the clinical observations about these archaic syndromes, we have yet to achieve any consensus about patterns of transference enactments in analysis that might constitute truly significant nosological entities. As a result, the contemporary psychoanalytic scene is characterized by a number of hostile schools competing for public favor, often on the basis of evangelical fervor rather than the presentation of reliable evidence. American psychoanalysis seems to be in danger of splintering into dogmatic camps: traditionalists who continue to insist that the emergence of archaic material in analysis is merely regressive noise, designed to mask the oedipal music; "self psychologists" who have enshrined Kohut's clinical generalizations as a superior and universal conceptual schema with which they would replace the framework of the traditionalists; "object-relations theorists" who view archaic enactments in treatment as the reliving of crucial early childhood relations with the caretakers, but who make no systematic effort to integrate this idea with previous psychoanalytic conceptualizations; and numerous idiosyncratic factions that resist such brief characterization.

If the threatened dissolution of the psychoanalytic community has to this point not eventuated, one bond that has countered the foregoing centrifugal forces is the fact that each of the rival schools continues to focus its attention on what it considers to be a crucial set of unconscious pathogenic fantasies.[1] Almost everyone, that is, seems to agree that the research agenda of our time is the exploration of the deepest layers of the unconscious mind: It is as though we have come full circle to the resumption of Freud's pioneering studies of the 1890s! This agenda implies that the differences of emphasis between the various schools are not truly fundamental from a therapeutic perspective; it may simply not make a great deal of difference whether one stresses the grandiosity implicit in archaic fantasy systems, as Kohut did, their primitive hostility, in the manner of the traditional viewpoint, or the distorted object representations that the fantasy systems embody. At the level of nosology, however, these subtle differences have led to varied schemata that do diverge in significant ways: There is no rational way, for example, to compare Kohut's (1971, Chapter 1) criteria for the diagnosis of "narcissistic personality disturbance" with Kernberg's (1975) criteria for the diagnosis of "borderline personality organization."

II

My own conceptual work (Gedo, 1979b, 1979c, 1981a, 1981b; Gedo & Goldberg, 1973) revolves around the attempt to elaborate an inclusive, hierarchical view of personality organization informed by a developmental perspective. I have tried to make this framework

1. It is true that each school hypothesizes that, in their original childhood occurrence, these fantasies subserve certain adaptive functions. Thus Kohut (1971, 1977) attributed the genesis of grandiose and/or idealizing fantasies to the psychological needs of the infant dependent on the ministrations of a "selfobject." From the standpoint of Kohut's conception of development, there is no possibility of any child avoiding passage through the phase of archaic grandiosity and primitive idealization; hence these archaic fantasies constitute the universal psychic material explored by Kohut's "self psychology." The very fact that Kohut viewed the acknowledgment of the legitimacy of the child's claims to "mirroring" confirmation and ideal parenting as an empathically curative measure demonstrates that his psychological system continued to accord primacy to archaic mental contents. This is the reason, of course, for Goldberg's (1978, p. 9) claim that Kohut advocated an analytic technique relying entirely on interpretations.

I believe that the other major schools of analytic thought have focused on fantasy content in an analogous manner. This reductionism has often been justified on the ground that the child's subjective experience is the crucial determinant of subsequent functioning. As I have tried to demonstrate elsewhere (Gedo, 1979b, pp. 21–23, 178–181, 202–217; 1981b), this viewpoint ignores the fact that the basic units of human behavior consist of obligatory reenactments—actions that Freud (1920) believed were regulated by a "repetition compulsion"—that transcend the realm of what we usually term the "psychological," that is, the realm of mental contents capable of symbolic representation.

broad enough to accommodate the entire gamut of clinical generalizations reported by psychoanalysts of all persuasions[2]; at the same time, I have employed conceptual categories general enough to avoid clashing with any of the major metatheoretical systems currently in use. This hierarchical model stresses the fact that psychological maturation involves the acquisition of competence with respect to a progressively expanding list of specific mental and behavioral skills. Although stressful circumstances may lead to more or less temporary regressive losses of these autonomous functional capacities, in an "average expectable environment" (Hartmann, 1939), most of these skills will be permanently mastered. Competence in the domain of certain crucial mental capacities enables an individual to confront the challenges of subsequent developmental phases. If, on the other hand, an individual is deficient with respect to certain requisite skills, this deficiency, even if only relative, may have to be patched over through external assistance. The need to find symbiotic partners who can render such aid leads to the manifold behavioral potentialities that I have labeled "archaic transferences" when they emerge in the analytic setting.

In my recent clinical work, I have concentrated on specifying the nature of the deficits in mental functioning that can be "filled in" through psychoanalytic efforts to the extent of rendering the pathological symbiotic solution unnecessary. In grappling with this issue, I have tried to leave behind the field explored with such excitement by the psychoanalytic pioneers of the last 25 years: In the spirit of those analysts who exploited Freud's conceptual advances of the 1920s to elaborate a psychoanalytic psychology of the ego, I want to emphasize structural considerations—the progressive consolidation of the "self-organization"—rather than fantasy content *per se*.

2. The complexity of the resulting clinical theory has bewildered certain commentators to the point that they simply cannot keep the entire schema in mind at the same time; on the basis of a particular fragment of the schema which they fallaciously equate with the entirety of my conceptualization, they proceed to condemn me for reductionism! Rangell's (1981, 1982) reaction to my work most clearly exemplifies this sequence. In his initial commentary, Rangell (1981) asserted that I propose to reduce psychoanalytic psychology to a matter of conflicting values as these are espoused by patients. (This particular misreading of my work has recurred in Richards's [1982] inadequately researched critique of various theories of "the self"; this is but one of a series of straw men Richards topples in his unrecognizable caricature of my views.) Following publication of my response (Gedo, 1981b) to Rangell's essay, he proceeded to charge me with reductionism of a different sort: He asserted that I believe "oedipal or castration conflicts are structures of the past" (1982, p. 864). This erroneous claim was published almost two years after the appearance of *Advances in Clinical Psychoanalysis* (1981b), where I described the specific role of oedipal conflicts in no fewer than 12 completed analyses (pp. 377–382)! It would seem that I am in no position to prove my innocence in these matters.

I should note in passing that Kohut (1977, Chapter 4) also made an effort to develop a structural dimension for his "self psychology." But his intention of spelling out the precise manner in which the "bipolar" self is formed was never carried out. Moreover, Kohut conceived of this "structure" merely as a combination of the individual's ambitions and ideals—in other words, as an enduring set of subjective wishes. Accordingly, his work always focuses on dynamic issues, generally (and commendably) within the transference. Self psychologists of Kohut's school invoke the structural viewpoint only when they explain certain regressive phenomena as consequences of the breakdown or "fragmentation" of the "self." Because the self psychologists have never provided a detailed account of the mechanisms of "transmuting internalization"—the process Kohut postulated to account for the structuralization of the self—they have merely given us a promissory note.[3]

In order to illustrate the structural dimension of my own approach, I would like to single out, almost arbitrarily, one general area of mental content and provide an outline of the structural possibilities associated with this content as they are categorized by the hierarchical model. The content area I will explore here concerns the relationship between masochistic behaviors and depressive moods— an issue hitherto poorly understood within the conceptual framework of traditional psychoanalysis. To put my intention differently: Masochistic phenomena invariably involve suffering as their ideational content and are often associated with depressive affects. In order to differentiate meaningful categories of these phenomena from one

---

3. In *The Restoration of the Self* (1977), Kohut himself recognized this state of affairs (see pp. 178, 186). In my judgment, his neglect of structural considerations followed from his refusal to concede, prior to *The Restoration of the Self*, that "self" could refer to anything beyond mental contents (see Kohut, 1977, p. 207n.). For the manner in which some of Kohut's students of the time pushed him toward his later views, see Handler's (1970) report of the meeting of March 1969 of the Chicago Psychoanalytic Society.

My own work on the concept of self stressed from the outset the *need* to view it from a structural viewpoint (see Gedo & Goldberg, 1973, pp. 63–69, where the work of previous authors who took similar positions is also cited). Largely in deference to Kohut's contemporaneous struggle with these issues, I did not attempt to fulfill my own promissory note until 1975: My presentation of the self-as-structure at the May 1975 panel discussion, "New Horizons in Metapsychology," has been reported by Meissner (in Panel, 1976). By then, I had abandoned my expectation that Kohut would develop a concept of self that transcended mental content. In fact, at the time, Kohut still maintained a view of self-as-content focused on the vicissitudes of narcissistic libido (e.g., personal communication, January 1969). Kohut's late conversion to a structural view of the self in *The Restoration of the Self* (1977) incorporated no acknowledgment of the fact that he was following in the footsteps of a number of theoreticians who had earlier advocated the conceptualization of personality structure in holistic terms.

another, our clinical theory must be expanded so that it can approach these phenomena from the structural viewpoint (cf. Rapaport & Gill, 1959). We must clarify, in other words, the nature of the typical regulatory mechanisms that determine behavior in specific modes of organization in the course of development, no matter what the dynamic issue of the moment may be. With this requirement in mind, I shall now review a series of masochistic behaviors arranged in a developmental sequence, beginning with those of later genetic origin. I shall then try to correlate these respective behaviors with the various "depressive" reactions that frequently accompany certain of their vicissitudes.

A developmental perspective toward the manifold phenomena we designate "masochistic" or "depressive" might well start with Freud's (1924) category of "feminine masochism." This formulation probably belongs within the conflict-free sphere of well-adapted behavior; in contemporary terms, we could reformulate Freud's idea as the capacity to make constructive sacrifices on behalf of others. Clearly, this virtue does not belong to one gender alone—Freud, for his part, obviously knew that men had their quota of "feminine" character traits. For members of both sexes, the typical response to disappointments associated with such a capacity is that of grief. I need hardly remind clinicians that grief is the predominant affect we are likely to experience if, through no fault of our own, fate interferes with one of our therapeutic enterprises—to offer an illustration from our own "everyday" lives.

In contrast to "feminine masochism," the masochistic perversions are referable to areas of functioning under the sway of the pleasure principle. More precisely, we must always make the appropriate distinction between erotic fantasies with masochistic content and the actual enactment of a masochistic perversion. The former often generate considerable shame or guilt, thus betraying the fact that these fantasies usually crystallize within the nexus of the Oedipus complex. With true masochistic perversions, on the other hand, any of a variety of earlier determinants may predispose the child to conceive of sexual relations in terms of suffering. Whenever masochistic wishes are implicated in structural conflicts of this kind, they are, of course, chronically frustrated, and this circumstance generally leads to severe difficulties in the sexual sphere in everyday life and occasionally to problems in broader areas of interpersonal relations. It follows, then, that one consequence of conflicts of this type is some degree of impairment in self-esteem, a chronic dissatisfaction that many people experience as a mood they term "depressive."

Freud's (1908) dictum that a neurosis is like a photographic negative whereas a perversion resembles the clearly printed "positive" image, should remind us that individuals who enact fantasies totally unacceptable to many even at the level of mere mental content are, in certain fundamental respects, "different" in their personality organization. Of course, simply to label them defective in ego or superego structure, as exclusive reliance on the structural theory formerly obliged analysts to do, hardly clarifies the actual manner in which they function. If they have problems in self-esteem, these problems are not demonstrably related to their perverse behavior. More often than not, they regard their sexual activities—probably not without justification—as the best part of their lives. This point was brilliantly made a few years ago in the motion picture *Belle du Jour*: The appealing heroine subjects herself to sadistic tortures in a brothel. When, upon the departure of a particularly nasty customer, a fellow employee expresses pity for her plight, she responds with fiery indignation, "And what do *you* know about it?!"

This caveat notwithstanding, Arlow (1981), among others, has recently observed that when a person with an overt masochistic perversion is analyzed, the content of his or her sexual enactments is generally found to be referable to the same oedipal issues we uncover in neurotic patients. Freud's photographic metaphor, in other words, proves accurate as long as we limit our concern to the nature of the patient's sexual wishes. But such a narrow focus belies the psychological meaning of the perversion in its relevant developmental context. As Loewenstein (1957) has pointed out, overt *perversions* are formed when a predisposed child struggles to deal with oedipal problems that have become overwhelming by virtue of impaired development. In accord with Loewenstein's insight, it is widely recognized that patients with overt masochistic perversion tend to become clinically depressed when the opportunity to practice their perversion is lost. By this statement, I do not merely mean that these patients undergo a darkening of mood, but that a psychobiological illness actually ensues which may involve disturbances in appetite, sleep patterns, sexual desire, and the like.

The observation of the foregoing correlation has become a commonplace, to the extent that it has become tempting to conceive of perversions as home remedies devised by severely traumatized children to patch over their "disorder and early sorrow." I suspect that Kohut and his collaborators are probably alluding to the same correlation in claiming that childhood sexuality is, to an appreciable degree, employed to overcome subjective states of deadness or devitalization (Kohut, 1977). Although I view such a generalization as entirely too broad, I believe that eroticism *is* often used effectively as an antidote for childhood depression, presumably depression precipitated by a variety of severe losses. There of course remain alternative solutions to such early childhood problems, and, in any given instance, the choice of a particular symptom must be explained in terms of its adaptive advantages in a specific set of circumstances. I have tried to illustrate these issues with reasonably detailed case material in *Advances in Clinical Psychoanalysis* (1981b, Chapter 12).

Having identified the type of depression associated with masochistic perversion as the recurrence of childhood prototypes, I must acknowledge that I feel much less qualified to illuminate "infantile depression." In the large category of patients who have erected no successful compensatory or defensive barriers against recurrence, we tend to attribute its emergence in adult life to "moral masochism" (see Berliner, 1958; Bergler, 1961). I do not doubt that children who have fallen into such an abyss must be disappointed in their parents, but I am not ready to follow Kohut (1971) to the conclusion that their difficulties are *caused* by frustration of a putative need for parental perfection.

At the levels of regression represented by the repetition of such experiences within an analytic transference, we are at the boundary (if not actually within the domain) of behavior regulation which is "beyond the pleasure principle"—I am thus inclined to believe that many of these syndromes do indeed originate in biological proclivities. In trying to understand them, I am disinclined to dichotomize the conceptual field into issues of drive gratification and issues of object relations (as Rothstein did at a recent panel [1983] on this very topic). As I have argued elsewhere (Gedo, 1979c), early psychobiological events leave their mark on patterns of affectivity; they do not influence drives or object relations as such. It follows that our most useful conceptual option is to focus on the earliest subjective, that is, *affective*, states of the child himself, for these states tend to be endlessly repeated in ever new versions throughout life—a phenomenon Freud termed the "repetition compulsion."

If, as I believe, such early experiential states constitute the building blocks of the motivational system of every individual, then "moral masochism" may be viewed as nothing more than active repetition of certain subjective states that the observer would not choose to seek for himself. We find ourselves in the shifting quicksands of personal value judgments if we assume, for example, that a commitment to saintly self-abnegation is *prima facie* "pathological." (For a more detailed consideration of this important issue, see Chapter 6.) To be sure, there are certain individuals in whom such behaviors do indeed constitute mere reaction formations against hostility and selfishness. When this eventuality obtains, however, we may rely on the method of free association to lead us to the childhood conflicts that fuel the underlying angry self-assertion.

In instances where we deal not with the outcome of conflict, but with repetitive behaviors which, for the patient himself, help define the core of his personal identity, any therapeutic pressure to induce the patient to abandon his "maladaptive" activities will, if successful, lead to a state of empty bewilderment—to *l'espace blanc*, as our French colleagues would put it. More often than not, such covertly nonanalytic efforts on our part are not successful; instead, our analysands become unpleasantly negativistic or, even worse, suddenly slip into "negative therapeutic reactions" that restore their former equilibrium. It was not for nothing, after all, that Freud insistently warned analysts against excessive therapeutic ambitions! The appropriate analytic approach in such contingencies is to *explain* to the patient the functions served by his painful habits in his overall adaptation. I consider such psychobiological explanations to be noninterpretive interventions, but the fact that the provision of such explanations parallels the interpretation of unconscious mental contents is, I hope, readily apparent. In many cases, the knowledge that an apparently maladaptive enactment serves to affirm or restore a sense of coherent self-organization is usually sufficient henceforth to maintain the patient's equilibrium without the need concretely to repeat the enactment in question. Even in the domain of these archaic transferences, in other words, verbalization of the issues may lead to the substitution of recollections for repetitive enactments.

Perhaps I should add the cautionary note that I am by no means confident that the decision to designate all of these phenomena as "depressions" is really justified—here, the poverty of our clinical vocabulary perhaps encourages us to construct illegitimate homologies out of disparate materials (cf. Basch, 1975). At the same time, I am certain that the varieties of "masochism" we heuristically differentiate in the context of such a discussion may coexist in one and the same individual. Thus, the repressed perverse fantasies of our neurotic patients probably represent the oedipal version of their archaic fixation on painful subjective states. As corollary to this conviction, I contend that, for optimal therapeutic results, it is not sufficient to deal with these phenomena in their oedipal guise; ideally, they should also be worked through in terms of their more archaic determinants (see also Gedo, 1981b, Chapter 14).

III

The foregoing material about the various possible correlations between masochistic and depressive phenomena can also be assembled into a simpler graphic presentation (Figure 1) in terms of the hier-

THE HIERARCHICAL VIEW

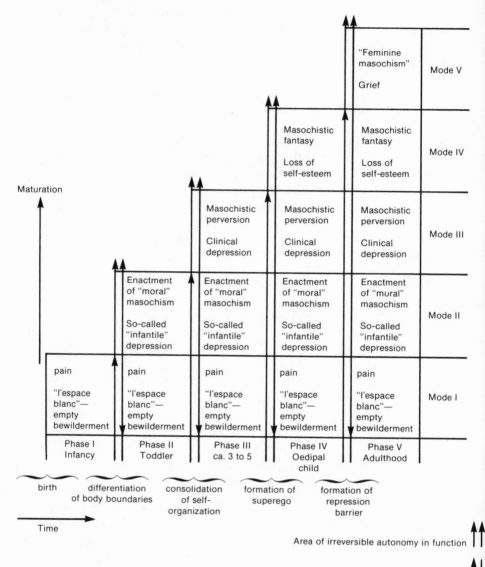

Figure 1. The hierarchical model: Correlation of masochistic behaviors and depressive moods.

archical developmental model I originally devised in collaboration with Goldberg (1973). Instead of explicating this diagram verbally—an exercise that would duplicate the descriptions in *Models of the Mind*—it will be more useful at this point to spell out the advantages of ordering psychoanalytic observations in this manner.

Let me begin by noting that this all-too-complex hierarchical organization categorizes essentially homologous mental contents into five major subgroups characterized by differing structural modes. Within this framework, we see that all the masochistic phenomena and depressive moods with which I have dealt (and which, to the best of my knowledge, include the entire array of these psychic experiences as we encounter them clinically) are characterized by similar ideation and affect. I have tried to establish meaningful distinctions within this class of phenomena by assigning each of these experiences to a set of alternative modes of behavior. Each mode is acquired in the course of a different developmental phase, but each remains potentially available at all times thereafter; the various modes differ from one another in terms of the capacity of the organism in a particular mode to turn the contingencies of life to adaptive use.[4]

By processing psychoanalytic data within the conceptual framework of a hierarchy of modes of functioning, we shift our emphasis from the realm of mental content or unconscious fantasy life to the realm of enduring adaptive patterns, that is, from the consideration of dynamic issues to that of psychic structure. When we recast the problem in this way, it becomes apparent that we have surmounted the need felt by contemporary theoreticians to choose between a

---

4. Although my historical survey does not require a detailed discussion of the specific adaptive solutions characteristic for each of the five modes, a cataloging of these various possibilities is perhaps of sufficient interest to warrant a brief detour from the principal thesis of this chapter. Starting at the most archaic end of the spectrum, we may conceptualize the adaptive possibilities of mode I as a resort to the biological resources of the organism; from a strictly "psychological" viewpoint, in other words, experience in this mode is endured passively. The child has acquired the capacities I associate with mode II when, as a matter of routine, he or she can actively recreate a subset of subjective experiences. Similarly, mode III is attained when the child's characteristic response has changed from the automatic repetition of specific experiences to a holistic program of action. (In the illustration I have expounded in this chapter, this synthetic capacity permits the integration of the compulsive repetition of painful experience into the child's strivings for pleasure through the "erotization" of pain.) Mode IV, in turn, signifies that the individual need no longer process typical experiences through concrete enactments; instead, he or she can mediate them through the channel of fantasies. In Freud's terms, this adaptive potential means that the "positive" image which metaphorically stands for perverse behavior has changed into the "negative" image that represents a neurosis. Finally, in mode V, people characteristically make use of their nuclear fantasies in a creative manner as blueprints for constructive activities.

psychoanalytic psychology centering on intrapsychic conflicts and one highlighting functional deficits. Such a choice is based on an unnecessary dichotomy: These differing theoretical approaches are merely efforts on the part of the observer to impose some manageable conceptual order on his data; which of these alternatives happens to be more useful in a particular context is merely a question of heuristic convenience. Viewed from the perspective of the hierarchical modes of functioning, however, conflict psychology and deficit psychology are actually complementary aspects of the same observational field (see Gedo, 1981b, Chapter 14).

Although the gain in conceptual clarity achieved by using the hierarchical model consistently to categorize psychoanalytic observations is an important matter in itself, the therapeutic implications of such diagnostic refinement are even more crucial. I entitled my volume of 1979 *Beyond Interpretation* in order to stress that, by articulating the contents of hitherto unconscious intrapsychic conflicts in secondary-process terms, that is, via interpretations, we bring about their resolution only in selected instances—more often, additional therapeutic measures are required to overcome them. These noninterpretive modalities of treatment are therapeutically necessary in view of the fact that patients who suffer from structural deficits referable to earlier developmental phases are unable to master their conflicts unless they first acquire those missing psychological aptitudes and skills whose absence rendered them unable to deal with these issues in the first place.

The task of identifying psychological deficits, of bringing them to the attention of the analysand, and of assisting the latter in learning to function in the area of deficit, devolves primarily upon the analyst. These therapeutic tasks "beyond interpretation" constitute analytic operations formerly designated parameters (Eissler, 1953). My work of the past decade in the realm of the theory of technique has been an effort to systematize these essential but hitherto neglected aspects of analytic procedure. Illustrations of such measures in specific analytic contingencies will be offered in the remaining chapters of Section I and, in greater detail, in the two lengthier case histories that constitute Section II. Here, it may be useful to exemplify the use of noninterpretive analytic modalities more schematically by returning to the clinical problems used for illustrative purposes throughout this chapter. I am referring to the principles involved in dealing with masochistic phenomena in analysis.

Until relatively recently, patients selected for analysis on the basis of stringent criteria of analyzability were, at least in principle, likely to present us with masochistic issues only in the form of unconscious transference fantasies brought forth from repression in the course of the analytic process. In such instances, the conflict generated by this unacceptable mental content is generally resolved on the basis of appropriate genetic interpretation. Placing these affect-laden ideas into the childhood context within which they originated—usually that of an infantile misunderstanding of sexuality—is usually sufficient to integrate them with the patient's concurrently acceptable erotic repertory, perhaps as an aspect of foreplay.[5]

Analysts who have broadened their clinical efforts to encompass the treatment of individuals engaged in masochistic perversions (or self-damaging enactments) have generally found that these activities will not cease on the basis of genetic interpretations placing the dynamics of the transference into a childhood context. In order to render the recourse to perverse (or self-damaging) behaviors unnecessary, it is usually essential to create a "holding environment" (Winnicott, 1960; Modell, 1976)—that is, to enter into the patient's life as an auxiliary who can supply psychological skills unavailable when the analysand is left to his own devices. If such assistance is rendered with reasonable consistency, perverse or other masochistic enactments generally disappear without specific interpretation of the

---

5. Although the subject transcends the boundaries of this survey of analytic methods for dealing with masochistic phenomena, this may be an appropriate place to offer some brief comments about a related topic, the issue of *mis*interpreting patients' altruistic efforts in masochistic terms. (For a detailed discussion of a specific, albeit nonclinical, example of such an interpretation, as well as of the alternatives I would propose, see Gedo, 1983, Chapters 7 and 8, where the life of Vincent van Gogh is reviewed from this vantage point.)

Analysands who present significant altruistic commitments tend to be morally scrupulous, so that they do not take interpretations about unconscious aspects of their motivations lightly. When they are told that certain aspects of their sacrifices on behalf of others, or in the service of some ideal, have specific unconscious determinants that they themselves look on as aggressive or narcissistic, they tend, at least provisionally, to accept the interpretation; at the same time, they lose one of the essential buttresses of their self-esteem. If this misunderstanding of one major facet of their selfhood goes uncorrected indefinitely, such a treatment approach is likely to lead to regressive behaviors. Depending on the specific nature of these iatrogenic reactions, such patients may also show depressive side effects of various types. Analyses mismanaged in this manner are often interrupted, sometimes with much bitterness.

Lest these comments be taken to mean that I oppose making interpretations about "reaction formations," let me restate that we must always differentiate constructive sacrifices from defensive efforts of the kind I have in mind. Even if behaviors with primary defensive aims have changed their function (Hartmann, 1939), for example, it is entirely feasible to point out that they also serve to disavow hostility; simultaneously, one can acknowledge the social value of the defensive effort. But my point goes beyond this issue: I am trying to call attention to the fact that altruistic activities do not always have their genesis in defenses against sadism. The need to be helpful may originate as a primary identification with an admired caretaker, to give only the most obvious illustration of an alternative explanation.

meaning of their psychological content. Needless to say, such inter-pretations are often possible, and they do carry the analysis forward in various ways; but the crux of the matter as far as the acting out of masochism is concerned does not lie in that direction. It consists rather of explanations of the adaptive functions of these behaviors in various psychological emergencies (see Gedo, 1981b, Chapter 12).

Such adaptive explanations will often lead patients into more consistent reliance on the analysis as a source of help, in lieu of sexual or other forms of acting out (for an illustration of this sequence, see Chapter 4.) This consolidation of the therapeutic relationship may subsequently permit identification of the specific deficits which impel the patient to require symbiotic assistance; ultimately, these deficien-cies may be repaired by instruction, in or out of the analytic setting.[6]

In point of fact, analysts willing to do psychotherapy have long advocated such "ego building" techniques as a preparatory phase in the sequential treatment of patients who need interpretive assistance but cannot tolerate it in pure culture (e.g., Rappaport, 1960). It has often been assumed, without further evidence, that performance of such "preparation for analysis" impairs the capacity of the analyst to evoke and/or to resolve through interpretation the transferences that derive from the infantile neurosis. My clinical experience of three decades flatly contradicts this assumption, and I shall offer examples that support my position throughout the clinical portions of this volume.

To recapitulate: In formulating the progressive development of the self-organization in terms of a hierarchy of functional modes that give the maturing individual an expanding repertory of adaptive potentialities, I have attempted to focus clinical psychoanalytic theory on the issue of structuralization. If my work gains the attention of the psychoanalytic community, this effort may duplicate the historical sequence whereby Freud's structural hypotheses of the 1920s were the culmination of the pioneering explorations of the unconscious that preceded them. We may have reached the same stage within the cyclical development of psychoanalysis because the most recent gen-

---

6. I trust that my synoptic account of such a sequence of therapeutic transactions suffices to demonstrate the difference between the approach I recommend and the therapeutic stance of Kohut (1971, 1977, 1978). As I understand him, he conceived of these matters in terms of the establishment of an idealizing transference. In his view, it is the analyst's failures in the role of "selfobject" that provide sufficient opportunity to bring the idealizing need to the attention of the patient. Because Kohut viewed this state of affairs as an expectable way station on the road to self-formation, he con-cluded that interpretation of this need automatically led to its resolution through "transmuting internalization." Unfortunately, Kohut never adequately explained the meaning of this inspiring expression.

eration of analysts has once again focused its interest on the investigation of the human depths. The hierarchical model of mental functioning (Gedo & Goldberg, 1973) has generated a complex theory of analytic technique that I have consistently applied to my clinical work over the past decade. I believe the flexible clinical posture that derives from this model has enabled me to obtain superior therapeutic results in a wide range of adaptive disturbances.

2

A Psychoanalyst Reports: Fifty Consecutive Cases

I

A number of years ago, realizing that I had passed the midpoint of my career as a clinical psychoanalyst, I published a report summarizing my generally successful experience over the course of two decades of analytic work (Gedo, 1979a). In large part, I was stimulated to produce that piece of publicity for the analytic cause[1] out of the conviction that the prevailing pessimistic impression about the potential of psychoanalysis as a therapy was largely due to the inclusion of a disproportionate number of inexperienced analysts, generally candidates in training, in formal studies dealing with the outcome of analytic treatment (e.g., Firestein, 1978; Schlessinger & Robbins, 1983). In the interval, however, Erle's surveys (1979; Erle & Goldberg, 1979) have undermined the basis of my original conviction: Reasonably matched patient groups treated by respected senior analysts and by candidates supervised by the faculty of a well-regarded training institute fared no differently in terms of treatment outcome.

If the outcome of my own clinical efforts appeared to be much more positive, it would therefore seem that this fact can hardly be accounted for on the ground of experience alone—although, to be sure, the original review of my work did document the fact that I was least effective as a therapist during my initial years of unsupervised activity as an analyst (Gedo, 1979a, p. 647). It appears more likely

---

1. When Janet Malcolm published *her* report about our "impossible profession" in *The New Yorker* (subsequently expanded into Malcolm, 1981), I sent her a reprint of my article as an antidote to her downbeat attitude about analysts. She replied most courteously, pointing out that I was the third person to send her Gedo (1979a) in order to accomplish that end!

that the technical innovations I shall highlight in the following chapters and have described more systematically in earlier efforts (Gedo, 1979b, 1981b)—measures that have to some extent characterized my approach to analysis all along, if at first only preconsciously—have played the most significant role in accounting for my clinical results.

If this inference is valid, it will prove instructive to bring my midcareer clinical report up to date and to change the earlier focus, highlighting more effectively the various consequences of the nontraditional analytic techniques I have employed. In this context, I wish to stress that I construe the "traditional" method of analysis as an eminently reasonable procedure; in expounding my viewpoint, I will not invoke a straw man, such as the indefensible caricature of "classical" analysis Peterfreund (1983) has pilloried in a recent book. I believe it is fair to equate the currently accepted tradition of analytic technique with the clinical use of an inductive procedure based on observation—that is, the technique Peterfreund himself would advocate—but a procedure in which noninterpretive interventions are kept to an irreducible minimum (cf. Gill, 1981).

Although the nature of my clinical data scarcely lends itself to sophisticated statistical treatment, it will clarify matters in certain respects if I quantify subgroups within the patient population; in order to simplify the arithmetic, I shall limit my report to 50 consecutive attempts to use the psychoanalytic method over the course of more than 25 years. As a matter of fact, this series happens to include every patient I undertook to analyze prior to the latter part of 1980, that is, every patient about whom some reliable estimate of outcome can be made. If this list were brought further up to date, it would entail the addition of only a very few cases. Parenthetically, it is worth noting how pitifully meager the individual analyst's total exposure to humanity remains, even if he commits himself, as I did upon "graduation" from the Chicago Psychoanalytic Institute, to the exclusive practice of psychoanalysis proper.

One reason for my earlier opinion that favorable clinical results might be linked to a technical mastery that can be achieved only through constant practice was my impression that relatively few colleagues devote much of their professional time to the conduct of analyses after they have completed their training, usually when they are in their early 40s.[2] Hence, the "average" analyst's clinical skills

2. A recent survey by the American Psychoanalytic Association revealed that this impression was, if anything, an understatement. The respondents, clearly the more active fraction of the membership, had an average of 3.8 patients in analysis at the time. A full-time analytic practice actually permits eight to ten analyses to be conducted simultaneously. Possible explanations for the alarming extent of this "idle capacity" in the analytic community will be discussed in Chapter 12.

probably do not fully ripen until he (or she) reaches his late 50s, by which time he may have dealt with about a dozen patients altogether! In view of these realities, a series of 50 analytic cases actually represents an unusual amount of experience with our Sisyphean tasks.

A brief demographic survey will help define the specific nature of this experience. The 50 patients I have seen were almost evenly divided with regard to gender (24 men/26 women). They represent a relatively narrow segment of the sophisticated, urban, professional, and academic elite of late-20th-century America; they are exclusively white and—surprisingly, in view of my own audibly "European" background—native born. Although very few were deeply religious, half (50%) were nominally Protestants whereas more than a third (36%) were Jewish; only a few were Catholics (12%) and still fewer subscribed to other religious faiths. Members of all these groups tended to intermarry and/or to move from fundamentalist/orthodox positions within their religious communities into more prestigious, "mainstream" ones. In terms of vocation, almost one-third (30%) were mental health professionals,[3] another one-third (32%) were in academic life, either as faculty members or as graduate students, and a quarter (26%) consisted of a scattering of lawyers, journalists, artists, and other professionals. The remaining 12% of my analysands were well-educated people who had no settled occupation when they started treatment; they were mostly women married to men in the professions listed above. The age range of my patients at the beginning of analysis stretched from the early 20s to the late 40s, but more than half fell into the crucial decade from the late 20s to the late 30s. It should also be noted that 20% of my patients had had some previous analysis before beginning treatment with me, sometimes for extensive periods; invoking a fairly encompassing definition of the term, well over half had tried psychotherapy of one form or another.

From my vantage point, analysis was invariably undertaken to deal with the consequences of severe and complex disorders of character. Most patients had only decided to undertake this demanding therapy following serious adaptive failures in the vocational sphere, in family life, or in both areas; the proximate cause for seeking help was therefore almost always a severe loss of self-esteem. The presenting clinical picture was often alarming: depression, suicidal preoccupations, frantic perverse activities, some form of psychosomatic decompensation, confusion, or panic. Whatever the symptoms, my

---

3. When I wrote my previous report, this group comprised only 25% of my practice. This increase represents a sharp restriction of my clientele: This is the price one pays for the privilege of serving as a "training analyst."

unvarying policy was to accept for analysis anyone seriously committed to achieving self-understanding, provided there did not appear to be any serious risk of a psychiatric emergency requiring hospitalization (cf. Appelbaum, 1981).

As to the specific crises that led these patients to seek help, more than a quarter (28%) had just been forced to acknowledge the failure of a marriage or sexual relationship of equivalent importance. An even larger number (32%) were struggling to salvage a desperately strained relationship that seemed destined to rupture unless one or both partners could change drastically; in the natural course of events, most of these relationships were eventually dissolved, either during or after the analysis, occasionally without recourse to official changes in marital status.[4] Nearly another quarter of the patients (22%) consisted of people who had begun to realize that their characteristic mode of dealing with others would forever prevent them from forming stable relationships, much less establishing families. Even among those few analysands (18%) whose need for assistance was primarily unrelated to such issues, it is difficult to find instances of stable and truly satisfying intimate relationships. At the same time, about 60% of these patients had either reached a dead end in their careers or were seriously dissatisfied with their professional progress. In sum, then, overt adaptive difficulties accounted for the decision of all but five patients (10%) to undertake analysis with me. These five patients, of whom four were mental health professionals, complained of subjective discomforts alone.

In terms of administrative arrangements, the analytic procedure was invariably carried out in the so-called "classical" manner. I have insisted throughout on a minimum of four sessions per week (at this frequency, my schedule allows about 160+ sessions per year) but have almost always recommended five weekly appointments (i.e., 200+ sessions per year). Most of my patients have undertaken at least a significant portion of the analytic work at this greater frequency.[5] I have rested content with four weekly sessions only in certain specific circumstances: in the earlier phases of work with certain obsessional and paranoid characters who tend to respond to a daily schedule of appointments with increased negativism and, perforce, in rare cases where insoluble logistical difficulties prevent a fifth meeting. With very few exceptions, analyses that reach a successful conclusion require more than 600 sessions, often as many as 1200, spread over a

---

4. Such relationships underwent real improvements only in those instances in which the spouse also undertook analytic treatment *and* this turned out to be successful.

5. My sessions are routinely scheduled to last 45 minutes, but I allow enough time between visits to permit specific "hours" to extend to 50 minutes.

period of three to seven years.[6] Patients who have interrupted treatment generally did so relatively early, mostly within the first year of work. In only a single instance did a patient decide to leave "prematurely" at a later stage of the analysis; this event occurred early in my career and was almost certainly the result of my lack of experience in handling an unusually difficult clinical contingency.[7] By contrast, cases that end in stalemate usually drag on fruitlessly for a number of years; ultimately, one comes to the reluctant conclusion that an analytic process simply cannot be set in motion between the participants, and a radical change in therapeutic plan thereby eventuates.

Regardless of outcome, the actual decision to dispense with my services was always left entirely to the patient.[8] In my judgment, the analyst's task under such circumstances is confined to the provision of timely information, that is, to the rendering of expert opinion about what remains to be accomplished and what the chances of reaching specific therapeutic goals might be. In Chapter 8, I shall attempt to demonstrate that the duration of treatment does not seem to be related to severity of psychopathology; rather, it appears to depend most directly on the pace at which meaningful communicative channels between analyst and analysand are established.

Obviously, this latter task is most difficult with patients whose disturbances are genetically rooted in that early phase of development in which language skills are acquired (for a clinical illustration, see Chapter 8). Yet, cultural differences in themselves may also contribute to difficulties in communication. To take one example, I was conspicuously unsuccessfull in my efforts to work with three patients whose parents came from impoverished European peasant stock. Long ago and far away, I was raised to despise such people, and I have never been successful in treating their descendants.

---

6. The most dramatic exception in my personal experience was a treatment I have previously described in detail (Gedo, 1979b, Chapter 8). This analysis was concluded in less than 15 months with excellent results that have seemingly endured. At the other extreme, I have conducted one analysis for ten years and another for over 11; as one might expect, these difficult cases had more equivocal outcomes.

7. I had occasion to discuss these matters with this person almost 20 years later, and we reached an amicable consensus about them. No further analysis had been attempted, and the adaptational results were surprisingly satisfactory!

8. *Seeming* exceptions to this rule were several instances in which I was obliged to outline certain minimum conditions patients have to meet in order to continue with the analytic work, for example, the avoidance of certain delinquent enactments. Patients do occasionally leave under such circumstances, but they generally try to project responsibility for their decision onto the analyst. I believe contingencies of this sort should be classified as analytic stalemates leading to failure. See Chapter 7.

I have already observed that my work over a span of almost three decades has scarcely remained uniform in quality. In addition to the expectable growth of clinical skills over time, general progress in the field leads to modifications in one's approach. Insofar as my own theoretical work has led me into promising clinical ventures with patients generally regarded as very difficult to treat (cf. Segal & Britton, 1981, p. 268), colleagues have tended to refer even more challenging problems to me. Predictably, then, successful outcomes in recent years have usually been very dearly bought.

With the exception of one analysis described in *Beyond Interpretation* (1979b, Chapter 4) for which I subsequently arranged a formal follow-up (as part of the study reported by Schlessinger & Robbins, 1983), my assessment of the therapeutic outcome of my work is obviously subjective and impressionistic. But this caveat notwithstanding, what I reported previously (Gedo, 1979a, p. 647) still appears to obtain: Without deliberate efforts on my part, relevant information about former analysands continues to come to my attention. Many former analysands, after all, are mental health professionals in my community whereas others have intimate friends or relatives in the analytic world. Former patients occasionally return for a consultation about crises in their own lives or in the lives of family members; others may get in touch to communicate a piece of news generally related to some accomplishment. I have on occasion received such information through the newspaper. As a result of these actualities, I have learned something of the long-term results of most of the analyses I have brought to a successful, that is, to a mutually agreed upon, termination. By contrast, my information about patients whose analyses failed or were interrupted is much scantier.

II

The rate of mutually agreed upon analytic terminations in this series of 50 consecutive cases is 80%.[9] There is a startling discrepancy between this figure and the disappointing results Erle (1979) reported about the proportion of successfully completed analyses by candidates of the New York Psychoanalytic Institute (27.5%) and selected senior clinicians (24%). Although these results were apparently based on criteria similar to those I am using here, it is possible, of course, that they are not strictly comparable. Mutual

9. The rate in my earlier report (Gedo, 1979a) was 28 out of 36 or 77.8%.

agreement about terminating psychoanalytic treatment, after all, may come about on the basis of widely divergent transactions. At the very least, however, there is probably some consensus that a satisfactory termination implies that the major defects in adaptive capacity which prompted the decision to seek analytic help are no longer in evidence.

In this regard, favorable results in my subgroup of 40 patients who terminated with mutual agreement have been particularly striking with regard to career problems. To the best of my knowledge, these people have invariably done well in the sphere of work; they have often achieved impressive public success. In crude financial terms, their analyses proved to be sound investments! A number of patients, including some married women who were previously unemployed, launched new careers. On the other hand, several women were able to devote themselves to the rearing of children with enthusiasm and satisfaction. It is of course difficult to substantiate my claim that these changes grew directly out of the therapeutic work; but the fact is that certain of the happy mothers were, prior to analysis, too afraid of such childrearing responsibilities even to have children, that certain of the distinguished professionals had formerly wasted themselves in delinquencies and addictions, and that certain of the career women had been under the thumb of tyrannical husbands, and the like. Their new achievements seemed to follow changes in personality effected through psychoanalytic treatment. To my knowledge, only *one* of these 40 individuals has had a subsequent problem of major dimensions in the sphere of work: Excessive ambition led this person to attempt more than he was qualified to achieve. I shall return to the limits of this particular analytic result below.

It is more difficult to assess therapeutic outcome in the sphere of the capacity for intimacy and mutuality. The establishment of gratifying family life is generally a good criterion for favorable change in this regard, but the absence of such an external development may, after all, only betoken unfavorable life circumstances. For women over 35, opportunities to forge stable new ties seem to be realistically poor. Based on the knowledge I have obtained, at least nine of the 14 male patients and seven of the 14 women who were unattached while in treatment have subsequently made satisfactory family arrangements. Conversely, I know of three men and two women whose postanalysis bachelorhood was a matter of conscious choice based on what I believe to be realistic assessments of their priorities: In several instances this choice entailed the acceptance of *de facto* celibacy. One woman in her 40s made the compromise of entering a difficult marriage in preference to a life of solitude—a choice not all that different from those of certain patients who elected to continue in less than happy family situations as the lesser of two evils. I believe, however, that the beneficial results of analysis are more clearly demonstrated by the fact that *all* of the desperately strained sado-masochistic modes of relating that brought so many of these people into treatment were overcome as a result of the analytic work. If, in a few of these patients, these pathological enactments gave way to creative activities instead of significant love relations, this correlation merely buttresses Kohut's (1971, 1977) clinical impression that the expectable course of certain analyses which deal primarily with problems of self-esteem is in the direction of enhanced "creativity."

At any rate, the analyses that both analyst and analysand regarded as *complete* where characterized, as a group, by extensive and favorable adaptive changes in the capacity for productive work and, with somewhat lesser regularity, in the capacity for gratifying personal intimacy.[10] I do *not* assume that the permanent disappearance of any of the more threatening *symptoms* (behaviors which, after all, merely betoken regressions to relatively archaic modes of functioning in situations of stress) could have been accomplished only through analytic methods. I *do* believe, however, that the results I am reporting should be regarded as specifically psychoanalytic because they betoken actual new learning with respect to specific mental functions that subserve the patient's adaptation. Insofar as this is the case, therapeutic results are presumably sustained because the analysand has achieved effective self-regulation in areas of previous deficit.

Whether improved adaptation in particular cases has come about as a result of new learning of this kind or simply because the relationship to the analyst has provided a source of reliable, ongoing assistance is quite difficult to determine as long as treatment continues. This issue should ideally occupy the forefront of analytic attention during the termination phase of treatment; unfortunately, it is all too often trivialized and sentimentalized in practice, as if the analysand's reaction to termination were merely a question of a disappointment in love. Actual termination should only be decided on, of course, if there is reason to believe that the favorable adaptive changes achieved during the analysis will be sustained after cessation of the collaborative work because the analysand has acquired the requisite psychological skills to assume the burdens of self-inquiry and self-regulation (see Gardner, 1983). I shall try to illustrate how such capacities are actually acquired in the course of analytic work in

10. It may well be possible to obtain comparable adaptive results through other psychotherapeutic methods, as Dewald (1981) asserts in his pedantic critique of my work, but in my years as a psychotherapist (before completing my psychoanalytic training) I was never able to do so (see Gedo, 1964, and 1981b, Chapter 1).

the two detailed case reports that make up Section II of this volume and, in more passing fashion, in the clinical material introduced throughout Section III.

In the consulting room, it is invariably a matter of judgment whether the analysand has succeeded in making his own the insights and previously missing psychological capabilities that have become available through the analytic work. Obviously, only formal follow-up studies conducted by impartial judges could determine the validity of the decisions at which my patients and I jointly arrived in specific cases. The analyst is ever tempted to believe that, in the absence of information to the contrary, the very fact that expatients do not contact him is evidence of their ability to maintain therapeutic gains on their own. If I continue to trust this untested assumption, it is because the vast majority of my successfully terminated analysands do feel free to notify me in situations of difficulty or, more generally, when something noteworthy occurs in their lives.

It should be noted that, in discussing "successfully terminated" analyses, I am adhering to criteria for measuring the progress of the therapeutic *process* from a technical point of view. As we know, however, invoking here the analogy of surgery, the operation may be successful without significant long-term benefits for the patient. In addition to process criteria, in other words, we must examine therapeutic results from the vantage point of a set of independent criteria of *outcome*. In this respect, favorable impressions gained at "follow-up" are difficult to correlate causally with the treatment, although information that has negative connotations may certainly highlight various limitations of the therapeutic results.

Perhaps the clearest indication of such limitations is the subsequent necessity to resume analytic work. In three instances, former analysands have returned for a second period of treatment with me.[11] Another patient had moved to a different city in the interval and requested a referral to an analyst there. Two former analysands who sought a second analysis with someone else were young psychiatrists whom I treated before I became a training analyst; both subsequently entered "training analyses." The only other patient who, to the best of my knowledge, needed further assistance was the person to whose later vocational difficulties I have already alluded. Even before getting into deep water by pursuing unrealistic career goals, this patient returned less than six months after termination to tell me with considerable bitterness of his intention to consult some-

11. Two of these patients have "successfully" terminated these second analyses. In the 50 cases reported in this series, each of these individuals has been counted only once.

one else. At the time of this announcement, this person was afflicted with subjective discomforts alone; the adaptive breakdown that actually led to his resumption of treatment occurred some years later.

Other cases that required reanalysis were more unusual. The former patient who had left Chicago went from success to success in every sphere of life and eventually returned to consult me because of severe anxiety about this unprecedented state of affairs. Following my referral, I was kept informed about the progress of the reanalysis and learned that the issues which had arisen in the context of a new situation were quite different (at least to the patient) from the issues we had dealt with during the "lean years." Two of the three patients who returned to me for their reanalyses also did so in circumstances of emotional prosperity unprecedented in their experience. For these patients, one of the "sleeping dogs" (cf. Freud, 1937) we had been unable to awaken during the first period of treatment was an intolerance of surfeit that had subsequently become a source of renewed conflict.[12]

I believe it is pertinent to note here that awakening the sleeping dogs of potential conflict is one of the functions of the therapeutic activities "beyond interpretation" that I now advocate. To be sure, repeatedly challenging analysands about the need to give up those behaviors through which potentially conflictual life circumstances are avoided has been an accepted part of analytic work for a very long time: Freud's own heroic efforts to mobilize the "Wolf Man" (Freud, 1918) from his comfortable lethargy is the earliest published instance of such an effort, albeit an unsuccessful one. On the other hand, continuing emphasis on the primacy of interpretation in the model technique of psychoanalysis has discouraged the clinical use of such noninterpretive measures. In every one of my cases that eventuated in a second analysis, I had been overly reluctant during the initial analysis to throw my weight into the balance with a patient hesitant to alter certain habits. From the standpoint of these and subsequent clinical experiences, I have come to conceptualize such contingencies in terms of the persistence of certain unexamined illusions on the part of the analysand—in the examples I have cited, these were mostly childhood illusions of a self-depreciating variety—and I now regard vigorous efforts to overcome these illusions by challenging the patient's view of reality as an absolute analytic necessity (cf. Gedo, 1979b, 1981b).

12. The remaining patient who came back for a second period of treatment had clearly terminated analysis prematurely—a calculated risk we had accepted in view of an unexpected financial crisis.

III

At the time of termination, analysts tend to view their therapeutic results with optimism; it is always easier to detect the limitations of treatment at a later time, when distance has created an opportunity for greater objectivity. In spite of this necessary caveat, I believe that, over the past 15 years, my personal capabilities as a clinician have more or less coincided with "the state of the art." I make this claim in order to stress that I began those of my analyses which ultimately failed to reach a successful conclusion with some awareness of the potential difficulties that lay ahead. All of these patients would have been turned away as unpromising by any analyst primarily intent on demonstrating his therapeutic competence, whether to himself or to others. Indeed, many of these patients might have been deemed "unanalyzable" by colleagues who use conservative criteria in selecting their analysands; I suspect that virtually any experienced clinician will accept my judgment that, in these cases, analytic success necessarily hinges on exceptionally fortunate circumstances.

To illustrate both the anticipated difficulties and the simultaneous indications for choosing psychoanalysis as the preferred treatment modality, I can cite the instance of one of my patients who broke off the analytic effort. This woman was severely suicidal when she consulted me after arriving at a confusing impasse with her previous analyst. When, with my encouragement, she subsequently confronted him on this issue, the therapist admitted that he had consistently absented himself from the consulting room for significant portions of most of her sessions. Episodes of confusion and disorganization continued to occur during the early stages of my work with her as well, especially when holidays or other obligations on my part interfered with our schedule. After about a year of steady work, this turbulence gradually subsided, so that I was actually unprepared for her sudden flight from treatment. The patient rationalized her decision on the ground that the improvements she had achieved through my assistance had more than satisfied her original goals in seeking help and, in a literal sense, her contention was probably true. When the patient subsequently returned for a brief psychotherapeutic effort, however, we were able to explore further the basis for the abrupt analytic termination. We found that our therapeutic "alliance" had been ruptured by my unwillingness to concur with her delusional view about her position within her religious community. This unrealistic attitude about herself had emerged only in the course of her free associations. Because, during the analysis, I had refused to share her conviction that she was an evil heretic, unable to live by the rules of the religious sect that defined her adult existence, I had become evil incarnate in her eyes. Only through the method of free association could I get detailed information about the "heresies" about which the patient was assailing herself. When she was obliged to spell out for herself that her "sinful" activities were direct reflections of her authentic private beliefs, I was able to form and articulate the judgment that these personal convictions were just as worthy as the dogma of her community; although she temporarily fled from treatment, my support of her prerogative to live in accord with her own standards proved to be decisive in freeing this person from a slavish subjection to arbitrary authorities. But this provision of support did not provide the basis for a genuine analytic result: In trying to treat a Prophetess through the psychoanalytic method, I had been trying to extend analysis beyond the range of its conventional applicability.[13]

Viewed as a group, the ten patients with whom my analytic efforts were not successful might best be characterized as faced by overwhelming problems, the solutions to which were inconceivable without the maximal opportunity for insight afforded by the analytic procedure. Yet, poor prognostic signs were not always apparent early in the treatment. One patient who eventually required hospitalization for a psychotic decompensation, for example, originally presented herself in a manner that misled me into viewing her as a hysterical personality. When, several months later, the fragile nature of her integration became apparent, it emerged that she had been given the diagnosis of hysteria by a previous consultant. Thoroughly familiar with the phenomenology implied by the term, this desperate person at the brink of a loss of self-cohesion reorganized herself temporarily by enacting the part of a model hysteric. Needless to say, none of the patients whose analyses were successfully terminated had problems of this magnitude stemming from such archaic developmental levels.[14]

To my knowledge, only one of these ten patients decided to undertake a second analysis with someone else, a course of action I actively supported because I concurred with the patient's judgment that my subjective responses to his behavior were far from optimal.

13. This clinical encounter is described in some detail in Gedo (1981b, pp. 165–171, 178–183). For further discussion of the issue of value judgments in psychoanalytic practice, see Chapter 6.

14. In Chapter 7, I shall describe three cases that came to grief as a result of an overwhelming combination of delinquent propensities, extraanalytic symbiotic attachments, and covert disorders of thought. In a previous discussion of the current limits of psychoanalysis as therapy (Gedo, 1981b, Chapter 3), I have provided a detailed description of the treatment of the pseudohysterical patient to whom I have just alluded, along with two other analyses that failed after lengthy efforts, mostly, I concluded, as a result of covert delusional thinking.

He made arrangements to resume analysis in another city, and I never heard from him again. I did hear from an influential colleague, however, about a set of slanderous accusations of misconduct on my part that this former patient had conveyed to one of his patients, knowing full well that these accusations would come to the attention of her analyst. This colleague proceeded to inform me that our patients had been involved in a clandestine affair of which I had never had knowledge. My conscious discomfort during my work with this patient had been based only on the corrupt arrangements he had made to finance the analysis and his righteous indignation over my efforts to inform him about the undesirable consequences of this fraud. In this case, as in the case of the pseudohysterical young woman, I had no inkling of the true extent of the underlying psychopathology when I undertook the treatment.

Despite the signs of severe characterological difficulties that stood in the way of analytic success in this case, I suspect that the patient was in some measure correct in blaming me for the failure of our collaboration: My shock and corresponding inability to accept his corruption might not have been present with a patient whose professional activities were not so closely related to my own. To put this matter differently, it cannot be a coincidence that six of the ten patients with whom I failed were either nonpsychiatric physicians or mental health professionals. Is it more difficult for these institutional rivals to "submit" to psychoanalysis than for other people? Or is the problem my own? In all probability, the poor results in these cases stemmed from a combination of both factors.

It should also be noted that the failure of an analytic effort does not end the therapist's medical responsibility. On the contrary, such an outcome may constitute a potential emergency inasmuch as patients may well react to it with a sense of catastrophe—with panic, depression, and paranoid feelings of having been mistreated. It is imperative to deal with these contingencies in an appropriate therapeutic fashion. The treatment of these complications may require considerable time and effort, and I have never avoided assuming these psychotherapeutic responsibilities as long as they were required. If analysts demonstrate their continuing availability as therapists, the acute symptoms of unsuccessfully terminated analysands generally subside and treatment may gradually be tapered off.

IV

How far can the satisfying results of my clinical work be attributed to the specific technical innovations I have been advocating for the past decade? In my judgment, such questions are meaningless, for my published technical recommendations have, I believe, merely attempted to codify and systematize what competent clinicians have actually *done* all along. It is probably true nonetheless that, as I have tried bit by bit to articulate the nature of my successful procedures, the act of clarifying my rationales has gradually strengthened the courage of my convictions; this is to say that whatever skills I have gained with increasing experience have been incorporated into my writings on the theory of psychoanalytic technique as I have become explicitly aware of what these skills consist of operationally. I began to publish case material of this kind in the mid-1970s[15]; yet even the three lengthy clinical illustrations in *Beyond Interpretation* (1979b) justifiably struck most reviewers (e.g., Rangell, 1981) as relatively conventional—although Gill (1981) did note unusual features in my handling of one of these analyses.

To put this matter into historical context, in my writings to date I have been at pains to emphasize the continuity between my procedures and the "mainstream" of psychoanalytic tradition—a *vital* continuity, I would still assert. The clinical section of *this* volume is devoted to a more detailed demonstration of those aspects of my analytic technique that differentiate it from generally accepted practice.[16]

Wherever I have presented my case material, orally or in writing, experienced clinicians have seldom argued that my recourse to the noninterpretive measures I have described constituted departures from optimal therapeutic actions. Many would agree with Dewald (1981), who asserted that the acknowledged necessity for such technical departures from purely interpretive methods has transformed the treatment procedure from a "psychoanalysis proper" into a sophisticated form of psychoanalytic psychotherapy. Kernberg (1975, 1976) is another influential author who has vigorously espoused the position that the patients he classifies as "borderline" are most optimally treated by means of various "psychotherapeutic" procedures.

In my judgment, Kernberg's own treatment proposals are often best conceptualized in terms of the schema of therapeutic modalities Goldberg and I developed in *Models of the Mind* (1973) as a guide to psychoanalytic procedures. Perhaps, in fact, it is fatuous to argue about the specific designation we assign to such a treatment, especially

---

15. These papers (Gedo, 1975, 1977) were later revised and included in *Advances in Clinical Psychoanalysis* (1981b).

16. I shall offer two lengthy case histories (comparable to the trio of illustrative cases I used in *Beyond Interpretation* [Gedo, 1979b]) as well as briefer descriptions of the treatment of several other patients. If the clinical accounts in my other work (Gedo, 1981b, 1983) are added to this list, my four books contain reasonably detailed narratives about well over half of this series of 50 analyses and shorter excerpts from most of the rest.

given the fact that we are all in agreement about the difficulty of conducting such a treatment skillfully. I believe that the management of archaic transferences requires psychoanalytic skills of a higher order than the management of the transference neuroses, that is, than the management of those oedipal transferences to which the classical technique of psychoanalysis is entirely adequate.

At any rate, by introducing the notion that psychoanalysis as a therapeutic procedure employs a series of modalities beyond interpretation, I believe I have begun to answer the challenges to our theory of technique posed by Bergin and Lambert (1978), among others. In their skeptical assessment of therapeutic outcomes, these authors conclude that many forms of psychotherapy are effective, but that differences in outcome between various forms of treatment are difficult to demonstrate. Bergin and Lambert infer that factors incidental to the explicit technique purportedly employed by the therapist are therefore responsible for patient improvement. In their view, technique in general merely provides "a believable rationale and congenial *modus operandi*" for the participants of all forms of treatment. They conclude that "these considerations imply that psychotherapy is laden with nonspecific or placebo factors . . . *but these influences, when specified, may prove to be the essence of what provides therapeutic benefit* (Bergin & Lambert, 1978, pp. 179-180; emphasis added). I have striven to specify a number of these hitherto neglected influences in the particular case of psychoanalysis.[17]

17. This may be the appropriate place to comment briefly on another, more radical critique of psychoanalytic theory, that of the epistemologist Adolf Grünbaum (1979). I hope to reply to his views at greater length elsewhere; here, I merely wish to note that Grünbaum's objections to the evidential value of analytic outcomes are probably unanswerable if we persist in the claim that the *sole* curative factor in our work is veridical interpretation. Obviously, I have repudiated this reductionistic view of the mode of action of psychoanalysis—without, however, abandoning the belief that accurate interpretation of unconscious conflicts does indeed possess therapeutic value. The seeming discrepancy between the psychoanalytic claim of superior therapeutic effectiveness and the widely varying systems of interpretation used by the competing schools of psychoanalysis (Joseph, in press) is best explained, I believe, by postulating that these favorable results stem, in each instance, from the common use of the non-interpretive modalities I have described in my previous work.

3

On Some Therapeutic Side Effects
of Dream Interpretation

Sigmund Freud looked upon the interpretation of dreams as the royal road to the unconscious, a judgment that succeeding generations of psychoanalysts have generally accepted with little difficulty. To be sure, in the psychoanalytic situation the clinician is seldom able to pursue the latent meanings of dream material with the devotion Freud lavished on the specimen dreams that fill his masterpiece of 1900. We can therefore be much more confident about the adequacy of our *methods* of interpretation than we can be about the adequacy of any specific effort to decipher a particular dream in a clinical setting. The possibility of reaching a false consensus with the analysand has long been recognized; as early as 1931, Edward Glover called attention to seemingly beneficial therapeutic results brought about on the basis of inexact interpretations.

In this chapter, I wish to consider the converse of these circumstances, namely, various paradoxical effects of dream interpretations the validity of which we have no reason to question. By stating the issue in this manner, I am of course implying that agreement has been reached about the expectable results of an accurate and well-timed interpretation. There may, in fact, be certain differences of opinion about most items on a list of such results, whether they focus on transference developments, the expansion of genetic understanding, alterations in typical defensive operations, or improvements in the adaptive sphere. Rather than discussing this matter in the detail it actually deserves, however, let me proceed on the assumption that analysts could ultimately reach a significant degree of concurrence about what kind of responses to a dream interpretation constitutes analytic progress. I trust that my own views about what we generally expect will become apparent from the nature of the "paradoxical," unexpected effects I shall now describe. Needless to say, these effects will only be selected examples that hardly exhaust the manifold possibilities of surprising responses to the communication of analytic insights about dreams.

In order to reduce this bewildering variety to manageable proportions, I shall, for the most part, focus the discussion on instances when these responses are therapeutically favorable. However, I will begin with the most nonspecific and, at the same time, most disruptive of these unexpected developments: the occurrence of an immediate affective storm, most frequently in the form of an attack of anxiety. With certain patients, these dramatic untoward events *only* take place in response to correct interpretations; in contrast, messages that miss the mark generally leave them cold, if somewhat bewildered. It is natural to assume, at first, that the patient's reaction has to do with some specific, perhaps unintended, meaning of the analyst's communication. It is only after carefully reviewing a series of such traumatic episodes that the analyst may be forced to the conclusion that such an analysand is initially unable to absorb valid interpretations about anything whatsoever.

Patients with a wide variety of personality types may well evidence these responses, but in my own clinical experience those who have done so most dramatically have been afflicted with chronic traumatic neuroses. In one instance, the neurosis had been established before the child began school, in the context of repeated sexual assaults by an adult. Although the gross overstimulation had traumatized her, the patient was, for a number of weighty reasons, very attached to her molester and an eager participant in the affair. Hence, as we subsequently learned, every report of a dream was, for this woman, an act of seduction, and every interpretation of a dream signified success in inducing an act of phallic penetration. The royal road to the unconscious sometimes conceals amazing land mines! Childhood sexual traumata will be reenacted in the transference, no matter how abstinent the actualities of analytic technique may be. A successful interpretation may occasionally even lead to spontaneous orgasm, although the repetition of traumatic childhood anxiety reactions is much more common.

The highly condensed and schematic excerpts from the case I have just presented actually illustrate the well-known technical precept that, in all of our therapeutic activities, we must continuously monitor the fantasies stirred up by the unavoidable human interactions that constitute the treatment as a reality event (cf Gill, 1981;

Gedo, 1981a). I now proceed to an example of how the nature of these unconscious fantasies tend to change in the course of the analytic process, producing ever novel "side effects" in reaction to dream interpretation.

Having mastered the propensity for traumatization that masked other features of her pathology, the patient I have begun to describe went on to develop a profound archaic transference (Gedo, 1977) through which she relived the rageful transactions that had characterized her early relationships with both parents. The analysis was truly painful and difficult for both participants; the patient was almost always quite pessimistic about her prognosis and often threatened (I use the word advisedly) to interrupt treatment. In spite of numerous enactments bluffing such an abandonment of the analysis, the first indication that she was seriously considering an eventual termination emerged after five years of work, in connection with the following dream.

The patient found herself in an elevator in a high-rise building; it might have been the building in which I work or perhaps the one where she was living with her husband. She pressed the button for the floor on which their apartment was located, but the elevator proceeded to go out of control, wildly ascending and falling over and over again, without stop. She was terrified, but then heard instructions from people sent to her rescue: In order to get home, she would have to go through every phase of her analysis, as the textbooks prescribe. Her associations focused on her feeling trapped at the same time as she was determined to leave me; I responded by interpreting the dream as an indication of ambivalence about termination, that is, as the persistence of her symbiotic attachment to me.

The result of this transaction was a negative therapeutic reaction —one of a seemingly interminable succession of these "elevator accidents," to use the patient's dream metaphor. This disruption lasted for about ten days and was resolved when she recounted a reprise of the dream. In its second version, she had just left the elevator in a high-rise building and walked up to the door of an apartment she wished to enter. She was distressed to see that it was covered with eviction notices. Her associations revealed that the apartment simultaneously represented her marriage and her analysis. We now came to the realization that she felt trapped in the treatment because it protected her against developing primitive transference reactions toward her husband, thereby safeguarding her marriage. (Prior to the development of the archaic transference in the analysis, she had been forced to protect the marriage by keeping her husband at a safe distance.) At the same time, it became clear that she experienced *every* valid interpretation as a step bringing her closer to eviction from the analysis. Need I add that this woman had lost her primary caretaker before the age of three? Or that I precipitated the next negative therapeutic reaction by summing up the situation with the phrase "Home is where the heart is," that is, by announcing that I had come to assume the place of her beloved lost nursemaid in the analytic transference?

The nature of the two illustrations I have provided thus far might suggest that successful therapeutic use of a dream is likely to produce regressive side effects. Although this is indeed frequently the case, it is by no means universally true; in principle, such a transaction may just as readily promote paradoxical reactions without regressive connotations. I shall refrain from giving detailed examples of such contingencies, which are familiar to all analysts. For example, any sign of competence on the part of the analyst is likely to evoke phallic-competitive responses in the analysand, with attendant castration anxiety and/or narcissistic mortification.

II

Instead of spelling out the obvious, I should like to address myself to a different set of unexpected consequences of dream interpretation, namely, those beneficial therapeutic results of dream interpretation that transcend the effects of the valid insights which the interpretations may have produced. Sometimes these paradoxical effects take place in addition to the mutative results of the new understanding reached by means of the analyst's secondary-process communication; on other occasions, insofar as one can determine in the confusion of a clinical encounter, the unexpected response is the only one produced. I will again illustrate this latter contingency with an incident from the analysis of the young woman who experienced her treatment as if it were a rollercoaster ride on an elevator.

As I have already mentioned, the first several years of this analysis dealt for the most part with the elucidation of an archaic transference that reproduced the intense symbiotic needs of a child abandoned by her primary caretaker in the third year of life. Well into the fifth year of our collaboration, in the context of bitter complaints about her continuing lack of self-esteem and her disappointment in my capacity to repair this defect through direct action, I discerned for the first time indications that this material had meanings beyond the repetition of the early experience of a neglected child: The patient was now feeling worthless in comparison to certain other people. She reported a crucial dream at this time: She was walking around on the lower level of the Field Museum (the local museum of natural history) and was just about to walk up the stairs to the main floor when she heard a tremendous roar. Before she had a chance to flee, an enormous lion leaped upon her and pinned her to the ground. She then awakened in a panic.

Associations led to latency age memories of visits to the museum with her mother to sketch the zoological exhibits and to her sense of awe at her mother's superior skill in these endeavors. She also had some thoughts concerning my wife, whose activities as a lecturer at the Art Institute had recently come to her attention. I reminded her that the official symbol of the art museum is a pair of bronze lions that flank its entrance, so that the dream seemed simultaneously to portray her competitiveness with both current and past female rivals, particularly her fears of retaliation for daring to emerge from her lowly status, that is, from the lower level in the dream.

The subsequent course of the analysis was to confirm the central importance of this nascent oedipal conflict and its attendant fantasies in preventing my patient, who had previously been fixated on a symbiotic way of life, from resolving her dilemma. Not only was she afraid to risk *any* impairment of her relationship to her parents during the phallic phase of development which immediately followed the traumatic separation from her beloved nursemaid, but this inability to tolerate the anxieties of triadic situations had persisted throughout her life.

In spite of the validity of the interpretation, which the patient ultimately acknowledged in so many words, the analytic material that followed, marking a turning point in the treatment, had no direct connection with the purport of my message. What the patient responded to instead—probably in part as a defense against processing my meaning—was a very restricted aspect of what I had said: For the first time, the *concept* of competitive hostility became comprehensible to her in an affectively charged manner. She immediately expressed joyful excitement about the many diverse areas of her life which, previously not understood, were suddenly illuminated by this new cognitive tool. And within minutes, she turned her attention to one of the most important of these areas—the issue of her mother's poorly controlled competitiveness and the circumstances in which this competitiveness had impinged on the child. I shall not describe here the fascinating details of the manner in which this vital information emerged in the course of the next half-a-dozen sessions. Suffice it to say that the recovery of these essential aspects of her childhood experience was made possible by a decisive shift in her view of her mother brought about by an aspect of my dream interpretation that I regarded as incidental and self-evident.

Let me try to restate my understanding of the foregoing clinical transaction on a more general level and in terms of some appropriate conceptual categories. Having worked through most of the sequelae of a traumatic separation from the primary caretaker in the third year of life, this patient began to experience a progressive developmental thrust. This new development constituted the transference repetition of tentative efforts in the phallic sphere which she had made several times, abortively, in her childhood. Her fears of talion punishment for her aggressive impulses emerged in the dream of the lion in the museum which I have discussed. My attempt to direct her attention to this conflict miscarried, probably because certain traumatic aspects of her relationship to her mother were even then insufficiently understood. The same material was to emerge again after that issue was worked through, and my next interpretation of this patient's oedipal conflicts was accepted without any difficulty. This subsequent intervention on my part constituted the *successful* interpretation of a dream, and I shall therefore return to it in the concluding section of this chapter.

Although my use of the dream of the lion turned out to be premature as an interpretation of the focal unconscious conflict, it nonetheless brought about a dramatic therapeutic breakthrough. This progress did not involve any alteration in the conflict I was trying to bring into consciousness; it concerned instead the collapse of one of the patient's childhood illusions—the elimination of a reaction formation through which she had tried to overcome her disappointment in her mother. This disillusionment came about as a result of an aspect of my intervention that was incidental, but served to increase the patient's cognitive repertory. Undoubtedly, she had been prepared for the acceptance of this piece of reality by numerous transactions in the prior course of the analysis that had either diminished her need to idealize her mother or helped to reconstruct her underlying disappointment. In other words, this particular dream interpretation was by no means the initial incident in that lengthy process which, with Arnold Goldberg, I have designated "optimal disillusionment" (Gedo & Goldberg, 1973). In terms of the hierarchical schema of mental life we outlined in our work of 1973, the dream actually formed a nodal point between two modes of personality organization that were both represented in it: the more advanced realm of structural conflict (which was the one I had attempted to interpret) and a contiguous but separate manner of existence that was mainly characterized by disavowed illusions.

Nor was the task of mastering the "pseudoidealization" (cf. Gedo, 1975) of her mother completed simply because the patient finally perceived the competitive aspects of the latter's behavior. I should like to underscore this point by reporting a pair of dreams that constituted the next dramatic incident in this analysis, approximately six weeks after the events I have just recounted. In contrast to the unintended effects produced by the interpretation of the earlier dream, the results of my intervention on the second occasion were the predictable ones—perhaps for the very reason that I continued to focus on the more archaic aspects of the material. Before returning to this point, I must present some relevant clinical data.

In the course of a brief period of unusual well being, the patient began to read Barbara Tuchman's popular history of the 14th century. She became increasingly enthusiastic about the book and its intellectual power; her associations then focused on the personality of the historian, whose capacity to empathize with her subjects impressed her most favorably. She began to spin a fantasy around what a sweet woman Mrs. Tuchman must be. I interjected a comment about her need to attribute perfection to a person whom she admired for a specific and limited set of activities, a tendency that created a considerable risk of subsequent disappointment. The patient was visibly upset by these remarks, but managed, before the end of the session, to let me know that I had somehow missed the point of her thoughts about the historian. This transaction was literally without precedent in our relationship; in the past, she could only disagree with me in an indirect manner that invariably ended up in an attack of uncontrolled rage.

It was in the next session that she reported two dreams. In the first dream, she was an adolescent and was still living with her mother. She was helping to pack their belongings in preparation for a move. With a keen sense of surprise, she noted for the first time that her mother's house was in severe disrepair, her possessions in a mess. In the second dream, she was a married woman, paying a visit to some legislative body. As a matter of courtesy, she decided to sit among the Republicans, although she did not agree with them. She then found herself in an argument with a woman who pointed to the patient's wig and accused her of wearing one at all times. Despite being very distressed by this unprovoked assault, she decided to set her accuser straight: She pointed out that she only wore wigs on special occasions.

Her associations centered on her assumption that I must be a Republican. She went on to make the connection between the course of the previous session and the argument in the dream. The wig reminded her of the fact that, historically, the Republican party had replaced the Whigs on the political scene. She then explained that I had been perseverating on the dangers of idealization on the stage of everyday life: It was true that she had denied her mother's limitations, but, as the first dream clearly stated, she was now able to see them; she was, in fact, on the move! I then pointed out that, in the dream as in the reality of the previous session, she refused for a long time to articulate her disagreement as a matter of "courtesy"—in her mother's time, she had actually disguised herself as a Whig. She had seemingly idealized her mother, that is, but this outward attitude, adopted to spare her mother distress, had not represented her deeper feelings. When the patient indicated that she understood these issues in similar terms, I went on to explore the repetition of this pattern of relating to people in the analytic transference.

I should like to note that my intervention on this occasion did not constitute an interpretation of these dreams at all. The most obvious infantile wish portrayed in them was that of righteously being able to accuse me of an injustice toward her—an issue I chose to leave for elucidation on a later occasion.[1] In terms of reconstructing the relevant childhood antecedents of these dynamics, the material capped by the parliamentary dream might be summed up as follows: The patient had, indeed, suffered injustice at her mother's hands because of the latter's poorly controlled competitiveness; this flaw in her mother's character had caused the most painful disappointment for the child, but she had concealed her disappointment, even from herself, by erecting a false idealization of the mother and by identifying with the latter's faults. In this way, if she ever complained about her grievances, it would be a question of the pot calling the kettle black.

In my judgment, successful analysis of the patient's own competitiveness was contingent on prior removal of her sense of grievance about being undercut by maternal figures. This therapeutic accomplishment, in turn, required that the patient's need to erect illusions about such people be overcome.

But this is not the place to spell out further the rationale for my therapeutic tactics. Suffice it to say that, in this instance, I deliberately undertook to expand the process of "optimal disillusionment," especially within the transference proper. To put the matter differently, I applied the lesson I had learned from the patient's unexpected response to the interpretation of the lion dream by making use of the second set of dreams in a noninterpretive manner to modify a system of illusions that underlay her structural conflicts. I suspect, by the way, that most clinicians would classify such an intervention as an

---

1. As it happened, the opportunity to deal with that issue arose in connection with my next vacation. Not that she considered that in itself to be an injustice; on the contrary, she was flooded with guilt because she looked upon her own anger about the interruption as an injustice toward me. We then discovered her identification with her mother's devices for coping with guilt conflicts about her own aggression, namely, the latter's propensity to externalize her own self-criticisms. Ultimately, then, the lion that pinned the patient to the ground was her mother's skill in claiming that the child was unfairly reproaching her—when no such reproaches had in fact been made!

"interpretation," but, as I have elsewhere argued in detail (Gedo, 1979b, 1981b), we gain in conceptual clarity by narrowing the definition of that term to the translation of unconscious material into discursive language. Hence, I believe that my comments in this instance are best classified as attempts to clarify the actualities of the therapeutic relationship by continuing to use some of the metaphors the patient had provided to characterize these matters in the dream. This was the "shared language" that eventuated in the patient's optimal disillusionment and promoted the work of analysis.

III

The illustration I have just given demonstrates only one of the categories of unintended results that can follow an attempted dream interpretation: alteration of the analysand's systems of illusion. A category of similar importance concerns matters even further removed from the realm of conflicts about unacceptable infantile wishes. I refer to nonspecific responses to the analyst's communications that usually involve beneficial changes in tension levels, mitigating either stimulus deprivation or overstimulation. I do not mean to imply that such vicissitudes significantly promote the chances of ultimate analytic results. The matter is, rather, the other way around: In patients who lack the capacity for adaptive tension regulation, the repeated occurrence of disruptive crises may lead to therapeutic failure. Leo Stone (1954, 1961, 1981) has written extensively about the deleterious effects of rigid adherence to a climate of "abstinence" in cases of this very type. In my experience, it is only by helping such patients achieve more effective tension regulation on a long-term basis that analytic success can ultimately be reached.

In practice, excessive stimulus deprivation is generally avoided because analysands usually bring up a fair amount of material suitable for interpretation; much of this material, of course, takes the form of dreams. In the natural course of events, then, we have no way of differentiating the therapeutic effects of dream interpretations related to their verbal content from the effects produced by their paraverbal qualities—or, if you will, by their psychoeconomic consequences. On occasion, however, we come to perceive over time that our interventions have created a "holding environment" (to use Winnicott's [1960] term) without producing any lasting residue of insight.

Similarly, analysts are all familiar with certain patients who, driven by the compulsion to repeat, behave in a manner that forces the analyst into temporary inaction. Such patients then experience this circumstance as a catastrophic threat, often pleading for voice contact without regard to content. In such circumstances, we are not likely, in my judgment, to jeopardize analytic success by providing these patients with unconscious gratification of their oral receptive (or other infantile) wishes by talking too much. If we note their responses to our interventions, we can easily correct for such errors of overindulgence. On the other hand, we are prone to cause real damage in these patients by depriving them too drastically of the exogenous stimuli to which they are addicted, engendering panic in the process. In either case, of course, these issues must ultimately be brought into the analysis interpretively as matters of *central concern*.

I suspect that the utility of dream interpretation as an acceptable safety valve against the excessive frustration of stimulus hunger is, in fact, widely understood. I may be venturing into less familiar territory, however, in discussing the converse of these circumstances, namely, the *pacifying* influence of well-timed interventions ostensibly dealing with the latent meanings of dreams. I began this chapter by describing untoward incidents in which dream interpretations lead to storms of affect, not in response to the verbalized message but to the unconscious meaning for the patient of the very *act* of interpretation. I now wish to focus on similar events that lead in a direction that is exactly opposite to my earlier examples, that is, that lead to a diminution of tension rather than to its exacerbation.

Although such contingencies may have a number of diverse dynamic and genetic roots, I will confine myself to the eventuality which I believe to be most frequent. This is the circumstance in which the analyst is endowed with omniscience and magical healing powers (occasionally overtly so, but more frequently without conscious acknowledgment). Such a primitive idealization usually transforms interpretations into putative agents of cure for whatever happens to be amiss: If the patient is overstimulated, they effect pacification. These conditions may be quite difficult to discern as long as the patient continues to need such illusions. If we succeed in overcoming this obstacle, however, the analysand who is in the process of giving up magical ideation may produce material that retrospectively sheds light on these attitudes. I have previously published a detailed example of a clinical encounter of just this sort (Gedo, 1975, pp. 500–502) and will not duplicate that account here. I will merely repeat that, at this critical juncture, my patient's dreams gave clear evidence that she valued the analysis most of all because of my assistance in forestalling her propensity for almost hypomanic excitement. It was also evident that my interventions had gained this power because the patient viewed me as a magician: In one dream, for instance, an enormous airplane in which she was the only occupant was safely brought to the ground after a great deal of dangerous stunt flying.

Perhaps I have now described a sufficient variety of unintended consequences of dream interpretation to permit consideration of some of the general inferences we can make from such clinical findings. In my opinion, the most important lesson to be learned from them is the reminder that all psychoanalytic interventions—including the failure to intervene—have simultaneous consequences on multiple levels. In this chapter I have illustrated three of the separate modes of functioning that are routinely implicated in the responses to interventions. As I have emphasized for many years (Gedo & Goldberg, 1973; Gedo, 1979b, 1981b), there are in reality at least five major modes that the analyst must consider at all times. The modes I have previously described but omitted on this occasion involve the mode in which uncoordinated subsets of personal aims coexist, on the one hand, and the mode of conflict-free existence, on the other.

If we define interpretation as the translation of infantile conflicts encoded in the primary process into discursive language, we must expect that the result of a valid intervention of this kind will be the achievement of insight. This is such a dramatic event that its occurrence may easily screen additional consequences referable to the other modes of functioning, that is, to modes not characterized by structural conflicts. Nothing could be more reassuring and pacifying than the empathic understanding implicit in the valid interpretation of a dream—or a better guide to those perplexed by the multiplicity of their disparate goals! The multiple appeal of our interventions is therefore easy to overlook, and this circumstance has led to widespread disavowal of the importance of those aspects of psychoanalytic technique that are beyond interpretation.

IV

Lest the foregoing remarks be misunderstood, I will conclude by reiterating that valid dream interpretations continue to provide the optimal way for preparing analysands to undertake the burdens of self-inquiry. This statement will perhaps be looked on as a truism 85 years after Freud's masterful demonstration of its validity, but still another illustrative example will not overburden this chapter, if only to underscore the difference between a successful interpretive intervention and the noninterpretive transactions I have described to this

45

point. For this last vignette, I will return to the dream of the lion that opened the examination of oedipal issues in the analysis from which I have taken most of my clinical evidence.

A few weeks after the resumption of work following a vacation that proved to be less disruptive than previous interruptions of the analysis, the patient signaled the restoration of her equilibrium by reporting a vivid dream. She summed up the dream by characterizing it as a variation on the ballet *Petrushka*. It will be recalled that the protagonist of this ballet, Petrushka, is a puppet who possesses human qualities: He falls in love with the ballerina and is dismembered by a jealous rival. In my patient's dream version, there were two puppet slave girls in lieu of the hero; they had strange, tightly curled black hair. She understood that these figures represented the two aspects of her character: her conscientious and mature behavior at home versus her angry demandingness within the transference relationship. At the same time, the story of the ballet referred to her childhood love for her two maternal caretakers (her real mother and the nursemaid who actually raised her until the patient was almost three), as well as her efforts to deflect her anger from whichever of the caretakers was present onto the one who happened to be absent. I commented that her identification with Petrushka confirmed our previous conclusion that she had, in childhood, transcended the state of symbiotic dependence on mothering figures and entered the arena of triangular love relationships. She confirmed that the threatening rival for the mother's love, represented by the violent Moor of the ballet, had been a jealous older sibling. I then inquired about the meaning of the peculiar quality of the puppet's hair in the dream.

It was the chain of associations initiated by this question that permitted interpretation of the latent content of the dream. The hair turned out to be cut in the way poodles are clipped; the patient proceeded to recall that I had once alluded to this breed as particularly appealing. This association led to the sudden realization that she had recently heard from her mother that the latter's cat had died. The incident was quite remarkable to the patient because her mother was so openly and genuinely upset. She could only conclude that her mother had more feeling for this animal than she had ever had in a human relationship. The patient was at that point able to discern that, in the dream, she was expressing the childhood wish that I prefer her over all others; it remained for me to interpret that, in the present, she actually occupied the position of the jealous older sibling who wished violently to attack her rivals. In this way, the analysis of this dream opened the way to mastery of her oedipal jealousy. The dream she next reported represented a social relationship between us in which she displaced an older sibling figure; her affect in the therapeutic situation while working on this material was that of rage.

As these latter examples show, in the last year of this prolonged but dramatically successful analysis, dream interpretation finally assumed the role it has traditionally been assigned—that of the royal road to the Unconscious. In the terminal phase, the confusing effects of kaleidoscopic transference reactions could always be overcome by turning for ultimate guidance to the evidence of thoroughly analyzed dreams. For instance, the particular nature of the patient's subjective experience during the phallic phase of childhood emerged with increasing clarity in a series of dreams that continued the imagery and thematic content of the "Petrushka" material. One important signpost of this progressive evolution was a joyful dream in which the patient saw herself as a ballerina, lifted high over the head of her dancing partner. Her associations dealt with her frequent reactions of humiliation, anger, and helplessness within the analytic situation, even when our work was, in my judgment, going quite well. Indeed, she was perhaps most likely to feel that way when I was satisfied with my performance. It was subsequently possible to reach consensus on the fact that she could only derive satisfaction from our collaboration when it lifted her to a superior position.

In connection with this dream of joyous elevation above her partner, the patient was still unable to acknowledge that the underlying issue might be her need to turn the tables on men who had the power to humiliate her, especially in terms bearing on genital anatomy. Several weeks later, these issues found a reprise in a dream in which she was riding the Elevated (municipal transit) by standing on her seat. Opposite her, a man of the lower class was sniffing his own armpit and discussing the merits of a deodorant named "Seasick." She associated this dream imagery with morning sickness (sea sickness = *mal de mer; mal de mère* = morning sickness) and with certain manifestations of female vanity (e.g., the use of cologne) recently adopted by men of fashion. We were thus led to the reconstruction of her childhood conviction that women are stinky and diseased. At long last, we were able to understand her habitual hopelessness when she found herself in competitive situations involving men, a circumstance most likely to arise in her adult life in the vocational arena.

I have reviewed excerpts from the later stages of this analysis in order to demonstrate that the paradoxical side effects of dream interpretation tend to disappear if the issues giving rise to the more archaic aspects of the transference have been adequately dealt with earlier in the analysis. The solution of archaic conflicts (cf. Modell, in press) and the acquisition of competence with regard to hitherto deficient mental functions (see Gedo, 1981a, 1981b) permit new integration of the typical dilemmas of oedipal experience. Under these circumstances, dreams become amenable to traditional interpretation, and the resulting insights frequently make it possible to terminate analyses without falling into therapeutic illusions.

V

I have presented the foregoing clinical material from the vantage point of the surprise in store for the psychoanalyst who approaches the task of treatment—in the instances cited, the specific technical challenge of using dreams in an optimal manner—from the traditional perspective of invariably interpreting latent meanings. Clearly, this choice has somewhat obscured the actualities of the analytic process in the course of the treatment from which all the examples (with one minor exception) have been taken.[2] In order to avoid leaving the reader with a false impression, it will be useful briefly to review its therapeutic course.

As I mentioned previously, the analysis initially revealed and gradually helped the patient master the traumatic aspects of her chronic need to establish erotized relationships with men. A lengthy period of work followed in which, within the wider context of an archaic idealizing transference based on the infantile relationship to the lost nursemaid of her early childhood, the patient reexperienced the severe disappointment and loss of self-esteem accompanying each disruption, however temporary, of such a sustaining relationship. She relived states of empty depression, as well as the adaptive maneuvers she devised in childhood to transcend them: escape into grandiose illusions, self-stimulation through either sadomasochistic or erotized enactments, regression into symbiotic relationships (in

---

2. In a discussion of these data at the First Franco-American Psychoanalytic Encounter in Paris (March 1983), François Roustang proposed an overall conception of the analytic transaction in this case as a theoretically based indoctrination of the analysand to ascend the ladder of the Gedo-Goldberg hierarchical schema—in the manner recommended to the patient by her rescuers in the nightmare of the falling elevator. In other words, Roustang disregarded my manner of organizing the data altogether; he assumed that, contrary to the thrust of my report, I clinically operate from a preconceived framework that obliges the analysand to reexperience a specific sequence of developmental phases in analysis. I believe that Roustang is excessively suspicious about the constraints of any theory on the analyst's freedom to respond appropriately to the spontaneous unfolding of the transference. Obviously, in this chapter I actually intend to support the point Roustang overstates: that rigid application of theory does lead to the difficulties he postulates. I trust that, in practice, I generally managed to avoid these errors with this particular analysand. Further data from this treatment will be included in Chapter 9, where one such error will be described in some detail.

the course of which she experienced herself as the double of someone else), and negativistic struggles to avoid being enmeshed in the narcissistic world of the unreliable caretakers who, in childhood, had tried to undermine her sense of reality in order to protect their own self-esteem.

Reliving these archaic transferences in the analysis was, however, insufficient in itself to effect major therapeutic changes. As long as the patient could not rely on her assessments of reality, especially when such assessments involved the motivations of others, she was unable to maintain her self-esteem in the face of actual or fantasied hostility. Consequently, her competitive strivings had to be disavowed to avoid the risk of retaliation (ultimately, the threat of abandonment), and her (negative) oedipal constellation remained intractable while her symbiotic needs continued. These latter needs were transcended only when the patient learned to trust her own sense of reality; until then she could avoid confusion only by eliciting reliable judgments about her human situation from a benign and dispassionate helper such as the analyst.

After learning about the nature of the foregoing deficit in her psychological armamentarium, the patient investigated its origins in the context of the systematic "gaslighting" (Calef & Weinshel, 1982) she had undergone as a child. The understanding that followed these genetic inquiries henceforth permitted her to trust her own judgments. Following this improvement, she was able to risk the experience of oedipal involvement within the transference and gradually to give up her idealization of the analyst in manageable increments. Such "optimal disillusionment" (Gedo & Goldberg, 1973) led to spontaneous relinquishment of the analytic relationship.

The improvement in this patient's capacity for human intimacy as a consequence of the lengthy analysis was truly startling. I shall refrain from providing clinical details about these changes, however, for I have been concerned in this chapter only with matters of analytic technique, and have not described the patient in sufficient depth to make such details truly meaningful in any event. In Section II, I shall remedy this shortcoming of the foregoing presentation by describing two complete analyses at length and laying special stress on the very issues I have neglected in this account.

CASE ILLUSTRATIONS

4

A Turtle's Progress

Sheldon M., a clinical psychologist in his early 30s, consulted me about undertaking an analysis upon his return after a period of military service. To be more precise, he had wished to resume working with the senior woman colleague who had treated him before he was drafted; when he contacted her by letter from overseas, she informed him that the state of her health was too precarious to permit the assumption of long-term clinical responsibilities, and she suggested that he discuss a referral with another analyst who ultimately steered him to me. He took these steps shortly after settling his family in the suburbs and obtaining a staff position at one of the mental institutions in the area. He explained his need for treatment by recounting the saga of his recent efforts to buy a pair of shoes: Having allowed a salesman to give him short shrift by selling him an ill-fitting pair he did not like, he had returned to the store several times intending to ask for an exchange, only to be fobbed off with promises that a bit of stretching would take care of the problem. To my later chagrin, it did not occur to me that the story might also refer to his prospective experience in analysis.

In contrast to this tale of obsessional ineffectiveness, the patient exuded optimism and self-confidence about his professional prospects and his marriage. In part, these feelings were based on the positive evaluation of his former analyst, confirmed by the brief written report she sent at my request. But he had impressed most people quite favorably wherever he had been: His faculty advisor in graduate school was still assisting him with the problems of reentry into civilian life, his peers in the field were encouraging his ambition to seek psychoanalytic training at one of the institutes that cater to nonmedical candidates, and the director of research at his hospital

53

seemed to be grooming him to become his deputy. He was, in addition, setting up a part-time private practice on the strength of a number of promises of potential referrals.

With regard to the marriage, he felt that certain minor difficulties had been settled during his prior analysis as a result of confrontations about lack of consideration for his wife. During the years they spent in Europe while he was in the armed forces, she was apparently happy and productive in a civilian job on the base; she had in fact pushed him into reenlisting and was disappointed when, apparently because of his interest in his career, he finally decided to return to civilian life. He was unconcerned about her reluctance to resume her former existence as a housewife and mother. They had two children, with whom he had a somewhat distant but essentially untroubled relationship that need not concern us in this account. What did seem significant was the fact that he regarded the extramarital affairs he had begun overseas as a sign of increased integration; he felt so "confident" about his marriage that he had proposed switching partners with another couple—a plan which his wife had not rejected, but that fell through for adventitious reasons. One of his mistresses, an army wife, had also returned to this country, and he was planning to continue the affair by arranging to take periodic vacations near her home.

Despite his prevailing complacency about these matters, the patient had, in fact, sought analysis while he was in graduate school because of difficulties with his therapeutic responsibilities. Although he was quite vague in his efforts to recollect those upsetting events, I gathered that some of his clinical supervisors had been sharply critical of his approach, rating him poorly for inactivity or the failure to make conceptual efforts. I could not learn whether these deficiencies had been overcome, and if so, whether his former analysis was instrumental in such an improvement. At any rate, there was no question about the intellectual rigor of his dissertation, and his graduate program had not required its graduates to demonstrate their competence as therapists. His work in the army had not challenged him in this area, and I had the impression that one reason for his eagerness to resume treatment was his unspoken anxiety about his plan to begin private practice as a therapist.

The first analysis had lasted less than two years, and it was clear that its interruption was arranged in advance by the patient. This amounted to the enactment of an unconscious fantasy: The patient had been draft-exempt as long as he remained a student, so that he began the analysis *knowing* he would enter the service on graduation, an event that would take place within a couple of years in the normal course of his progression. Part of the meaning of this enactment

54

could be dimly discerned from his report that he had actually given up hope of getting anything from the treatment (and experienced a mild but unmistakable clinical depression as well) several months before the "interruption," apparently as a result of a chance occurrence—his realization that one of his fellow students had also started analysis with his own analyst. Given her prestige among analytically oriented psychologists in this area, this "chance" event actually had a high probability of taking place within the two-year time span.

It seemed reasonably certain that his dramatic reaction to this information echoed his feelings during the earliest event he recalled from childhood, a hospitalization at the age of six, ostensibly because of a fever of undetermined origin. The outcome of this two-month stay in the hospital was the pediatrician's recommendation that the patient's mother stop working and take personal charge of the boy when he was out of school. This prescription was followed for some time, and he remembered the subsequent months as a period of serenity. Later on, as far as his hazy memories went, his mother resumed her major commitment to the family business, and he tagged along after his only sibling, a brother five years his senior who was something of a playground hero. In adolescence, this brother became a ladies' man, and the patient was still dogging his footsteps when he took his dates to the movies. Sheldon subsequently chose the college his brother had attended, joined the same fraternity, went out for the same sports, and aspired to "screw" similar broads. When he was in high school (and his brother was already out of college), he discovered that he could surpass the latter academically, so that he was never tempted to emulate his choice of a career in management. His interest in clinical psychology was stimulated by the excellent results of the psychotherapy of a male cousin who was his closest companion in adolescence. By trying to become like the psychologist who impressed the entire family so favorably, he hoped to outdo them all; in most respects, however, he continued to feel inferior to his brother, especially in the sexual sphere. In the analysis, he soon confessed, with enormous humiliation, that he was afraid to compete in cocksmanship because he was certain that his penis was very small. Thus, he had stayed away from the kind of glamorous girls his brother preferred and tried to compensate for his "handicap" by exploiting his intellect with intellectual types. He was very proud of his wife's incisive intelligence, and he was just as ambitious for her as a potential scholar as he was for himself.

Unfortunately for him, the only family member who valued intellectual accomplishment was his mother. She had aspirations of becoming a writer before her marriage. Everyone else in the family espoused practical aims; from their viewpoint, even clinical psychology was suspect as eggheadedness. Although they earned their livings in various independent business enterprises in the setting of a medium-sized city in the Great Lakes region, the most incomparably important aspect of their lives was athletics. The patient's father had been an amateur boxer of some note in the near-legendary past, and his cousin's father was one of the first Jews to succeed in professional football. The latter's prestige was overwhelming, and the family ethos demanded that all the boys compete actively for similar achievements. While his older brother starred in phallic swordsmanship, Sheldon actually challenged their uncle on his own turf: He tried out for the high school football team. He experienced parental opposition to this venture as a stunning betrayal and dismissed his father's explicit concern about the risk of serious injury (because the boy weighed only 135 pounds) as a rationalization for envy and an unfair devaluation.

The outcome of this venture proved to be the high point of the patient's life: He turned out to be a brilliant scat-back who earned the nickname of "Shelly the Bombshell." He tried to perpetuate this intoxicating experience in college; to nobody's surprise but his own, the coaches would not even give him a chance. In desperation, he took up boxing, only to sustain some severe beatings. Shortly thereafter he dropped out of his fraternity, redoubled his academic efforts, and began to acquire the surface polish he felt he would need to tackle graduate school and life in big cities. His success in an elite psychology training program filled him with a sense of triumph over his entire family, and he contemptuously stayed away from all family members as much as he could.

It was striking that I could obtain very little additional information about the patient's childhood though, to be sure, I did not push this line of inquiry because he was clearly embarrassed by the haziness of his recollections. He could talk about living among working-class non-Jews or joining the softball team of a nearby Catholic orphanage, but even the family's domicile during his preschool years was unknown to him. Around the time of his hospitalization, they moved into an apartment building owned by his maternal grandmother, a formidable lady universally known as "the Colonel." Needless to say, both boys avoided her as much as possible. When the sandlots or playgrounds became deserted at dusk, they went to the parents' business premises (a motel located a half hour away by bus) and ate dinner at the adjoining restaurant. Then they went home by themselves, and so to bed. This story was told matter-of-factly, as if such a way of life were the most routine imaginable.

This same quality of taking things for granted characterized the patient's account of his courtship and marriage. In college, he had been keenly interested in another girl, a sophisticated person who introduced him to upper-class mores and social attitudes, but did not reciprocate his romantic feelings. He met his future wife after he accepted the hopelessness of his ambition to win this girl. The new relationship was more sober and prosaic: After he proposed in the spring, for example, she promised to give him an answer when school resumed in September, and they did not keep in touch during the interval! Similarly, she was slow to follow him to Chicago when he was about to start graduate school, spending *that* summer with her parents, even though they had been married for over a year. Sexual life was satisfactory for both, although the patient found that his mistresses were somehow more enthusiastic and therefore more exciting than his wife. He attributed his wife's low-key attitude in these matters to her superior breeding and intellect. She was seriously interested in pursuing an academic career in one of the social sciences and viewed his therapeutic ambitions with some disdain. She had consistently refused to associate with his fellow students in graduate school, a fact he thought may have been a by-product of her disappointment in having to postpone her own studies because of the children. Her pregnancies were allegedly unplanned but accepted by both of them as a matter of course.

In spite of the first analyst's optimistic report, the discrepancies between self-assessment and the reported actualities alerted me to the possibility that the analysis of this complex personality might present certain difficulties. Nonetheless, I was largely unprepared for the technical problems that emerged. Most surprising to me was the extreme guardedness and discomfort with which the patient approached the task of free association, the painful slowness of his speech, and his intolerance of any effort on my part to inquire about the nature of his experiences. The difference between this initial reaction and the *Gemütlichkeit* that had characterized the (probably) maternal transference in the previous treatment was too striking to be assigned to adventitious factors; ultimately, we came to view it as the second half of the reenactment of a childhood abandonment—the repetition of the subjective sense of having fallen into the power of untrustworthy caretakers. Indeed, his profound and instantaneous transference reaction could only be described as paranoid, an impression reinforced by the fact that he could see nothing untoward about it. Much later, we would learn that he regarded such suspiciousness as entirely appropriate because it reflected the habitual attitude of his father, especially when confronted with the unfamiliar.

Sheldon's scarce and superficial associations were occasionally augmented by the report of a dream. Although he tended to regard his narratives of such subjective events as if he were reporting on the perception of external "reality," he was familiar enough with Freud's procedures to produce some relevant associations. It did not escape him totally, for example, that a dream about being engaged in a murderous struggle with a bear who was threatening his wife might somehow refer to the analysis by way of the fact that the local adversaries of his favorite football team had been the Chicago Bears! On another occasion, it was the Palestine Liberation Organization terrorists who were trying to murder her during a bus tour skirting the shores of the Dead Sea—details associated with commuting to his office and mine in terms of the topography of downtown Chicago. But perhaps the most graphic portrayal of the analytic dilemma occurred in a dream about a football game in which the pigskin was being carried inside its carapace by a large turtle. The beast was moving inexorably downfield, but at a rate that rendered its progress almost imperceptible. The opposing players were completely fooled by this stratagem, however, and did not impede the turtle. Sheldon eventually grasped that the armored ball-carrier was a self-depiction, but his willingness to consider additional meanings of the dream could only proceed at a snail's pace, to mix our metaphors.

From the perspective of the analytic process, the most troublesome of these meanings turned out to be his determination to prevail, in what he perceived as a competitive struggle, by withholding vital information. His attitude in this regard paralleled his views concerning extramarital sexual adventures: Why would any sensible person reveal such information to people who might disapprove? He was sufficiently committed to the analysis not to *falsify* his associations, but he withheld many of them, and his thoughts themselves were often full of a self-deception that enabled him to deny the obvious with manifest sincerity. The material he divulged with the greatest reluctance concerned his propensity to become sexually excited in the course of doing psychotherapy. He was struggling against impending erections much of the time, and he could not prevent overt excitement whenever a female patient showed any positive regard for him or when a male recounted the details of some actual sexual involvement.

Sheldon had never "confessed" these problems to his supervisors during his training; moreover, he did not regard them as obstacles to the conduct of adequate therapy. He wished to conceal these matters simply because he was humiliated by what he viewed as the betrayal of his vulnerability to stimulation. I was later to learn that he and his brother had savagely mocked each other for any "weakness" in the realm of overt affective expression: The brother had called Sheldon a cry-baby if he showed any longing for his mother whereas Sheldon, for his part, had depreciated his brother because the latter was afraid of the dark and actually sought reassurance from Sheldon's presence during their solitary evenings at home as little boys.

Any attempt on my part to discuss these findings in a matter-of-fact (and, I believe, nonjudgmental) manner was perceived by the patient as a confirmation of his fears that I would be his persecutor. I did attempt to focus his defensive use of projection (e.g., by trying to elucidate the meaning of the recurrent hostility toward his wife in his dreams). These efforts were unsuccessful for a very long time, and I was progressively obliged to lower my interpretive goals to what he could tolerate before he was able to accept my interventions as helpful. The fact that I could not go beyond *naming* his reaction to his over-excitability as "humiliation" finally alerted me to the probability that the image of a turtle was a valid predictor of a very long analysis. For Sheldon, armor plating was necessitated by an extraordinary over-sensitivity to narcissistic injuries; a turtle's shell also designated a tough Shel[don]. And our work, scheduled at a minimum frequency of four sessions per week, continued for almost nine years, that is, about 15 years beyond his initial commitment to undertake analysis.

Although my tentative attempts to comment on my observations hardly ever involved conjectures about *unconscious* meanings, the very fact that I chose to intervene implied to Sheldon that I had detected some flaw in him, and he generally reacted with injured bewilderment, often followed by a dream in which he was able to transcend the laws of nature. Perhaps as a result of his familiarity with contemporary psychoanalytic writings that emphasize such themes, the manifest content of these dreams generally focused on feats of levitation. In the beginning, he would portray himself as a Superman, flying unaided by mechanical devices. Later in the analysis, when he acknowledged the sense of helplessness that gave rise to these grandiose fantasies, his dreams might find him sitting on a magic carpet (to which he associated the Oriental rug in my office). In moments of unusual sobriety, he could even dream of being a passenger in a private airplane; the magical thinking in the airplane dreams emerged in associations about impossible guiding devices that would permit stopping in midair, and so forth.

At the behavioral level, these wishes to deny and/or to overcome limitations were expressed in rash attitudes that occasionally had serious consequences. He was involved in a series of minor accidents, invariably brought about because he underestimated the risks in activities such as driving, skiing, and water sports. On occasion, his lack of prudence even endangered other people, and some of these incidents involved his administrative responsibilites at work; his cavalier decisions undoubtedly contributed to less than optimal results in a number of cases. But the most fateful of his thoughtless actions was his decision to undertake treating some of his private patients by means of psychoanalysis. He asserted with some arrogance that he could purchase excellent analytic consultation from various practitioners not affiliated with organized psychoanalysis. My efforts to connect his certainty in this matter with the disavowal of his self-doubts were characteristically experienced as depreciating, like his father's questions about the advisability of his playing football. In everyday life, alas, he acted more like the foolish hare than the wily tortoise. To be sure, he was able to read the relevant literature and master its concepts, but he experienced unending anxiety about the possibility of public humiliation in the competition with regular psychoanalytic candidates. Moreover, the prospect of actually seeing a patient in analysis soon filled him with enormous dread.

Nor was this belated recognition of his lack of readiness unjustified, as any sensible observer could have told him if he had only been able to listen. Not only was he still afflicted with the consequences of having erotized the "power" he fantasied possessing as a therapist; what was even more serious, his inarticulateness in the analysis proved to be one of the many symptoms of a very widespread limitation in his capacity to use and comprehend complex symbolic systems of communication. To give only one concrete example of the practical consequences of this deficit, he was generally unable to follow the implications of the manifold messages encoded in a motion picture. When he went to the movies, he invariably asked his wife to review for him the purport of what he had seen and, more often than not, he was startled to discover that he had grossly misunderstood even the plot. He needed similar assistance with most situations involving social interaction, as his presenting story about his inability to buy a proper pair of shoes already demonstrated. His confusion in dealing with people, or in grasping how they deal with each other, stood in startling contrast to the clarity of his thinking in the realm of abstractions: His best work in school had been in the history of ideas.

For more than a year, the yield of the analytic work was confined to the gradual elucidation of this deficit and the manner in which the patient had been able to adapt more or less successfully in spite of it by using his wife as a living prosthesis. This state of affairs was summed up in a reprise of his dream about the football-playing turtle: In the new version, he perceived that the beast was actually like a papier-mâché prop in a play, manipulated from the inside by two stagehands. His associations led to the secret competitive advantage he derived from having such a perceptive spouse. His anxiety about doing therapy was caused by her absolute refusal to take any interest in his work; she would not listen to his accounts about patients, so that he could not get her to assist him in the professional arena.

As best we could discern from the analytic material, Sheldon did not react with any resentment to his wife's limits with respect to her willingness to involve herself with his troubles. In fact, he did not feel *entitled* to her aid, but believed, on the contrary, that he was obtaining it by stealth. The unconscious hostility toward her that he wished to project onto me proved to be related to her controlling, not to say tyrannical, behavior. She had a quality of unyielding stubbornness about certain issues, and when these issues arose, she would ruthlessly disregard the feelings and even the very physical welfare of anyone else. As Sheldon was prone to injure himself, so his wife had a tendency to injure others, both literally and figuratively. From his point of view, the most bitter wound she had inflicted was her bland acceptance of his obscene suggestion that they be mutually unfaithful to each other; he now realized with real surprise that unconsciously he had desperately wanted her to refuse with indignation.

His infidelities, which continued well into the analysis and only gradually ceased as he gained explicit understanding of their meaning, had been attempts to find the empathic acceptance she could not offer and to do so without precipitating a confrontation at home. Thus, his affairs constituted fantasied revenge and, at the same time, the silent despair of a neglected child determined not to inflict his grievances on those who caused them. The issue was most poignant in relation to his wife's propensity to cling to her children (as long as they permitted it) and then abruptly to leave them to their own devices. When she insisted on intruding upon the youngsters, Sheldon was troubled with dreams of hatred for "spoiled suburban Jewish kids," like the well-cared-for children he had secretly envied and overtly despised in the past. However transparent the meaning of such productions, he received interpretations about them with incredulous detachment. It was somewhat more feasible to gain his concurrence about his outrage when the children were neglected, especially when his wife callously disregarded their distress in such circumstances.

No matter how clear he became in his own mind about his objections to various specifics of his wife's behavior, Sheldon was utterly unable to do anything about it. Generally, he could not even discuss such differences with her as disapproval of encouraging their daughter to climb into bed with them at night. When he did try to register his doubts about her procedures, it was with such diffidence and vagueness that she was justified in brushing them aside. Although his "passivity" in the relationship was obviously characterological, he had also chosen a spouse whose rigid personality meshed with his own in a symbiotic bond with a sadomasochistic flavor. Occasionally, she went too far in her unilateral control over their common destiny, and he would then become aware of feeling as if he had been kidnapped. At these times, his flying dreams turned into terrifying nightmares of helplessness, with manifest content such as having been shot from a cannon. Indeed, his wife was a colonel of artillery!

I made some efforts to correlate these issues with the recurrent dreams he had reported in which someone made a murderous attack on his wife, but he was unable to grasp that he was projecting his own hostility toward her onto these "enemies." Even more troublesome was his tendency abruptly to shift his view of their transactions into conformity with hers, so that my interpretations, based on his former reports of feeling mistreated by her, were suddenly turned into fantasied assaults upon them both. Gradually, I realized that his entire view of the world was organized by the cues he received from her; if she denied the importance of certain of his perceptions, he was unable to use them. Because she was vehemently opposed to introspection and a psychological approach to human affairs in general, whatever he learned in the analysis was undone when he came into contact with her. Well into the second year of our work, it seemed that we had reached the kind of impasse that often ruins attempts to treat children whose parents' integration depends on the maintenance of the "patient's" pathological adaptation (several examples of impasse based on such a dilemma are described in Chapter 7). I was extremely concerned about having blundered into a stalemate or even into a travesty, a pretense of being "in analysis" for the sake of the professional advantages this entailed for Sheldon.

These suspicions fortunately proved to be unjustified. Although he was most of the time trapped in a zombielike condition under his wife's influence, Sheldon's motivation for treatment was genuine, and his wish to become his own man did keep him in the analytic arena for the better part of 15 years. In this sense, his precipitous need to mimic the activities of a psychoanalyst (as well as his sexual escapades) signified that he had preserved some islands of independence from his wife, even though he needed external support to maintain them. I shall omit spelling out the details of the childhood precedents for these patterns of behavior that were already present in latency: the need for symbiosis with some caretaker and the countervailing wish to assert his adequacy and autonomy.

Ironically, then, Sheldon got his opportunity to escape the influence of his wife because of her contemptuous disinterest in his difficulties with therapeutic responsibilities. As his private practice grew and he undertook to analyze patients with only token supervision of dubious quality, his need to receive assistance with his cognitive deficit increased. He was still incapable of revealing his handicap to his consultant—quite the contrary, he tried to create as favorable an impression as he could by impersonating an urbane, sophisticated, and knowing professional. As a result, the supervisor was seriously misled about what was happening in Sheldon's transactions with patients, so that his comments, as Sheldon related them to me, were generally too far off the mark to be helpful. When an attractive young woman became panicky about the possibility that Sheldon would approach her sexually, for example, this was explained as a function of her infantile neurosis instead of being understood as an indication that, as the core of truth at the center of this delusion, she had preconsciously recognized his own sexual excitement. She was consequently misdiagnosed as a hysterical personality, and her more alarming difficulties were never explored.

In the context of skating on such thin ice, Sheldon became increasingly anxious and developed a new symptom: Whenever he had to face his supervisor or what he anticipated might be a difficult session with one of his patients, he would have a run of multiple bowel movements verging on diarrhea. In such circumstances, his analytic material would focus more and more on the specifics of the therapeutic transactions he had failed to understand, and his unconscious wish for direct assistance from me became unmistakable.

At this juncture, I made a crucial technical decision: On the assumption that we were facing behavior organized in an archaic mode as a result of the patient's multiple cognitive deficits, I altered the principal modality of treatment. In terms of the schema of therapeutic possibilities introduced in *Models of the Mind* (1973), I switched from an interpretive technique to one focused on the task of "optimal disillusionment." In this context, I undertook to demonstrate to the patient his actual disabilities. To put the matter differently, in order to gain therapeutic leverage I entered into this patient's psychological world as an instrument essential for adaptation. In practice, I chose consistently to intervene when he presented his bewilderment about his work by supplementing his cognitive capacities sufficiently to clear up his immediate confusion. To give only one illustration from innumerable instances, I responded to his report that his "analytic" patient actually thought he was about to attack her sexually by calling his attention to his failure to consider her loss of reality-testing during that transaction: Although Sheldon *was* sexually aroused, there was no question of his losing control to the extent of actually approaching the patient. In response to such monitoring of his cognitive processes, he was eventually able to correct many of his misperceptions and thereby overcome his sense of helplessness with his patient. As a result, his sexual excitement in her presence also abated.

Sheldon's attitude toward these transactions with me was quite complex. He never informed his consultant about them, claiming full credit for any improvement in his work. At the same time, some of his dreams indicated that he was fearful of being disqualified for "cheating"—in the manifest content he was a golfer who loses his own ball in the rough but illegitimately plays the ball of someone else. I pointed out that it was his refusal to discuss his difficulties candidly and not his willingness to use what he could learn from me that constituted a delinquency. Several years passed, however, before he realized that such concealment was not really to his own advantage either. The most important aspect of his reaction to my active assistance seemed to be a shift in his view of me: Instead of depreciating me as hostile and untrustworthy (in the "paranoid" manner that had characterized the beginning phase of treatment), he began to regard me as a reliable resource. To put this shift in terms of childhood precedents, I no longer reminded him of negligent babysitters or of the brother who mocked him for needing assistance; I now qualified as a coach who would train him to become a football star.

The foregoing statement would be misleading if it were understood to imply a sudden shift in Sheldon's attitude. The change was, in fact, very slow and gradual, and not without reversals and regressions; the old misperceptions kept recurring for years. Nonetheless, the area of his life which he tried to organize in accord with my perceptions of reality steadily expanded, and his use of the perceptions of his wife diminished in proportion. For the most part, she apparently experienced this withdrawal as a welcome relief. In those specific instances where it impinged on her, however, she continued to be unyielding. For example, she insisted that his plan to come to his sessions in preference to going on a brief vacation with her did not represent his own wishes but only unwarranted compliance with my directions. In such circumstances, he became literally confused; his inner state was graphically represented in dreams filled with anxiety and disorientation. The most memorable of these dreams involved his being lost at night in a vast maze of railroad tracks, desperately looking for the right train to board but without knowing where the ones passing him were headed, then being caught between two trains moving in opposite directions and panicking about being crushed.

If, during the first two years of this treatment, it seemed dubious that *anything* constructive could be accomplished, the next period of approximately four years appeared to be an endless struggle to establish a regime of truth, rationality, and common sense in the life of a person held prisoner in the proverbial Chinese cookie factory. I persevered in the face of these frustrating difficulties partly out of my own stubborn interest in pursuing whatever we could accomplish and partly because Sheldon was slowly learning to decipher the meanings of his encounters with the world as a result of the instruction I was providing. This latter fact suggested that my effort was clearly justified, although in an analytic context the process was highly unusual, to say the least. These therapeutic interventions often went beyond the effort to provide "optimal disillusionment," such as the instruction I provided Sheldon about his lack of understanding of his delusional patient. In many instances, the required treatment modality was "unification of the self-organization" or even "pacification"—measures, that is, designed to deal with contingencies stemming from sectors of the personality even more primitive than those giving rise to the "narcissistic" issues involved in the task of surrendering infantile illusions (see Gedo & Goldberg, 1973, especially Chapter 11). To give only one illustration of such an intervention, I consistently tried to bring to the patient's attention the correlation between his bouts of mucous colitis (to use his internist's diagnosis) and his repetitive pattern of overburdening himself with responsibilities that he could not adequately discharge. When he grasped this point, I proceeded actively to instruct him on how to avoid such self-induced tension states by more prudent planning: by discussing his difficulties in managing his clinical responsibilities with his consultant, for example, rather than using the latter only as a source of narcissistic gratification by trying to impress him favorably by concealing these problems. When Sheldon learned a relatively small number of comparable "common sense" measures, he was able to avoid attacks of diarrhea most of the time. From the *psychoanalytic* viewpoint, however, the most important effect of these changes was not the direct improvement in adaptation; what proved to be more fruitful was the exploration of the childhood roots of his *lack* of "common sense." That effort, of course, was by no means simple and did not succeed until later stages of the analysis.

At the stage of our work I am now discussing, the deleterious influence of Sheldon's symbiosis with his spouse was steadily narrowing, not only because therapeutic success begat success, but also as a consequence of alterations in the marital relationship that were initiated by her. To be specific, if Sheldon needed analytic support to buck his wife's objections to his obtaining better clinical training (or the excuse of professional ambitions to justify getting the treatment that could help him overthrow her tyranny), this was not necessitated by any *actual* opposition to his plans on her part; in other words, it was scarcely her fault that he was "kidnapped" by her opinions— even if she kept silent about them! She *was* tyrannical about many issues, but what he did professionally was not one of them. If anything, she preferred to accumulate a list of "grievances" (this is why

CASE ILLUSTRATIONS

she had concealed her indignation when Sheldon made his indecent proposals in Europe) in order to justify doing as she pleased about matters she regarded as vital. And her priorities had always been absolutely clear: She was impatiently awaiting the opportunity to resume her own schooling and was much too clever to object to Sheldon's professional activities under such circumstances.

Eventually, she made arrangements to begin graduate work in European history in the best department in the area. In this enterprise, she was entirely successful; her commitment gradually increased, and her interest in Sheldon and the children waned. As a result, her rigid demands shifted in the direction of forcing her family to adapt to her unusual schedule and the life style of a graduate student. She refused to dress in conformity with upper-middle-class standards, she became more and more reluctant to accompany Sheldon in leisure activities, and she became progressively less willing to serve as his prosthesis. In other words, my effort to disengage Sheldon from the symbiosis with her eventually succeeded by default. Yet, I am convinced that satisfactory disengagement could not have taken place if I had failed to make myself available to perform for him the essential functions for which he had needed her.

Nor did this task prove to be entirely practicable: We realized the full extent of her participation in his perceptual–cognitive processing only when she withdrew it altogether. At first, this occurred only when she left on trips. As she became involved in research for her dissertation, however, she absented herself more and more frequently, eventually spending several months at a time in Europe. In her absence, Sheldon became severely confused—except with respect to those of his activities structured through other external agents, such as his job or his work with his consultant. Elsewhere, he lost track of time, mislaid his possessions, forgot his commitments, lost his way, or made severe errors in judgment (leading to a new rash of accidents). The worst of his mistakes was his inability to admit that he was impaired or to acknowledge that he had any feeling of having been deserted. Not that anything he could have said would have had much of an effect on his wife—she was, at best, sullenly going through the motions of marital life. If she did not take the initiative to dissolve the household, this inertia seemed related to the fact that the status quo gave her the best opportunity to pursue her professional goals.

Consistent discussion of the phenomenology and implications of Sheldon's reactions to his wife's withdrawal gradually bore fruit: He began to anticipate the problems of having to cope on his own, to plan ahead so as to simplify his adaptive tasks, to make efforts consciously to monitor his activities with a schema of essential priorities in mind (or even written down!), and to apply consistently what he had learned in the analysis about using all available perceptual cues in order to make better sense of his experience. His skills in self-management slowly and steadily increased; it became clear that his former state of helplessness had been the result neither of constitutional defect nor the usual kinds of intrapsychic conflict—it had been based instead on inexperience and an arrogant inability to ask for assistance. As his false pride abated in the course of learning to acknowledge his difficulties, he also gained the capacity to solicit referrals from friends and colleagues, leading to a vast expansion of his private practice. But he learned most readily when I offered him *instructions*, that is, not merely a symbiotic relationship that compensated for his lacunae in functioning but, beyond such presence, verbal explanations of what he needed to learn and insistence that my interventions be apprehended as *examples* illustrating the general principles he needed to grasp. From this set of circumstances, we inferred that he had been gravely deprived in childhood of just such learning experiences. Presumably, the sitters who attended to his physical needs had not bothered to show him how to cope for himself. It turned out that even when his mother was not working, she seldom stayed at home because of her enthusiastic commitment to "community affairs." Needless to say, his wife's progressive withdrawal from the family closely echoed that childhood experience.

In parallel with these salutary developments at home, Sheldon's relationship to his work also began to change. His psychotherapeutic efforts became better planned and consistent because, for the first time, he tried continuously to *think* about what transpired and actively to *observe* the events as a participant, instead of allowing them to act upon him. Although his competence increased considerably, he was still overwhelmed by the burden of processing the free associations of his "analytic" patients. One of the latter quit the treatment in frustration, and Sheldon finally realized that his policy of concealing his difficulties from his consultant could only lead to such disasters. He cautiously began to take this supervisor into his confidence; predictably, his candor was correctly interpreted as a sign of improvement, and the supervisor's response was both understanding and helpful. But the supervisor's sharper perceptions of Sheldon's current capabilities in dealing with a difficult patient brought home to Sheldon for the first time how far he still had to go to become as adequate as he wished to be. When, as a consequence of Sheldon's greater comfort about the situation, his patient also became more candid about her dissatisfaction with his performance, he was able to face the hitherto unthinkable fact that he was poorly suited for analytic work. This conviction rapidly matured into the realization that he was subjecting himself to needless stress and frustration in pursuing an unattainable goal, that is, in seeking excellence in an area outside the limits of his considerable talents. It soon occurred to him that he could best bolster his self-esteem by setting his sights on professional achievements he would be more likely to reach. A decision to abandon these rash "analytic" adventures followed in due course.

This radical decision had immediate, dramatic consequences. Even before he altered his course with his patients (a matter of several months, in actuality), Sheldon came to the realization that renouncing his analytic ambitions would make it impossible for him to continue to tolerate the sterility of his marriage. He was able to achieve a number of related insights on his own: He saw that he had not needed affection or admiration from his wife as long as he held on to the fantasy that he would have a string of analytic patients who would fall in love with him. For him, any sign of positive transference on the patient's part signified such an erotic triumph; by the same token, his own feelings of attachment to me constituted a terrible humiliation. He was quite certain now that his only reason for staying in the marriage was uncertainty about his ability to manage properly without the assistance of his wife.

The other side of the equation involved a permanent shift in the quality of Sheldon's experience of his life as a whole. His mood shed its depressive cast, his bowel symptoms disappeared, and he became enthusiastic about the prospect of enjoying himself. Moreover, he found that, once relieved of obligations he had barely been able to fulfill, he was much better able to function adequately, without external monitors. Hence, it did not take him long to reach the conclusion that the potential advantages of having his wife in reserve for emergencies were far outweighed by the chronic frustrations of a loveless marriage. A few months after he discontinued the "analyses" he had tried to conduct, Sheldon arranged an amicable separation from his wife, to be followed in due course by an uneventful divorce. He moved to the center city and joyfully threw himself into new social and professional activities. Nor did he experience any significant disorganization from then on; his previous dependence on others for optimal performance was sufficiently overcome to reduce his reactions to "abandonment" to the occurrence of certain danger signals. The most prominent of these automatic responses recurred whenever the analysis was interrupted: He would return after such a hiatus in a state of subjective lassitude, his speech and thinking slowed to a painful crawl, his attention narrowed upon his own sensations.

This heightened vigilance about himself generally succeeded in preventing Sheldon from falling into ill-planned or dangerous activities. He was keenly aware of the importance of these changes and explicitly grateful for the therapeutic assistance he had received: He stated this as a conviction that the analysis had saved his life. His dreams also showed evidence that the basic organization of his mental life had shifted. His flying, for instance, was now represented in terms of warm-blooded creatures lacking in armor, such as bats.

I shall not elaborate on Sheldon's subsequent success in the professional sphere; suffice it to say that he carved out a respectable niche for himself in clinical psychology by specializing in activities he could perform well, such as the treatment of delinquent adolescents. His residual difficulties as a therapist involved his reluctance to be firm about his own rights and minimum requirements; we dealt with these issues as they affected his work in the larger context of their characterological significance, and that is how I prefer to analyze them now. What needs emphasis about Sheldon's professional life at this stage of the treatment is the startling diminution in the scope of his professional ambitions. He realized that he had tried to outdo his competitors through the magical influence of his sweetness, and he now faced the hopelessness of such a quest. His strivings for excellence became concentrated on his relations with women. One might say that Sheldon reverted to the more fundamental personal aims which, as an adolescent, he had abandoned in despair in favor of therapeutic ambitions. He seemed to have believed that those who can make it with women do so, and those who cannot become their therapists.

By shedding a marriage that simultaneously signified being a therapist and a patient—in Sheldon's distorted view, his wife was as desperately dependent on him as he was on her—Sheldon abandoned the identification with his "castrated" cousin and resumed the earlier one with his brother: He became a ladies' man. To his own surprise, he found that he had a great capacity for affection toward the women he dated; he was less interested in sexual adventures than in romance. As a result, of course, he became very successful indeed in the sexual sphere. In fact, on a number of occasions, his warmth and open-hearted intimacy proved to be more than certain ladies-on-the-town bargained for. He was exhilarated when he fell in love for the first time since his abortive interest in his earlier girlfriend in college. His retreat from that disappointment was not repeated in the present when, for one reason or another, his feelings were not reciprocated, although he was quite hurt on one occasion because the woman refused to believe in his sincerity. But he clearly saw this expression of doubt as *her* problem, and his self-confidence did not collapse as it had in college and, presumably, as a consequence of his mother's lack of interest in him in childhood. He went on to the next affair in a cocky way, and his enthusiasm for the new relationship equaled his ardor for the previous one. Nor did I ever again hear him complain about the size of his penis.

The fact that these improvements did not amount to a tenable solution of his phallic conflicts soon became apparent. The specifically sexual aspects of his grandiose fantasies of levitation now came to the fore in the form of a refusal to accept the impossibility of winning each and every woman. His secret formula, which he had applied in his marriage for more than a dozen years, was the demonstration of infinite patience and sweetness and a willingness to continue whatever the difficulties created by the beloved. As I have indicated, his therapeutic style was impregnated with the same repeated features. They turned out to constitute identifications with the outward behavior of his mother, especially her bearing toward her paranoid husband. Yet, it was evident from his dreams that he viewed these modes of operation as infinitely powerful tools; for example, he sent a rocket to a frozen planet, scored a direct hit, and melted its icecap. Short of achieving such miracles, he continued to feel inferior to his potential rivals, the present-day representatives of the admired older brother of his early childhood.

To a certain extent, this phallic competitiveness was displaced into the therapeutic arena. Thus, in the seventh year of the analysis, it became possible for the first time to detect a "transference neurosis" in the context of our work (in contrast to the earlier transference reactions we had successively witnessed). On the one hand, he compared his professional skills unfavorably with my activities as an analyst; on the other, he was constantly tempted to outdo me, either through renewed resort to his magical sweetness or by calculating defeat of my analytic efforts with him. This issue persisted into the termination phase, with recurrent dreams of warfare in which Sheldon and I were on opposing sides, and he was desperately fighting to prevent my final victory. On occasion, he was a conscript in my army who mutinied by going to sleep on the road instead of doing his duty. The principal area of struggle, however, continued to involve the power to manage women.

Indeed, it took Sheldon several years before he learned to become a winner in that regard. Over and over again, he chose partners who could not reciprocate his feelings, and he persisted in false hopes in the face of proofs of the hopelessness of his quests. He was unable and unwilling to articulate his needs and minimum requirements or to voice his objections when offended. Nor would he attempt to assess the motivations or personality of the women he met; his interest was aroused by the qualities his brother had appreciated as an adolescent: physical appearance, adherence to fashion, etc. If I called his attention to his disavowal of dissatisfaction and anger with these relationships, he responded as he had at the beginning of our work, when he had seen me as the embodiment of his hostility.

Thus Sheldon's relations with women simultaneously expressed his identification with his brother and attempt to outdo the latter, his wish to impose himself on people as his mother had been able to recapture his affection after his hospitalization, and his childhood resort to grandiosity in response to both oedipal and pregenital frustrations. But the development of the brother transference now took a new direction: Behind the hostile competitiveness, we began to discern a profound positive attachment. Sheldon was not only able to acknowledge gratitude for the past accomplishments of the analysis; with deep embarrassment, he realized that he was reluctant to give up the relationship. Like the tie to his brother in childhood, it was in fact the most meaningful aspect of his life. *He* had never been anxious as a little boy because his brother was there—and took care of the worrying! He now recovered numerous memories of emotional and physical closeness between them, their games and jokes and mischief in alliance against the whole world. As his anxiety about the homosexual implications of fraternal love diminished, Sheldon was able to reestablish affectionate contact with his brother who, by coincidence, had moved into the metropolitan area not long before. In parallel, his sense of humiliation about his "dependence" on me also disappeared.

Near the end of the eighth year of the analytic work, Sheldon harvested its ultimate result: He finally fell in love with a young woman who became just as enthusiastic about him as he was about her. As they cemented this relationship in the course of the next several months, the termination phase of the analysis began. At times, Sheldon thought about bringing it to a close before getting married again later in the year; more of the time, the theme of ending the work was not explicit. The day-to-day material did not differ very much from that of the last three years; it consisted mostly of detailed discussion of his dealings with his beloved (and, to a lesser extent, with his patients) and the usual analysis of dreams. The old patterns of compliance and passivity recurred in matters of smaller moment; sometimes Sheldon caught himself yielding to these temptations to fall into grandiose illusions, on the other occasions he simply waited for me to intervene, consciously unaware that this also constituted a *choice* of activity on his part until I called it to his attention. As had been the case over the entire three- to four-year span, his reluctance to adopt more rational programs steadily decreased. Moreover, it now assumed a teasing quality, thereby betraying its transference origins. The wish to draw me into this "game" was exemplified in dreams such as one in which Sheldon was watching a man about to set out on a trip in his car, only to fall onto the pavement because some practical joker "pulled the bottom out from under him." The tone of this material was an echo of the childhood relationship of affectionate abuse between the brothers. Associations led to the ludicrousness of his commanding officer in Europe who had not realized that Sheldon had arrived at his destination. For indeed, he had.

DISCUSSION

I have attempted to describe the essence of an analysis of over 1400 sessions which followed an earlier period of treatment elsewhere that served as a prelude. The analysand was a person of exquisite narcissistic vulnerability, severe impairment in a variety of perceptual-cognitive capacities, and a symbiotic way of life. Despite a difficult beginning characterized by a paranoid transference attitude, it was eventually possible to bring this analysis to a reasonably successful termination. Perhaps the most trying feature of the analytic process was the slow pace; for a number of years, we gained almost no knowledge of the patient's inner life, aside from indications about his inordinate ambitions. Because he organized his perceptions of the world in terms of his wife's cognitive capacity, he remained helplessly dependent on his relationship with her; his profound dissatisfaction with his wife's tyranny and the lack of emotional resonance in the marriage was disavowed or even projected onto those he enlisted to assist him. In times of crisis, moreover, it was acted out and rationalized.

The analysis remained in an unproductive stalemate as long as the patient's wife was willing and able to compensate for his handicaps to an extent that outweighed whatever assistance I was giving him (for comparable clinical instances see Chapter 7). Because we had no information about the first six years of the patient's life, it became possible only retrospectively to see the beginning phase of several years as a repetition in the transference of childhood reactions to inadequate substitutes for his mother. And it did not prove possible to deal with this issue or any other issue by means of verbal explanations of the operative dynamics: Whatever effects such interventions might temporarily produce were regularly undone by the overwhelming influence of the patient's wife, whose view of most matters was, of course, antithetical to any analytic formulation.

I decided that this impasse could best be overcome by offering in the analysis the symbiotic assistance that the patient required—and doing so without inflicting on him the unacceptable price he paid for such assistance with his wife. Because this program did not, in fact, clash with her best interests, she passively allowed it to succeed. The establishment of a symbiotic relationship in the analysis did not constitute a "corrective experience" any more than the relationship with his wife had, but it did allow for gradual repair of the patient's cognitive deficiencies through direct instruction. At the same time, it was only through the provision within the analytic situation of what the patient most urgently needed from his symbiotic partners that it was possible to establish a *truly* empathic ambience: Empathic intentions without provision of these missing psychological skills still leave such patients wallowing in their perplexity. But the most important finding of this therapeutic experience was the *spontaneous resolution* of the symbiotic need in parallel with the patient's acquisition of the psychological functions his symbiotic partner had had to perform for him.

As a result of this development, the realm of the patient's intrapsychic conflicts could be seen for the first time without the enveloping haze of primitive pathology that had previously obscured them. I do not mean that the emerging phallic competitiveness and its disavowed counterpart, the passive erotic attachment to fraternal figures, had ever been absent from the material, but only that neither of us had been able to focus on these issues effectively before the most primitive symbiotic needs were resolved. This final phase of the analysis, like its predecessors, lasted a long time but was otherwise essentially unremarkable.

We can approach this matter equally well from the opposite direction by noting how remarkable it was that my earlier departures from the usual activities of a psychoanalyst in no way precluded the successful analysis of these conflicts.

5

And I Will Gather the Remnant of My Flock Out of All Countries Whither I Have Driven Them*

*Jeremiah, Chapter 23-3

I

A number of years ago, I was consulted by a woman in her mid-20s to whom I had been highly recommended by friends well-acquainted with the local psychoanalytic scene. A pretty but overweight person with a winning smile, simultaneously childlike and seductive, the patient presented herself with expert dramatic flair that encompassed her clothing, her gestures, and the recital of her life story. She was seeking assistance because she felt herself in the grip of dark inner forces that skewed her behavior in undesirable ways and threatened to blight all of her enterprises. She offered the example of her relationship with the decent, sophisticated, and intelligent professional man who shared her life. Although they "loved each other"— as she understood the expression—they could not commit themselves to marriage, and she felt that she was compelled to spoil their life together by repetitively provoking conflict. They were also partners in a promising business venture that involved promotional work for cultural organizations, and she was comparably afraid that her interpersonal difficulties would interfere with the conduct of this complex project. Her most serious concerns, however, were subjective in nature: She was disturbed about her lack of self-knowledge, her inability to commit herself to long-term goals, and the puzzling volatility of her moods.

In contrast to the articulate presentation of her complaints, the patient's understanding of the origins of her plight was rather hazy.

She placed the greatest weight on the oppressive environment of her parents' household, which she had left behind on going away to college. She described an atmosphere of sterility and gloom created by her father's unceasing but private preoccupation with his tragic past as a concentration camp survivor. In actuality, both of her parents lived through the destruction of large families by the Nazis; they met and married in a camp for displaced persons somewhere in Germany after their liberation. According to the patient, they had never been willing or able to discuss the nature of their horrible experiences—possibly, they were seriously confused about the details of these unbearable events. Still conspicuously foreign after almost three decades of residence in America, they lived a constricted life in a Jewish neighborhood, managing to achieve a modest level of prosperity by operating a "mom and pop" clothing store at the edge of the black ghetto.

The patient was the second of four children. Her older sister, who had always taken life rather calmly, married straight out of high school. She now had a growing family of her own, although she remained close to the parents in every way. A sister almost eight years younger and a brother some ten years younger were still in high school; both were bright if socially inept students. Within the family, the patient had always stuck out as different: much larger than her siblings, seemingly more intelligent, but clumsy, fat, and beset by ill-health. In particular, she had a number of grand mal seizures in midadolescence; the resulting diagnosis of epilepsy had filled her with humiliation that was compounded when she grew dark facial hair as a side effect of her anticonvulsive medications. Her mother was clearly shamed by having a defective child; her father, by contrast, seemed infantilizing and overconcerned about this condition and other illnesses—allergies, bronchial asthma, infections—as well.

In spite of these handicaps, the patient did exceptionally well in school and became a leader in student activities. She had a number of friends, although she joined her mother in comparing herself unfavorably with more sophisticated and attractive girls. She also started to date, but her social life did not blossom until she went off to one of the state universities to work toward a degree in teaching. When she did become involved with someone, however, it was a boy from her parents' neighborhood; eventually she became engaged to this young man, planning to marry him upon graduation from college. As the wedding approached, she became more and more convinced that something about these plans was radically wrong; she broke the engagement practically at the last minute, despite her parents' disapproval of this decision. This event seemed to have been a turning point in her life: It not only signified a refusal to follow in her sister's footsteps as a middle-class housewife, but heralded a decisive break with everything that her family stood for.

A period of some confusion followed, during which she had fleeting involvements with a series of men, flirted with the idea of conversion to Catholicism, and moved about restlessly, all the while supporting herself as a substitute teacher. Her most stable relationship during this interval was with a "modern" woman more than 20 years her senior who became a loyal friend. Her time of troubles came to an end when she started the affair with her current lover, a serious intellectual educated at prestigious schools and professionally involved with the management of a musical organization. They rented a fine apartment in a sophisticated mid-city area and proceeded to furnish it in accord with contemporary good taste. In the context of moving once more toward a commitment to one particular way of life, however, the patient again found herself in the process of undermining the relationship. It was this realization that crystallized into her decision to seek psychological assistance.

On the basis of this information, I formed the impression that treatment would have to deal with a complex disturbance involving the organization of the entire personality. Because it was clear that the patient's financial resources were not adequate for an analysis at full fee, I kept my consultative role to a minimum and offered to find someone who would treat her under Institute auspices for whatever she could afford. She accepted a referral to a senior candidate of excellent reputation without obvious ambivalence. I was therefore quite surprised when she asked for another consultation within a few weeks. When she returned she announced her conviction that my young colleague lacked the experience and self-confidence to treat her; she had decided, therefore, to defer analysis until she could pay my regular fee, provided I was willing to work with her.

We agreed that she would contact me when she was able to start treatment on a schedule of at least four weekly sessions; the door was also left open for occasional visits during the waiting period if she felt the need to discuss any acute problem. As it happened, she notified me less than a year later that she would soon be ready to undertake analysis, and her only visit in the interval concerned the administrative arrangements we had to conclude. She explained that she had made the analysis possible by aggressively pursuing the purchase of appropriate health insurance; she procured such insurance by obtaining a job that carried the necessary coverage as a fringe benefit. Specifically, she went to work for a well-known local firm of educational publishers, helping to write textbooks for use in the primary grades. Soon after launching this new career, she was told that her ability to create fresh and interesting material suitable for very young children was quite exceptional. By the time I was able to accommodate her within my schedule, she had received a substantial increase in salary and some executive responsibility for the production of a series of "readers."

II

In certain respects, the analytic work began in an expectable manner, with increasingly dispassionate scrutiny of the patient's troublesome relationship with her lover. Now that she was bringing home a regular salary, he had given up outside employment and concentrated his efforts on their consulting business. Although he possessed the requisite expertise, somehow his efforts seldom came to fruition; even less frequently did they turn out to be profitable. The patient found herself monitoring his activities from afar, with mounting irritation. This phase of the relationship was usually followed by a crescendo of nagging and meddling on her part that produced only passive resistance on his. She might then increase the intensity of their bickering, lose her temper, and even resort to physical assault! She knew well enough that her behavior only served to demoralize her lover and render him still less effectual, but the seeming senselessness of this pattern of actions did not deter her. Although I did not convey my impression to her for some time, I gradually realized that she was enacting the role of a slave driver: The brutalities of Auschwitz were beginning to echo in my consulting room.

Needless to say, these strains had taken their toll on the couple's sex life. It is true that their sexual relationship had always left much to be desired—in fact, the patient had never reached an orgasm during coitus—but the poisonous atmosphere had gradually led to fewer efforts on the part of the man to initiate lovemaking. Instead, he spent more and more time stimulating himself by reading girlie magazines. His extensive collection of such erotica was provocatively strewn around the apartment as a humiliating reminder to the patient of her inadequacies as a woman. Her response to the punitive messages was vocal and emotive complaining—dramatic enactments of the suffering of an innocent victim.

She also compensated herself for these deprivations through orgiastic eating binges. These binges had the added advantage of fattening her up to a grotesque degree, so that her lover would be humiliated about living with a freak. To be sure, she was so ashamed of her appearance that she had to pretend to be invisible beneath her tentlike clothing in order to be able to leave the house. Yet, this shame notwithstanding, she was continuously tempted to stop shaving, so that she might become like the bearded women in the circus. Through these escalating masochistic enactments, the patient was able to create pseudojustifications for her cruelty. To take one example: Was she not the innocently injured party in view of the fact that she was lending herself to ever greater financial exploitation by subsidizing her lover's business losses? We soon learned, in this regard, that in her parents' house disputes often culminated in competing claims about who had borne the most extreme suffering. Her father, who spent almost five years as a slave laborer, generally could not be bested in this competition, but the patient had never ceased trying to do so!

Although we had hints of this kind about past precedents for various maladaptive behaviors in the present, for some months the analytic material generally remained at the level of reports about the patient's travails on the stage of everyday life. Because these extra-analytic enactments did not cease spontaneously, I decided actively to question their function in the patient's psychic life. In response to my queries, she was ultimately able to realize that she did not *love* the person with whom she was living out this drama; rather, she *needed* him to structure her existence. Whenever he failed to provide a superior program of action, however, she tended to slip into the mold of her adolescent struggles with her parents in her dealings with him.

I shall comment in greater detail below on the relevant past history shortly; here, let me highlight the crucial fact that as soon as the patient realized that her lover had only served a quasi-therapeutic function for her, she decided to dispense with the relationship and to rely exclusively on the analysis for psychological assistance. The relationship with her lover thereby lost its emotional intensity. They acknowledged that they could no longer regard each other as sexual partners, and a decision to live apart followed shortly thereafter. The fighting stopped, and they were able to stay in business together for several years, despite the fact that his methods of operation continued to obstruct profitability.

The relinquishment of this extra-analytic transference bond ushered in a phase of intense struggle in the analytic situation. In fact, it would be misleading to date the onset of this development to this time; the struggle had actually been present from the beginning of treatment, although it was initially masked by the patient's desperate effort to obtain help for her acute difficulties. As these problems receded, the patient's maladaptive behaviors within the analytic setting assumed more obvious forms. These manifestations were, from my point of view, entirely unexpected. In my judgment, it is their emergence—and the unusual technical requirements of their management—that lend special interest to the account of this analysis.

III

The simplest way to characterize the transactions I want to describe is to group them under the rubric of a paternal transference. The patient began to experience the analysis, in Freud's sense, as "after-education" (*Nacherziehung*), an ambivalently desired correction of her upbringing. It turned out, however, that before her father had lapsed into silence and introspective rumination in recent years, he had himself made serious efforts to correct what he had seen as his daughter's faulty upbringing, and her response to these hesitant homilies had been contemptuous and dismissive. The repetition of this pattern within the analytic transference took on the flavor of dealing with a particularly insolent and rebellious teenager. At the same time, this pattern of rejecting the instruction she needed left her with no more than meager skills that had alerted her father to the fact that he had to take a hand in her upbringing in the first place. In the analysis, we went through repetitive cycles of rebellion leading her to a state of bewilderment or confusion, followed by chastened appeals for renewed assistance that she would again refuse to accept.

As it happened, the analytic situation automatically brought the deficits in her psychological armamentarium into high relief. One way to approach the definition of these missing or faulty functions is to observe that the patient was utterly ignorant of the ground rules of human discourse. To begin with, she did not know how to listen to my communications. Before I had a chance to complete a sentence, she would begin to associate privately to whatever she had heard me say; even if she refrained from interrupting me by blurting out such associations, she would miss the purport of my message because of her preoccupation with her own thoughts. But, then, she was also ignorant of the need for the parties to a dialogue to take turns, so that she seldom hesitated to interrupt or even to shout me down. She did not attempt to rationalize these habits as efforts to follow the basic rule—she behaved in this manner everywhere. If she did pause long enough in her intense self-preoccupation to hear some of my words, she was just as likely to construe them in an arbitrary manner as to grasp their meaning by placing them into the context of the immediate transaction between us.

As one might expect, this inability to listen was paralleled by an equally grave deficit in the capacity to reach the listener, in marked contrast to the clarity of her exposition when she had the opportunity to prepare herself in advance. In spontaneous discourse, she could not keep in mind for more than a few moments what the listener might be in a position to follow, so that she often ended up talking past me. For her, conversation often lost its function of conveying reliable meanings; instead, she would lapse into talking to hear the sound of her own voice, like someone testing a microphone. Although she had no intention of falsifying information, she could and did say things that did not represent her own thinking, without indicating her personal attitude toward the ideas she was expressing. As with her inability to listen, these primitive behaviors were not simply consequences of regression in the analytic situation: She had always behaved in this manner, whenever and wherever she pleased. True, she had become aware of the fact that these habits were annoying to other people, but she did not feel impelled to change them. Indeed, she was convinced that they made her unique, fascinating, and daringly unconventional. Perhaps this assessment of her effect on others even had some basis in fact—many people did like her strange mixture of keen intelligence and childishness. But her manner of discourse completely prevented her from learning anything from her human contacts.

These deficiencies in human communication were by no means the only matters about which the patient's father had made futile efforts to inform and influence her; for expository purposes, however, they suffice as examples of the wide array of basic psychological skills that continued to be unavailable to her. They are suggestive, moreover, of the double dilemma with which I was technically confronted: Within the negative paternal transference, all of my interventions were aborted by the patient's contempt and negativism, but I could not make my interpretations of these or other transference reactions understood because of my patient's deficient communicational skills. It was therefore necessary to devise interventions that would overcome the obstacles to meaningful discourse and engender a shared language that could facilitate an analytic process; in the process of doing so, the patient's disavowed transference attitudes of hostile disparagement inevitably came into focus, and she was brought face to face with the system of childhood illusions that underlay her obstinate refusal to become socialized. These illusions consisted of the kind of self-aggrandizement I have already cited—including the patient's belief that her disruptive behavior would be appreciated by others as entertainment—and the parallel depreciation of her father and everyone else who echoed his views of social propriety.

Before I describe the specific techniques I used to circumvent the problem in therapeutic communication, it may be illuminating to spell out the steps that were sequentially employed to effect "optimal disillusionment" (Gedo & Goldberg, 1973, pp. 120, 164–168) in this area. It should also be noted that the change I will report only took place gradually, through a process of working through equally taxing for analysand and analyst alike. It was perhaps least difficult to establish that she always missed something of potential utility if she failed to register what I was trying to tell her; I also underscored this lesson by confining my remarks for some time to pragmatic issues that gave her trouble when she was on her own. Once my credentials as someone worth hearing out were established, I could begin cautiously to point out various matters about which the patient's naive self-confidence was unwarranted, such as her fantasy that her frigidity would not be a handicap in her relations with men. Still later, this process of countering her grandiosity (in hopefully "optimal" increments) was retrospectively extended into the past. The outcome of this exploration of childhood was a host of memories that radically altered our understanding of the patient's development.

IV

The patient's contempt for her father went back as far as she could remember, to the period before she started school. In later years, this contempt was confirmed and reinforced by her mother's open disparagement of his abilities and common sense, but it probably originated at the time of his incapacitation by a severe and poorly treated physical illness for a span of over two years, roughly between the patient's third and fifth years. (Eventually, his functional capacities were dramatically restored through appropriate surgical intervention.) The mother's complaints about the father centered on his allegedly joyless attitude to life, his passivity in business affairs (which had purportedly allowed a former partner to defraud him), and his inconsiderate sexual demands. But beyond these significant charges, there was a much graver indictment: The father was declared to be crazy because of his open and fervent espousal of Jesus as his Savior. Of this matter, the children could not be in any doubt: Their father attended church on Sundays, attributed his survival in Nazi captivity to his Christian belief, and looked upon the Holocaust as the mark of Divine displeasure with the Jews because of their rejection of the Savior's message.

As the patient reviewed these issues over a period of years with my encouragement, her mother's viewpoint came to lose its cogency. It was no doubt true that the father was a sober man who took his family responsibilities with unusual seriousness, but, as his vigorous sexuality demonstrated, he was quite able to enjoy the pleasures available to him under difficult circumstances. His business acumen was vindicated by the success of his store after he bought out his partner. As for his alleged propensity to let others take advantage of him, this appeared to amount to no more than a superficially accommodating bearing, in contrast to his wife's rash quarrelsomeness with customers and employees. He was, in fact, quite a shrewd operator who had already made a good living as a black marketeer in the Germany of 1945.

The father had always possessed unusual caution and foresight. At the age of 21, when he was deported to Auschwitz, he survived the week-long trip in a sealed boxcar because he carefully hoarded his supply of food and liquids in expectation of the great scarcity that was to follow. As a skilled construction worker, he was assigned to the crew that built and maintained the *Lager*, but his five-year ordeal ended only when he was at the point of death, reduced to a desiccated skeleton of 60 pounds. At some point within this time span, a kindly German soldier gave him a crucifix, with the promise that Christian faith would save him. It does not seem implausible to attribute to his ensuing religious conversion his capacity to endure the extreme hardships that followed without a collapse of morale. Thus at the time the Nazis evacuated Auschwitz, he claimed to be the only person on the journey to Germany still able to endure beatings for climbing under the moving train to ingest lubricants, in preference to engaging in the prevalent cannibalism. As I learned more about his story, I found it ever more moving and inspiring, and my reaction—which I never bothered to conceal from the patient—permitted her to see her mother's attitude toward him, and her past own feelings, as strangely inappropriate.

The mother was entirely unwilling and unable to deal with her own experience of the Nazi persecution, and she stopped her husband from talking about his experience, if necessary by mocking his martyrdom. If pressed to recollect her life in wartime, she gave a vague account, as if she had been the heroine of a romantic adventure. Her family lived in Lwow, a city occupied by the Russians in 1939, so that her exposure to the Germans, who arrived in 1941, was much shorter than her husband's. It took the Nazis some time to deport the Jewish population of this major center; as we pieced the story together, we determined that the patient's mother was in captivity for less than three years. Her entire family reached a transit camp from which her older brother escaped to join the Partisans. When the Germans threatened to execute the remaining family members in reprisal, the boy voluntarily returned to the camp and his death. The patient's mother idealized his sacrifice, which effectively saved his three younger siblings—herself and a sister and brother even younger.

Although they were separated from the parents, who subsequently disappeared, these teenagers were used as forced laborers and eventually found one another at the end of the war. The patient has never been able to learn anything further about these events from her mother, but the latter's younger sister, though equally reticent about other aspects of the story, volunteered with great emotion that her own life was repeatedly saved by the older sister's devoted vigilance during their captivity. None of the survivors was able to acknowledge that the parents had perished; they maintained fantasies that they would some day return from exile in the Soviet Union.

When the sisters married a pair of friends in the displaced persons' camp after liberation, they were able to stay together and subsequently move to the United States together. Once in this country, the patient's mother apparently reverted to the patterns of behavior that had characterized her as a young adolescent in Poland: She became "fun-loving," exhibitionistic, flirtatious, a "comedienne." She was preoccupied with the lives of movie stars and entertainers, and with the bodies of her daughters as commodities that might gain her entry into this glamorous world. At the same time, she made no effort to become Americanized in other respects, with the consequence that the patient was scarcely less humiliated by the mother's foreign speech and appearance than by her father's "craziness."

It took several years of analytic effort to put these facts into sufficient perspective to allow the patient to abandon her defensive "pseudoidealization" of her mother (cf. Gedo, 1975). Ultimately, she came to the conclusion that her mother was childlike, basically inoffensive, but utterly unable to contribute anything more to the upbringing of children than one would expect of a preadolescent babysitter: She was completely absorbed by the task of safeguarding them from the dangers that had threatened her little sister under the Nazis. As I saw it, this woman's thinking was frozen at the level of a myth about her own childhood so divorced from the actualities of current life as to render her essentially delusional. Specifically, she fantasized that her childhood had been a period when she was a cultivated, upper-class personage whose expectations of entitlement had been met by her environment. I have never been able to form an opinion about the likely onset of her state; it may have begun with the family's deportation, but it may also have been a preexisting condition. Some of the mother's American relatives, it should be noted, appeared to suffer from similar psychopathology.

On the basis of the historical information about her parents, we gained fresh understanding of the patient's failure to learn basic human skills such as the rules of conversation. On the one hand, many of these deficits actually constituted direct identifications with the style and behavior of her mother. As such, they tended to drop away as she gave up the defensive idealization of mother and faced the pain of her childhood disappointment in her. As the other side of the same coin, the patient's negativism also protected her from further identifications with the parents or their surrogates, for such new learning might well prove to be as unserviceable as some of the habits she had already absorbed at home. To give only the simplest of examples, she had never been taught the rationale of any household procedure. Matters such as the use of soap in washing dishes appeared to her to be senseless rituals enforced by the slave drivers who commanded the parental generation. Hence, by dispensing with such rituals, she asserted her refusal to join the parents in their servitude. To be sure, her father, as I have mentioned, had noted many of these eccentricities and tried to instruct her in more rational conduct. Whenever his views differed from those of the mother, however, the patient's unconscious rejection of the mother's ways was abruptly transformed into a conscious protective attitude that buttressed the reaction formations that defended her against this disappointment.

One way or the other, whether through identification with mother or the negativism that protected her against such identification, the patient remained astonishingly unprepared for effective functioning as an autonomous agent. Even before starting school, she had realized that she had to get away from home in order to become a person different from her mother and from the older sister who remained within the mother's orbit: At the age of four, she literally refused to be seen in public with her mother because she wanted to affirm her separateness.

But the patient's childhood efforts to assert her individuality only drew criticism from the mother, whose sole interest, as far as her daughters were concerned, was the cultivation of their sexual appeal. The patient's intelligence was never appreciated, as her older sister's conventional good looks monopolized the mother's attention. Hence the patient's failure to learn was also motivated by spite: Because she could not gain her mother's approval by improving her performance in most of the ways people generally consider important, she was filled with pain and anger for reasons which she could not acknowledge. Unconsciously, however, she retaliated by provoking her parents by disappointing their expectations: She remained fat and hirsute in order to distress her mother at the same time as she strove to be ignorant, incautious, disorderly, and rude in order to distress her father.

V

The patient's characteristic rudeness may be the best point of entry for a discussion of the technical measures necessitated by her enactment of the Babel of confusion that reigned in her family home. I must reemphasize, in this connection, that this pattern of behavior did not simply reflect the emergence of an archaic transference (cf. Gedo, 1977)—as the patient later explained, she had to exercise conscious self-control of the highest order to refrain from such behavior for more than a few minutes anywhere. She had been desperately worried about these barbaric outbursts on her part for some time. Indeed, it was the early occurrence of some outrageous piece of rudeness toward the student-analyst, accepted without comment, which convinced the patient that he would be unable to handle her problems. She realized that her violent scenes with her lover echoed her mother's uncontrolled behavior at home; moreover, the young man's passivity in response to her assaults—worse, his subtle retaliation in the form of humiliating her with his erotica—provoked her into paroxysms of fury, precisely because it failed to provide the kind of external control her father usually imposed on her and her siblings when he was witness to their misbehaviors. For instance, when, as a young teenager, she was cruelly teasing her little brother, age three, taunting him with being a girl rather than a boy, her father stopped her with a thunderous command to cease tormenting the child; he demanded for good measure that she acknowledge that the boy had "a cock"! A man after Freud's heart. . . .

In responding to the patient's violations of the usual rules of human discourse, I decided to follow the guiding thread of my own affective responses. For example, I might feel misused, like a slave laborer(?), if she failed to respond in any way to a direct question, such as, "I do not understand; what did you mean?" Under such circumstances, I would with great intensity and a purposeful display of the emotion I was experiencing, demand an explanation of the meaning of this behavior. If she expressed bewilderment about what I regarded as misconduct—this was generally the case at first—I might tell her that ignorance of the law would serve as an excuse only once; from that point on, I could hold her responsible for maintaining ground rules which we would then proceed to establish.

Would she agree that it was inadmissible to ignore a direct question from a collaborator? When pressed in this way, she would invariably agree with the dictates of common sense; henceforth, recurrences of the same behavior could be interpreted as the *acting out* of hostility or provocativeness that should preferably have been communicated in words.[1]

To give a further example of how I might deal with the patient's disruptiveness within the analytic situation: Whenever I became aware of the fact that she had failed to ask for clarification about some statement of mine that escaped *her* understanding, I would insist on immediate attention to this neglect on her part. On most occasions of this kind, she would subsequently acknowledge that she had dealt with a moment of embarrassed bewilderment by disavowing that it could be of any importance to learn what I had meant. I responded to such confessions in one of two ways: either by stressing the actual significance of the substantive issues she had tried to dismiss, or by underlining the personal outrage of a speaker whose views are treated so cavalierly.

In this way, she soon learned that the cost of protecting her self-esteem by depreciating others far exceeded the momentary strain of facing the displeasure of one's interlocutors. Through her refusal to pay heed to everything unfamiliar, she had actually managed to remain astonishingly ignorant of the world, for her policy shut off the most fertile source of information, that of oral discourse. Over time, this policy locked the patient into a vicious circle: As the lacunae in her fund of knowledge became more and more glaring as she progressed in life, it became ever more humiliating for her to acknowledge them. She was able to compare herself, accurately, to a successful photographer who employed her to tutor him to overcome his illiteracy—aside from herself, nobody knew of the man's inability to read, because it was simply too painful a secret to betray. Her own horizons remained limited to her personal experiences; she read neither books nor newspapers and confined her leisure-time activities to the world of pop culture.

Though consistent efforts to point out the self-damaging and objectionable aspects of her failures to communicate adequately, I

1. From the standpoint of the treatment modalities I have adumbrated elsewhere (Gedo & Goldberg, 1973; Gedo, 1979b), my insistence that this patient "explain" to me the meaning of her behavior partook of both "unifying" and "optimally disillusioning" therapeutic strategies. On certain occasions, that is, my insistence had a primarily unifying import in making her confront the fact that the same person who was being nonresponsive was the person who was allegedly interested in obtaining analytic assistance, which could not be effected on such a basis. On other occasions, my insistence was optimally disillusioning in making her come to grips with the self-destructive implications of what she was doing.

was gradually able to obtain the patient's consent to a set of reasonable ground rules to govern our discourse. This consensus did not end her rude behavior altogether, but it did reduce the frequency of such incidents. The patient adopted these ground rules as ideals to be followed; if, on occasion, she failed to live up to them, her behavior could henceforth invariably be construed in terms of unconscious aims in conflict with her wish to collaborate with me—as a function, that is, of ordinary transference vicissitudes. Our focus on her psychological deficits, in other words, gradually permitted her to acquire the skills she needed to become a workable analytic patient. Her interpersonal relations at work and in social life improved at the same time, leading to revolutionary changes in her daily activities.

One of the fruits of the exploration of the transference vicissitudes that continued to produce episodes of uncooperativeness in the patient's behavior within the sessions was an expanded understanding of her behavior disorder in childhood. Her rebelliousness had not begun in adolescence; it extended as far back as she could remember. Reliable witnesses (who were not members of her immediate family) testified to the fact that she had been an uncontrolled and ragefully imperious child even before she had learned to talk. These observers attributed her misbehavior as a toddler to her parents' failure to provide external controls for her. On the basis of the parents' own testimony, we concluded that there had always been an important distinction between the policies of mother and father. Her mother's attitude was one of negligent *laisser-faire*; her father, on the other hand, was excessively concerned and could not bear to let the baby cry. Because she apparently cried a great deal, partly as a result of frequent illnesses, he spent much of his time at home carrying her about in order to pacify her.

In retrospect, the patient was able to accept my judgment that the behavior patterns she had learned from her mother or developed in reaction to her family could justly be compared to the human degradation that Eugene Ionesco satirized in his parable of 20th-century man, *Rhinoceros*. Not that I could communicate such a conclusion to this young woman—if she no longer thought that anyone familiar with the name of such an author must be bizarre, she still would have shriveled up with humiliation at being needlessly confronted, once again, with her lack of knowledge. It was always safer to avoid using allusions in talking to her; by contrast, she was very quick to grasp the meaning of metaphors. Consequently, I dubbed her "the crocodile." Far from being insulted by this designation, she was both amused and challenged to acquire the virtues that would qualify her as fully human in my eyes. She made it clear that, if anything, she considered my verdict to be merciful, for the very decision to seek analytic help had started her on the path of repudiating selfishness and sadism, so that her behavior was already partially tamed when I met her.

VI

The patient's decision to separate from her former lover some six months after the beginning of the analysis produced a variety of beneficial results in everyday life beyond the crucial changes it brought about in the arena of transferences. Instead of pouring herself into the losing battle to transform this neurotic man into a "winner," she began to take over the functions he had formerly provided for both of them, if necessary by seeking instruction from appropriate people. She learned to keep her apartment clean and orderly, to manage her budget and her checkbook, to file income tax returns, to brush her teeth and wash her hair, and even to prepare reasonable meals for herself. This acculturating process was lengthy and gradual, marked by false starts, wrong turns, and angry retreats into her former ways. At length, it became possible for her to entertain cultivated people, to attend respectable public events, and to do business with executives in the communications industry. She lost enough weight to become attractive, began to dress well, to have her facial hair removed by electrolysis, and to avail herself of the best medical care available to bring her various health problems under control. She renewed contacts with her family, became helpful to her younger siblings who were attending college at the time, stopped fighting with her mother, and established, for the first time in her life, a respectful and trusting relationship with her father.

At work, she began to exercise leadership, instead of ingratiating herself with coworkers, including the clerical help, by exchanging inappropriate personal confidences. She had done well as a writer from the first, so that she was soon put in charge of a team engaged in parallel projects aimed at different grade levels. After less than a year of analysis, she was able to renegotiate her contract, receiving a level of remuneration commensurate to that of middle-management executives. She initially approached the writers whose work she was to coordinate and supervise as if she were their younger sister, but at crucial junctures realized that her responsibilities entailed the assertion of authority. Eventually, she became an effective team leader. The series of books the team produced, anonymously, was phenomenally successful, selling more than half a million copies within a year.

In view of these highly favorable developments, the patient's continuing subjective uncertainty about herself was a source of unending surprise to me. She was by no means committed to writing textbooks for children, nor did she consider herself more expert in this field than in any number of other fields. Occasionally, she toyed with the idea of obtaining an advanced degree in education, mostly as a public relations gimmick to buttress her bargaining power, only to realize that such paper credentials were now superfluous for her. Just as often, she made plans to attend a graduate school of business in the belief that her greatest talent would prove to be marketing. This plan was also laid aside because she already seemed capable of selling anything.

Periodically, she had a bout of enthusiasm about the business she still ran as a sideline with her ex-lover. If only his own psychotherapy would help him overcome his inability to earn a profit, she believed, they would be able to compete successfully as consultants to cultural organizations. From time to time, one of their projects made something of a splash, and she was tempted to launch similar—but profitable!—ventures on her own. Then again, her newfound realization of the recent tragedy of the Jewish people awakened her interest in the Zionist ideal, and she began to dream about moving to Israel, where her multiple talents would be *needed*, instead of having to be peddled for commercial purposes. She dreamed of becoming an Israeli political journalist or even a politician.

In some distant future, she could also see herself as a married woman, even as a mother, provided she could find a man sufficiently exciting to render worthwhile the requisite interruption in her career. The men she encountered in Chicago certainly never qualified; they were, in general, at least as disturbed as her former lover, but without his assets of intelligence and helpfulness. She tended to characterize them, drawing on her parents' Yiddish, as *Auswurfen* (scum). In this context, she began to appreciate that her father's moralizing disapproval of premarital sex was not simply a reflection of generalized anhedonia—perhaps there was really no point in having anorgasmic coitus with an *Auswurf*! She was very occasionally excited about a truly intelligent man, such as a glamorous television producer she interviewed, but she surmised that such people would only be interested in starlets of irresistible sexual appeal. She conceded that, on the grounds of intelligence alone, I seemed to be on a par with these people, but, to her own surprise, she consistently thought of me as utterly sexless, that is, as the embodiment of her father's Christian morality.

The chaos of the patient's mutually exclusive aims, each aim equally cherished but just as easily abandoned when something that seemed easier to attain came along, occupied the forefront of analytic attention for the better part of two years. There was a brief period of respite from this disorganization toward the end of the first year of treatment. Specifically, when I took my major vacation that year, she managed to obtain a place on a junket sponsored by the Israeli government for young Jewish-American "opinion makers." She returned from this trip fired with exaltation, largely because of the moving and impressive congress of concentration camp survivors that took place in Jerusalem at the same time.

In the aftermath of this trip, she was determined to conclude her analysis as rapidly as possible in order to emigrate to Israel. This plan also happened to serve the function of rejecting me at a time when she felt rejected as a consequence of my lengthiest absence to date. Furthermore, it perpetuated her repudiation of her father's preferences: He was firmly opposed to Zionism, advocating instead the assimilation of the Jewish people into the Christian civilization which, in his view, surrounded it. But these transferential elements did not constitute the strongest motive behind the patient's fantasy. Not only was she permanently captured by a Zionistic ideal that could assimilate her aggressiveness into its service; she also felt that in Israel her origins would be transmuted from the handicaps they had been in America into decisive advantages that would permit the realization of her highest ambitions. Golda Meir had returned to Zion with less!

To be sure, this inspiring program of action faded from her consciousness within a few weeks, despite my assurances that her analysis did not have to stand in the way of its realization. If it were most practical for her to go before our work was finished, I offered to find a competent colleague in Israel who could continue the analysis with her. Although she made it clear that she would prefer to postpone the move until the analysis was successfully terminated, the principal reason for her loss of immediate interest turned out to be different. During her trip, she had met a senior Israeli official who volunteered to show her around privately in the intervals between group activities. This dashing, middle-aged reserve officer seemed to single her out for attention and instruction about Israeli affairs because he formed the impression that she was a woman of superior abilities. In his judgment, her embarrassingly unfashionable figure was a negligible impediment to their relations, one about which he could speak with humorous candor. Although these negotiations had hardly passed the bounds of a mild flirtation, the patient expected to hear from her colonel imminently. As weeks went by without word from him, the glamor of Israel also faded in her eyes, and her usual chaotic planlessness returned.

Alerted by this sequence of events to the probability that the patient's failure to adhere to a coherent set of priorities was a consequence of disavowing an actual preference for a romantic attachment to an admired man, I subsequently began to focus my interventions on her refusal to work out any reasonable program of action. In other words, I attempted that unification of personal aims which, in my work with Goldberg (1973), was defined as the crucial task in personalities characterized by disorganization. Consistent attention to the patient's disavowed wishes to have a serious relationship with someone like the colonel soon led her to realize that she was, in fact, chronically lonely—that she wanted to be part of a family, to have a husband as well as children. Much to her father's relief, she solemnly promised him that she would meet his aching concern about her future by soon settling into the security of marriage.

As it happened, the patient's initial efforts to meet suitable men did not succeed. Although she was introduced to several people who became quite interested in her, none of them awakened her enthusiasm as had the man she met in Israel. The most serious prospect appeared to be a brilliant young Jewish professor of finance, who was dazzled by her guttersnipe vitality; in her view, however, he was dull and desiccated. A future of pouring tea for faculty wives in the drawing rooms of a university neighborhood filled her with horror. She compared herself to the Israeli Minister, Ariel Sharon, ill-suited for diplomacy but indomitable in leading his armored divisions into combat. In exploring these aspects of her deepest ambitions, she gradually became aware of the fact that comparing herself to Prime Minister Meir was no idle pleasantry: She wanted to lead and protect the Jewish people as she had always shielded her own mother, as her mother had reputedly saved her little sister, and as her mother's older brother had sacrificed his life to rescue his family from the executioners.

VII

As the patient thought through her priorities for the future, it became apparent that the Israeli colonel had excited her in an unprecedented way because a fantasy of sharing life with him could simultaneously accommodate at least two aspects of her early childhood goals and values that had until then remained irreconcilable: her identification with the one truly admirable aspect of her mother, the latter's combativeness in defense of her kin, and her disavowed love for her father and his family values. The colonel united these aims in his own person: He had fought well for his people, but his government had detached him from military service because he was even more skilled in the arts of peace. He was comfortable in his pride as an Israeli, but was able to value the Arab civilization that surrounded his country. Likewise, he was the devoted father of several children, but was able to let them take their own risks, in contrast to the fearfulness of the patient's own parents about the dangers of an alien community.

In the middle of the second year of analysis, while in the process of clarifying these matters, the patient received a message from Israel that the colonel was on his way to America on official business. If she would welcome him, he could arrange a couple of stopovers in Chicago; whatever she could do to publicize his mission would be of great help to the Israeli cause. She was galvanized into immediate action, not only setting up a series of meetings and interviews for him in Chicago, but phoning the responsible executives of national television networks and succeeding in arranging appearances for his delegation on a number of news programs. During his first visit, in the context of their mutual fervor about the cause, he declared that he was falling in love with her; before his departure for Israel, he told her that his feelings echoed those he had felt for his mother, who was murdered by Arab terrorists during his adolescence.

The patient was utterly unable to believe in the sincerity of these heartfelt, even poetic, declarations. In her eyes, she was once again disgracing herself with an *Auswurf*, this time with one who was married, for good measure! Her suspicions were heightened by the infrequency of the colonel's subsequent communications; she did not trust his explanations that he could not write an acceptable English letter and could seldom spare the money for international telephone calls. Whenever she did hear from him, he asserted with increasing conviction that he wanted her to move to Israel so that he could share her life, but she heard these appeals as the blandishments of an accomplished seducer. At the same time, she cast a pall of uncertainty over the nature of her own feelings about him. She admired his passion and eloquence, his wide culture, and his humanism, to be sure, but she questioned whether her infatuation was more than a displacement of similar feelings toward me. Was he not old enough to be her father, after all? Or perhaps she was simply luxuriating in the unprecedented narcissistic gratification of being desired by an *adequate* man.

The complex unconscious motives behind these obsessive doubts were gradually brought to light in the course of the next several months. At one level, she was simply too angry about the man's residual loyalty to his family to acknowledge that she wanted him. This denial, moreover, could be rationalized on the ground that he was simply too old to be taken seriously in the long run. In another sense, she had to justify her own deep reluctance to leave Chicago—

that is, her own loyalty to her family and, in the transference, to me. Her younger sister was now engaged to be married, and her brother's predictable success in a difficult technical vocation would require his departure from the Chicago area. Thus the task of looking after the parents in their approaching old age, she felt, really fell upon her. She now realized that, if anything happened to her father, her mother would be unable to cope with the complexities of American life. In fact, almost everyone in the family now looked to her, as the most competent among them, for advice.

She also felt guilty about appropriating the husband of a decent middle-aged woman who had borne the man a fine brood of children. She knew that her father's puritanism did not countenance adultery or divorce—in fact, her need to erect him into an externalized conscience was so strong that she was convinced that he would disapprove of her enjoyment of sexuality even in marriage. I expressed strong skepticism about this fantasy, and I challenged the patient to ascertain the facts about her father's attitude by discussing these matters with him. When she did so, her father did not conceal his personal distaste for violations of sexual morality as defined by conservative Christians (or in the lamentations of Jeremiah!) but he also expressed shock—even outrage!—at the thought that a grown person would ask someone else to sanction such personal aspects of her own behavior. This transaction had a decisive effect in inducing the patient subsequently to accept full responsibility for her own moral standards.

As for the "oedipal" guilt she experienced at the prospect of appropriating the colonel, she soon had to face the fact that he was no possession over which women could fight or appeal to King Solomon for judgment. He made it clear that his marriage had never meant much to him and had entirely ceased to matter years ago; as for his children, he expected the patient to accept them with affection, for he intended to maintain, even to increase, his commitment to them. Under the circumstances, she soon realized that guilt over "oedipal" fantasies was an effort to uphold an illusion of power in a situation of helplessness: The colonel was no more *hers* than I was, or than her father had been in childhood.

With respect to these conflicts, perhaps the most archaic of the infantile motives to emerge from repression was the patient's phallic competitiveness. She had dreams of swordfights with Middle Eastern warriors whose fearsome weapons reminded her of the colonel's impressive sexuality. These associations led her to the realization that joining forces with him in Israel would mean the renunciation of her political ambitions, at least for the foreseeable future, for his position in the bureaucracy required his companions to exercise absolute discretion and organizational loyalty. She had to face her reluctance to adapt her behavior to the needs of others and her continuing propensity to impose her preferences on those around her—family, coworkers, lovers, and analyst as well. We could now understand her former rudeness and misbehavior within the analytic situation as the enactment of a phallic duel.

During the vacation period that marked the end of the second year of analysis, the patient arranged to return to Israel in an effort to resolve her uncertainties about the plan to live there, with or without the colonel. She had a triumphant experience once again and resumed our work with the same determination to put childish things behind her that she had briefly evidenced a year earlier. It turned out that the colonel had really meant what he had been telling her: He was actively negotiating a separation agreement with his wife and purchasing his own living quarters in a different community. He planned to initiate divorce proceedings after taking possession of his apartment in the winter, and he hoped that the patient would be able to join him in the near future. If her personal affairs required her to stay in Chicago for more than another year, he was even prepared to ask for a leave of absence to spend time with her here. She also ascertained that she had a number of interesting employment alternatives in Israel, especially if she took advantage of the colonel's extensive network of friends. Moreover, he promised to arrange a year-end vacation that would permit him to visit her in Chicago so that they could firm up these plans.

Under the circumstances, the patient could no longer disavow the genuineness of the relationship with this man, and she made a decisive commitment to share his life. Instead of the oedipal and phallic concerns that characterized the months leading up to this decision, her anxieties now began to focus on separation and loss. On the one hand, she became fearful about the possibility of losing her lover through illness or death, the volatile political circumstances of the Middle East understandably fueling her concern. On the other hand, she became painfully aware for the first time that her plan involved losing me. The analysis, that is to say, now entered its phase of termination.

VIII

At first, the patient thought about going to Israel to be married as a remote eventuality, or one that might still be aborted by some calamity. She was not preoccupied, in this connection, with the extent of our unfinished analytic business; rather, she focused her growing anxiety on her new assignment at work, that of leading a team of writers in developing a second series of graduated curricular materials to parallel the successful books she had earlier helped to produce. The responsibility for this venture was exclusively hers; she had recruited the entire project team, whose livelihood now depended on her leadership. It was no coincidence, of course, that all of the writers were women and that the *esprit de corps* among them approached that of a sorority: The patient had recreated the emotional position of her mother in captivity. She experienced the intellectual challenge of her job as a matter of life-and-death, and she could not conceive of abandoning her friends to their fate by leaving for Israel before the project was completed.

Her conflict between loyalty to helpless women and heterosexual commitments was dramatically brought to a head by the colonel's eagerly awaited visit at the end of the year. As if to introduce her into the fabric of his life in Israel, he managed to bring along one of his best friends, a sober and pragmatic businessman who was able to give the patient much practical advice about her prospective move to their country. In the setting of this emotional reunion with her beloved, the patient's coital frigidity finally disappeared, and she could no longer maintain that she would have to postpone marriage pending the accomplishment of her editorial venture. She began to daydream about leaving Chicago in the course of the next calendar year. Moreover, she wanted to try out her ability to manage without analytic assistance before her eventual departure, so that a termination date preceding that event by several months seemed optimal to her.

The colonel's return to Israel then brought the other side of the patient's ambivalence to the fore. On one level, she dealt with her sense of loss by skipping a menstrual period and gaining some weight; she realized that she was disavowing the significance of "losing" a particular person by compensating herself through this transient pseudocyesis. On another plane, her lover's renewed absence led her to reexperience her childhood anger about the unavailability of her father during his period of ill-health. In this context, she felt subjectively insecure about herself for the first time in 25 years: She wanted me to confirm her judgments and turned to a number of friends for various kinds of emotional support. In other words, her reluctance to separate was not exclusively motivated by guilt and loyalty; she had to acknowledge her own symbiotic needs in an explicit manner at this time.

On the basis of the foregoing behaviors, we were able to reconstruct the vicissitudes of her oedipal conflicts: She had ultimately decided to throw in her lot with her mother because the latter was at least always *present*, in contrast to her father whose illness absented him during this crucial developmental period. In the transference, there were now overt indications of wishes for my love; there were also transient but intense episodes of vengeful regression in various aspects of the patient's day-to-day adaptation in response to the inevitable frustration of these infantile wishes. In connection with reliving this "return to the mother" during the oedipal period, the patient was also able to review her differentiated manner of responding to men and women in adult life.

She now realized that her attitude toward men tended to be both depreciating and unreasonably suspicious, in identification with her mother's unanswered barrage of accusations against the father. In contrast, she was characteristically timid, credulous, and submissive with women. When she encountered a situation in which she could not evade a difference of opinion with another woman, she actually had difficulty remembering her own point of view; in any case, she was unable to argue effectively. In the analytic situation, she enacted both sides of this pattern, depending on which parental figure I currently represented in the transference. These repetitive fluctuations ultimately enabled her to grasp the fact that arguing with her mother had always been useless; the latter would confuse the issue (and the patient) by diverting the discussion into a tangle of irrelevancies or by shamelessly insisting on falsehoods, as if she were matching wits with a Nazi interrogator. The mother's anxiety level with respect to any opposing viewpoint apparently led to violent disputes with her husband; hence the patient did not dare uphold rationality and common sense against her mother's arbitrariness.

As a result of these insights, the patient gradually mastered her anxiety about provoking the wrath of unreasonable and unscrupulous females. In part, this acceptance of increasing levels of tension took place within the analytic situation, where the patient's former tendency to tremble at the thought of my displeasure slowly disappeared. At the same time, she learned to assert herself on the job in actual disputes with authority figures. In this context, she gradually became able to assess the policies of her employers more critically and soon reached the conclusion that these policies would preclude the development of a product that could live up to her own standards. Under these circumstances, she notified the colonel that she would be ready to move to Israel by September (when he would be in a position to remarry, she thought). She now set a date to terminate the analytic work with me by early summer.

IX

The last portion of this analysis was, from an external vantage point, uneventful, for the patient's day-to-day life had assumed a satisfactory course. She prepared for her move to Israel through step-by-step agreements with her fiancé about the detailed arrangements to be made. On her job, she was able to persuade her superiors to approve the controversial and innovative proposals she had developed over the past year—a success that was contingent on her newfound ability to uphold her views in the face of hostile criticism.

Along the same lines, she was able to tell her parents about her plans for marriage despite their expectable disapproval. As it happened, the patient's mother accepted the news with equanimity, betraying in the process the hypocritical nature of her lifelong diatribes against sexuality: Her attitude about her daughter's success in bagging a glamorous officer was one of ill-concealed admiration. The patient realized, in this connection, that her mother's survival in captivity had, more than likely, depended on her capacity to manipulate potential male protectors through eroticism. The father's response, by contrast, was entirely predictable: Instead of speaking to the specifics of his objections to the colonel, he made one final effort to win the patient over to Jesus—adding a cautionary note to the effect that his personal views about such difficult matters could be mistaken.

In the analytic setting, the patient responded to these cumulative benefits attributable to her treatment with increasingly overt expressions of gratitude. She dreamt of termination as the regrettable ending of a movie she had loved—or as the departure of a Savior, similar to the Christ who had shepherded her father through the Holocaust. It thereupon became possible to focus interpretively on the archaic idealization that underlay her trust in the analytic relationship. She realized that she viewed her choice to end the treatment, that is, her decision to monitor her own performance from then on, as the renunciation of magical protection. In the midst of this process, she vacillated between turning to me with childlike certainty of my omniscience and acting as if she no longer needed or wanted my assistance at all.

Whenever she repudiated the wish for external magic, evidence of regression to personal grandiosity might crop up in her dreams. When she acknowledged how difficult it would be fully to master Hebrew, for example, she dreamt of her return to Israel by way of Egypt, with the Red Sea parting before her! Yet she was able to interpret this material for herself—as a reaction to the possibility of feeling helpless (like her parents, the enslaved Jews)—and she spontaneously connected the specific meaning of termination with the childhood experience of losing the reliable protection of her father when she was three years old. She even recalled her fantasies of becoming an omnipotent healer during his period of illness.

It was perhaps no coincidence, therefore, that we terminated our collaboration just 32 months after we had begun our regular work.

PROBLEMS OF TECHNIQUE

6

Saints or Scoundrels
and the Objectivity of the Analyst

I

Some years ago, I participated in a seminar on creativity in which Freud's (1910a) essay on Leonardo da Vinci became one pivot of discussion. Some participants accepted Freud's premise that Leonardo's pursuit of enterprises that took him away from creating art was the manifestation of a neurotic inhibition. Others, including myself, took the position that this judgment, ostensibly formed on clinical grounds, actually represented the imposition of a personal preference on the subject of our study. However much we may long for the master-pieces Leonardo might have created if his commitment to art had been more absolute, da Vinci did not owe posterity such single-minded devotion to his painting. It is very likely true, as Freud implied, that the artist's vacillation between his creative activities in the visual arts and his other studies was the behavioral manifestation of con-flicting personal aims. To acknowledge this fact, however, is merely to transpose the difference of opinion to which I have referred from the realm of a concrete clinical illustration to that of general clinical theory.

In conceptual terms, we critics of Freud's position are contending that intrapsychic conflict need not be pathological. Moreover, the determination of whether or not a specific instance of conflict is pathological is exceedingly difficult and can only be made on the basis of long-range observation in the psychoanalytic setting. Not only may conflict be regarded as an unavoidable dimension of human existence; more to the point, in certain respects it may be viewed as the essential stimulus nutriment that gives meaning to our lives. In this sense, the *absence* of conflict may be viewed as potentially patho-genic insofar as it generally leads to the cessation of further develop-ment. To be sure, this point of view is based on the assumption that psychological "health" can be correlated with the open-ended expansion of the individual's repertory of responses. In any event, we cannot avoid the conclusion that our viewpoint about such matters will necessarily be a function of our individual system of values. If, for example, I cannot accept the goal of living like a vacationer at a beach resort as a "healthy" program of action, this judgment cannot be attributed to my scientific knowledge—it is the expression of certain moral commitments.

It is interesting to recall, in this context, that less than 25 years have passed since Heinz Hartmann published his monograph *Psycho-analysis and Moral Values* (1960). This manifesto of the analyst's moral detachment asserted that psychoanalysis as a clinical procedure con-stitutes a technology without moral considerations. One might say that Hartmann took a position of absolute relativism in moral matters; he declared that psychoanalysts are only entitled to judge the behavior of analysands on the scale of its *authenticity*, that is, the degree to which it truly represented the values professed by the individual. I am afraid that Hartmann's claims about absolute analytic objectivity and exclusive adherence to "health values" now sound like the utter-ances of a voice from another age.[1]

Of course, Hartmann's position merely echoed Freud's viewpoint in his *New Introductory Lectures* (1933), where he disclaimed that psycho-analysis posits any values beyond those inherent in science as a whole. Perhaps we can understand such categorical assertions about matters that now strike us as enormously complex by recalling that they were made in the context of selecting patients for analysis on the basis of exceedingly stringent criteria as to the possession of what Freud called "good character." To illustrate what Freud recom-mended for the occasional "scoundrel" who consulted him, consider this remark from his correspondence with Edoardo Weiss: "One ships such people . . . across the ocean, with some money, let's say

---

1. The point of view Hartmann expressed a generation ago was based on an attitude about science as a whole. In an age characterized by the epistemology of positivism, Hartmann assumed that the analyst and analysand shared a common set of goals simply because they both lived in an "average expectable environment." This concept implied an average expectable culture and an average expectable superego as well. Because we no longer accept this assumption, epistemology itself has changed, and science no longer conceives of reality in such absolutist terms. Modern epistemologists (e.g., Polanyi, 1974; Polanyi & Prosch, 1975) assume that in any scientific enterprise the subjectivity of the investigator is a central issue that must be systematically explored.

to South America, and lets them there seek and find their destiny" (1970, p. 28).

The psychoanalytic attitude toward such problems has dramatically changed in recent decades. Freud and Hartmann both took for granted that analyst and patient shared a common system of values. It is obvious that we no longer can take this assumption for granted, and that the types of disagreement about basic values that might arise in a clinical situation can no longer be ignored in our consideration of technique. In large measure, of course, this fact follows from the broadening scope of our work, along with our changing concepts of analyzability itself.[2]

In the past 20 years, most analysts have become much more ambitious in attempting to apply the psychoanalytic method to a broad range of character disorders. With this significant expansion of the parameters of our clinical experience, we are no longer able to assume that most of our patients concur even with the "scientific" value system; with regard to many of our more personal values, there is even less chance of agreement. Personally, I have long suspected that many therapeutic failures in psychoanalysis have been caused, in large measure, by the covert adherence of analysands to antiscientific values such as dogmatism, reductionism, and the rejection of rationality. In my judgment, such personal commitments may well be present in personalities that do not otherwise differ from the "neurotic" character types that have traditionally been found to be most suitable for analytic assistance. At any rate, if the participants fail to recognize such fundamental differences in the course of their collaborative work, something that passes for analysis may transpire which, in reality, is nothing more than an argument about *Weltanschauungen*.

I cannot offer a more convincing illustration of such an impasse than the embarrassing failure I reported in *Advances in Clinical Psychoanalysis* (1981b, Chapter 3). I undertook to analyze a student radical at the climax of popular protests against the Vietnam War. Although the patient himself sought help because of his lifelong immersion in a masochistic perversion vis-à-vis male torturers, his actual problems in living during the treatment did not involve this matter, probably because this rapidly shifted from the stage of everyday life to that of attempted transference reenactments. In my judgment, the major problem turned out to be the patient's complacency about focusing

---

2. I have outlined my own convictions about the appropriate range of psychoanalysis as treatment on several recent occasions (e.g., Gedo, 1981b, Chapter 3); in this volume, the issue is only dealt with *en passant*. In Chapter 7, however, I shall illustrate the specific difficulties I have encountered in applying the psychoanalytic method to the treatment of "scoundrels."

his life entirely on the analytic situation: Although the treatment was financed by his family, he felt no need to continue his studies, to seek employment, or to adapt in any other way to the usual requirements of adult existence.

In the transference, this patient recreated his sadomasochistic universe through provocative arguments about the most basic issues generally taken for granted in our society. For example, he applauded the rash of contemporaneous acts of terrorism directed against major universities. Although certain of these communications had a slo-ganeering flavor, leading me to respond mostly to their function as efforts to force me to register disagreement, they turned out, in the long run, to represent the patient's actual convictions. As I recounted in my previous discussion of this case, I eventually realized that I could not reach consensus with this patient about those aims of a psychoanalysis Freud subsumed under the rubric of "science" when he told me about his understanding of Shakespeare's message in *The Tempest*. As the patient saw it, Shakespeare's hero is Caliban, that freedom fighter against the colonialist oppression of Prospero! In agreement with Herbert Marcuse, he regarded the reality principle as an illegitimate instrument of social control.

II

Meissner (in Panel, 1984) has recently suggested that many patients who enter analysis in this era of broader criteria of analyzability have an illness mostly in the sense of lacking an authentic set of values to guide them. I believe that in such circumstances the task Meissner sets for the analyst, that of divorcing his personal values from the analytic enterprise, becomes impossibly difficult. I believe, on the contrary, that analysts are increasingly confronted with situations in which they cannot be truly neutral—personally, subjectively neutral —about the material that their patients bring them.

The most dramatic occasion I recall of being confronted with this actuality was during a continuous case seminar conducted over 15 years ago. One of the psychoanalytic candidates reported an analysis in which the analysand, during the disturbances of the late '60s, voiced a serious intention of blowing up the post office. We had an animated discussion at the time about the appropriate analytic re-sponse to the communication of such a plan, with sharp disagree-ment among the participants in the seminar about how the analyst should respond. At any rate, the heat generated by this "technical" issue proved to everyone, I believe, that the analyst cannot remain morally neutral at all times, and that it is fatuous, in this context, to believe that he can conceal from the analysand the nature of his response: whether the response is simply one of waiting to see whether the patient will in fact blow up the post office (is it an actuality, or is it merely a fantasy like those of my provocative Caliban?) or whether the response is one of genuine concern, anxiety, and shock lest the patient involve the analyst as an accessory before the fact in a serious crime.

The foregoing example may be dismissed as so extreme as to constitute a negligible exception. But we are often confronted with similar dilemmas. In my personal judgment, the only way we can carry out Meissner's injunction is by communicating to the patient what is obvious to him in any event: If we are shocked, we must say so, and if we are shocked because of personal value judgments, I think we have no choice but to make clear that this is the case and to make the explicit separation between what is personal and what is part of the analytic enterprise in so many words.[3]

An example provided by Meissner (in Panel, 1984) himself aptly illustrates the fact that the analyst cannot conceal from the patient how he really feels. His patient, who engaged in provocative acts of vandalism, had correctly ascertained his analyst's identity: After all, Meissner's professional credentials include not only an "M.D.," but also an "S.J.," and his patients, well aware of this fact, will reasonably infer that a Jesuit priest is bound to be shocked by behaviors of certain kinds. I think it is simply unnecessary to conceal from analysands what is obvious to them in the first place. We can proceed to the examination of the meaning of the patient's behavior if we simply acknowledge that *of course* we are shocked by such behavior—*Personally* shocked! The patient in question obviously knew that Meissner would be shocked in the first place.

I am in further disagreement with Meissner's contention that issues of this sort tend to arise, for the most part, only with "borderline" patients. In fact, they may confront us in every analysis, regardless of the nature and extent of the patient's pathology. Let me give an illustration that belies Meissner's claim. A very well-structured individual had been seeing me in analysis for several years. He was very conflicted about his own hostility, very guilty, and tended to act out expiation of this guilt in various ways, including working an

3. In response to these ideas, Michels (in Panel, 1984) has raised the question of what the analyst should communicate to his patients about his personal subjectivity. This question transcends the topic of values, but it deserves serious consideration. In this regard, I think we have probably been too reticent in the past due to our preoccupation with guarding our anonymity. In fact, it is only in our verbal communications that we even undertake to maintain anonymity; we routinely betray ourselves—and our values —without saying anything explicit to the patient.

inordinate number of hours to the point of being exhausted and upset. I remarked to him one day, "You wear your profession like a hair shirt." He was utterly shocked, and we had a great deal of difficulty in the analysis for the next week or so. It turned out that the patient was shocked because he had discerned that I do not approve of wearing hair shirts. In an earlier commentary on this illustration, Michels (in Panel, 1984) has pointed out that my terse and allusive interpretation was quite ambiguous. It might have been heard as encouragement to the patient to abandon his ethical standards in favor of my own; on the other hand, it might have been understood as a communication that the meaning of work in the patient's life had certain unconscious aspects that did not fit into his own professed system of values. Michels concurred with the desirability of an intervention highlighting the conflictual nature of the patient's behavior. If the patient's work efforts were based on unconflicted attitudes, however, he submits that "Gedo was preaching and shouldn't have been doing it."

I completely accept this clarification; my intention, of course, was to highlight certain unconscious conflicts that implicated the patient's own value system. But I cannot hide behind this therapeutic intent as an alibi, because the patient clearly heard my remark differently, and he too was right. The fact that the patient did not hear my remark the way I intended it to be heard naturally told me a great deal about him, but the transaction also told him something about me, and his inference in this respect was perfectly correct. I had not intended to reveal my own moral values in the transaction at issue; after all, we are "only" dealing with a choice of metaphor! But the fact is that analysts are continuously betraying themselves through their choice of words and intonation, and their patients are generally intelligent people who hear their analysts with the same sensitivity that their analysts exercise, hopefully, in hearing them.[4] It follows that when a revelation about the analyst emerges inferentially, it is imperative that the analyst make it explicit. The particular patient I have mentioned, for many complicated reasons, was unable to disclose his accurate reading of my own values for over a week, and the analysis was disrupted until he reported hearing a sermon and proceeded to associate to his feeling that I was trying to convert him from his value system to mine.

This vignette further demonstrates the extraordinary way in which the psychoanalyst's very language is impregnated with values. To take another example, consider how often we hear that certain patients with developmental difficulties present with "superego

4. I shall elaborate on treatment as the development of a shared language in Chapter 8.

lacunae." What does this psychoanalytic construct actually convey about the functioning of the individual? It merely means that in terms of the analyst's own value system with respect to certain issues, a particular patient is closer to that extreme position on the axis of alternative possibilities that betokens a lack of values. From the patient's point of view, however, the analyst's attitude with respect to the same issue is closer to the other extreme on that axis, a position excessively loaded with those specific values. If we fail to recognize that all value commitments are ultimately arbitrary, it is all too easy to slip into scorn for those who do not share our position: "'Ban 'Ban, Ca-Caliban" (The Tempest, Act II, Scene 2)!

Whenever value issues of this kind become the central focus of the analytic material, analysts are likely to find themselves in the midst of a particular kind of transference configuration. The transference in question may not be referable to any particular stage of development; more likely, it may stem from any number of developmental phases. But the point is that the type of transference transaction involved will echo the acquisition of ideals and values in childhood from a caretaker or an institution to which the child had an important relationship. It follows that whenever the analyst engages in a discussion of his own values, as this task becomes necessary in the context of analyzing the patient's own value system (e.g., in the context of challenging whether the patient's value system is the only one possible, whether it is as unconflicted as the patient may believe it to be, and so forth), it is imperative that he follow through with a careful analysis of the transference implications of his intervention. But then this stricture of course applies to all psychoanalytic interventions (cf. Gill, 1981)!

III

Once the analyst begins to focus explicitly on the ways in which values impinge on clinical work, he comes to appreciate that values are a source of human variability of truly primary significance for a large number of patients. To give only one suggestive illustration of what I mean, I will refer briefly to a case I have dealt with at length in *Beyond Interpretation* (1979b, Chapters 8 and 9). This analysis achieved a dramatic and (to date) lasting therapeutic result, although the presenting picture was one of an ominous depressive reaction with suicidal preoccupations. The novel insights gained in the course of this treatment were concerned, for the most part, with the effects of two separate and *conflicting* systems of values on the patient's current behavior. The first system was a set of conscious precepts learned from the patient's father, beginning in early latency; the second system, largely disavowed but relatively accessible through the method of free association, had been embraced in earliest childhood from the patient's primary caretaker, an admired and beloved grandmother.

I wish to emphasize that, in trying to assist this patient in integrating these mutually exclusive subsets of values into one coherent hierarchy—a hierarchy, moreover, that could be serviceable in the future because it would be congruent with the patient's adult assessments of the realities of the world—the neutrality extolled by Hartmann (1960) with regard to value judgments was neither sufficient nor practicable. It would have been insufficient because one could challenge the patient's commitment to certain of these unrealistic but heretofore unquestioned ideals only if one offered the judgment that *no* human being could be expected to live up to them. To put this point differently, neutrality was impracticable because it was *imperative* to question this man about his reasons for categorically refusing to engage in certain self-protective behaviors; it was equally important to indicate disagreement with his a priori assumption that no other course of action was consistent with human decency. In fact, it was only by explicitly identifying a number of equally decent modes of conduct that I was able to make the patient aware that he was guided by a specific—and highly idiosyncratic—value system. Thus, he devalued exerting influence on others by opposing them, even via verbal disagreement; he tried to effect "influence" solely by setting a good example, without explaining how he understood the issue at stake.

Colleagues who have heard my views on these matters over the years occasionally recoiled from an implication they impute to the logic of my argument: They believe I might be advocating the contamination of analytic technique by an admixture of moral exhortation. On the one hand, such concern is based on a misunderstanding; I have never knowingly pushed any patient in the direction of my personal system of values. Rather, my activities have focused on clarifying the analysand's own commitments in this regard and, when possible, on providing assistance in resolving contradictions and establishing priorities among the various components of these commitments.[5]

---

5.   One of my values is my belief that the most radical position is necessarily the "best" one; I am constantly disillusioned with myself because I cannot be radical enough to outdo my colleagues! I would never go as far as Meissner in pointing out that a patient's value system is a "bad" value system. I would only go so far as to submit that it is one of several alternative possibilities, and that it is ultimately for the patient to endorse one value system over another.

On the other hand, I do believe it is fatuous for psychoanalysts to hide the shared values of the discipline itself from their patients because *these* commitments should clearly shine through every facet of their professional behavior. Can we, and need we, disavow our adherence to truthfulness, probity, reliability, and fairness to others? And do we "idealize" these qualities because they are pragmatically useful in order to get along in "this dungheap world" (to use Stendhal's phrase) or because we are moral beings.?[6] Of course, analysts continue to have the option, in emulation of Freud, of exiling the scoundrels who seek treatment by referring them elsewhere—preferably to disliked colleagues, thereby killing two birds with one act of candor and generosity! But once an analyst accepts such a patient for treatment, it is in the interest of the analysis to state explicitly that he finds the patient's immorality unseemly—or worse. In any case, there is certainly no hiding this fact if it is true; the attempt to do so is merely a bit of useless hypocrisy.

I shall try to illustrate some of the practical difficulties entailed in the procedure I recommend in the next chapter. Here I wish to comment on the other side of this same coin: the analyst's dilemma in undertaking the treatment of a would-be saint. I have in fact attempted analyses that amounted to efforts to do just that on a number of occasions. And, of course, one of the things that one *cannot*

6. I shall devote Chapter 10 to consideration of the theoretical divergences among psychoanalysts, including those I attribute to their differing value systems. Because that discussion will be confined to conceptual issues, it may be appropriate to pause here to assess the most serious challenge to the psychoanalytic consensus on the rationale of therapeutic technique, the position of Heinz Kohut (1975a, 1975b). In his critique of Freud's exclusive emphasis on ascertaining the psychological "truth" (or in the language of customary analytic discourse, the analytic reliance on insight) as the vehicle of cure, Kohut proposed an alternative based on a different hierarchy of values. It is not that Kohut was opposed to truth-seeking as one goal of analytic work; in instances where this aim came into conflict with the maintenance of an empathic ambience, however, Kohut unequivocally preferred the provision of empathy to that of accurate information.

On one level, of course, this shift in emphasis merely reflects our contemporary skepticism about the possibility of reaching ultimate truth, a point of view most clearly articulated in the psychoanalytic realm by Schwaber (1981) and Spence (1982). To this extent, the shift in emphasis corresponds to the end of the era of positivism on the general cultural scene. Yet, Kohut went beyond calling attention to the inevitable influence of the observer's subjectivity on the formulation of psychoanalytic insights. Although these implications of his position were never spelled out in his writings, the overall thrust of his communications (especially his spontaneous comments in numerous personal discussions) points to his belief that the nature of reality is simply not worth arguing about, especially with children. He held that nothing in human affairs can be as important as the appreciation of the individual's point of view. But exactly how irreconcilable viewpoints can simultaneously evoke empathic responses to all the participants in a transaction remains unexplained in Kohut's work.

do in such circumstances is to begin with the assumption that the ambition to be a saint is "bad" or illegitimate and that a goal of analysis is to induce the patient to abandon such a crazy ambition. Any effort based on this assumption is impregnated with personal values because the analyst's implicit aim is to weaken the authority of the values that impel the patient toward sainthood. I never formulate the goals of treatment in such terms, and I have therefore been able to make significant progress with those would-be saints whom I have analyzed. Of course, a variety of other issues make analyses of this sort very difficult, often including a value problem to which Michels (in Panel, 1984) has alluded: the difference between the value system of psychoanalysis, with its emphasis on the individuality of the patient, and the value system of the would-be saint, with its customary emphasis on the value of the collectivity. In fact, it is this obstacle that has accounted for the failure in those analyses of would-be saints in which I was not particularly successful (see Gedo, 1981b, Chapter 6, for one illustration).

I think there is agreement on the fact that the primary task of the psychoanalyst is to facilitate the patient's comprehension of his mental life and behavior. What remains uncertain is how best to work toward this goal. In the context of the issues raised in this chapter, the following question presents itself: What happens if there is some difficulty in continuing with an analysis because of an implicit disagreement on values or a collusion on values. At this early stage of our collective professional examination of this question, no analyst can commit himself with total confidence to a particular strategy for coping technically with such circumstances; in general, we have to date thought so little about such matters that we have no rules of thumb about what works best. My tentative conclusion, however, is that the analysis is promoted if we analyze and lay on the table not only what the contretemps means to the patient, but also what it means to the analyst.

IV

The last issue I will consider is the influence of the analyst's personal values on his individual preferences within the realm of psychoanalytic theory, a topic I shall approach from another perspective in Chapter 10. Here, I will confine myself to the bare outlines of the problem. Briefly, I am convinced that largely unconscious values strongly influence the analyst's choices in the areas of clinical theory and metapsychology alike. Such unconscious commitments involve profound aspects of the analyst's core identity; hence, his ideological positions on seemingly objective matters tend to assume the narcissistic flavor that Rothstein (1980) believes to be an important characteristic of theoretical controversies in the field. With respect to clinical theories, I have previously noted that "in the aftermath of Victorian prudery, Freud taught the victims of the discontents of a civilization simultaneously moralistic and prurient that one must live one's life within the body. . . . Through this revision of moral values, Freud effected a major change in the very fabric of our culture, one that decisively altered our conception of reality . . . [he] elevated the goal of appetite satisfaction to a position of relative primacy within the hierarchy of acceptable aims in life" (Gedo, 1979b, p. 259). From an analogous perspective, alternative clinical theories that have been influential in psychoanalysis have codified the significant meanings of human existence in terms of the primacy of different sets of values. The system of Melanie Klein and her followers, for instance, may be characterized as "a doctrine teaching the need to make reparation for man's constitutional wickedness," whereas the self psychology of Heinz Kohut stresses the value of "man's entitlement to an affectively gratifying milieu" (Gedo, 1979b, p. 261).

I believe that most clinicians have found each of these guides for systematizing the bewildering variety of psychoanalytic material to be extremely valuable in specific contingencies. Yet the vast majority of analysts have singled out one or another of these clinical orientations as the *sole* organizing principle of clinical theory. In my judgment, such nonrational choices derive from individual preferences about the values inherent in the respective emphases of different theoretical viewpoints.

At the level of metapsychology, the psychoanalytic community is splintered into groups adhering to a variety of mutually exclusive assumptions about the nature of things. It is essential to keep in mind that these a priori epistemological commitments are not subject to empirical validation. Moreover, psychoanalysts are hardly alone in splitting into such antagonistic philosophical schools; the same divisions characterize every intellectual community. One way to describe the various psychoanalytic schools is to focus on their respective attitudes on the mind/body problem—monism, dualism, or a denial of the relevance of the problem that I am tempted to label nihilism. Another approach to these a priori commitments is to assess their underlying assumptions about the extent of human malleability; the range, in psychoanalysis as in other disciplines, is bounded by extremes of utopian optimism and fatalistic pessimism. I trust that it is apparent that the psychoanalyst's preferences in matters of this kind stem from his most basic value commitments—commitments that, in fact, antedate morality itself. Hopefully, the nature of these archaic preferences will constitute a subject of continuing discussion in the profession.

7

On the Therapeutic Limits
of Psychoanalysis:
Delinquent Enactments

I

One chapter of my recent book, *Advances in Clinical Psychoanalysis* (1981b), was devoted to "the current limits of psychoanalysis as therapy." I focused there on two sets of constraints that may defeat psycho-analytic efforts, however far we may go in adapting treatment tech-nique to the individual requirements of given patients (cf. Gedo, 1979b). The first boundary of our therapeutic effectiveness is the occurrence of regressive episodes in the course of which the analy-sand loses the capacity to cope with the exigencies of everyday life, thus necessitating placement in a sheltered environment. The second boundary is the covert presence of delusional convictions, particularly when these unalterable beliefs concern the acquisition of valid knowl-edge. Patients afflicted with this variant of omniscience mistrust whatever new information they have the opportunity to acquire in their analysis, even though their unwillingness or inability to change false beliefs may often hide behind a screen of verbal assent.

At this time, I wish to focus attention on other aspects of these boundaries of the therapeutic scope of psychoanalysis. I should state at the outset, however, that I am by no means certain that the psycho-pathology I will delineate actually differs from the adaptive deficits described in my previous work on this topic. In other words, I merely wish to shift the point of view from which we approach this subject, concentrating now on the unfavorable significance of delinquent enactments within the analytic setting for the final outcome of treatment.[1]

As I have previously tried to show via clinical examples (Gedo, 1979b, 1981b), it *is* feasible to establish an effective analytic process with delinquent individuals, at least with those who do not exceed the analyst's anxiety tolerance through criminal or other dangerous activities. In my experience, most patients of this kind are well able to tolerate forthright statements about the nature of their behavior, including, if necessary, candid avowals on the analyst's part of the manner in which such activities conflict with his personal system of values (see Panel, 1983). Generally, it turns out that at bottom the patient has been in conflict about his delinquent propensities, and, as I pointed out in Chapter 6, that the analyst's implicit or explicit endorsement of codes of conduct based on responsible mutuality often opens the way to some form of idealizing transference (Gedo, 1975).

It is precisely the exceptions to this generalization that constitute one of the subgroups of patients for whom psychoanalysis has little to offer. In my own practice, I suspect that I screen out most prospective patients thoroughly committed to corrupt values through early and explicit insistence on their acceptance of precise business arrangements, especially with respect to schedule and fees. I can recall several instances of patients with delinquent propensities who decided against working with me, following extended exploratory consultations that seemed promising, after I made it clear that I would not look upon unilateral interference with my procedures *merely* as analytic material to be processed with detachment. Perhaps the clearest negative response to my policy occurred with a professor of law (!) who reported a first dream in which he was participating in a hockey game against the local Chicago team. At the decisive moment, he picked up the puck and carried it to the opposing team's goal, like a runner scoring a touchdown in football. When I commented on his wish to be exempted from the ground rules of analysis,

---

1. Individuals whose behavior betrays gross defects in integrity—criminals and psychopathic characters of other types—probably continue to be excluded from the practice of most psychoanalysts. Still, the steadily "widening scope" of the personality disturbances treated by means of the analytic method has inevitably confronted practitioners with an increasing number of patients whose delinquent propensities do not become apparent until the therapeutic regression induced by the psychoanalytic process has been set in motion. Many of these contingencies simply follow from the misleading information such individuals are likely to provide in the course of initial consultations. There are other instances, however, in which the delinquent behavior is in fact without precedent in the patient's adult life—it represents a return to modes of organization that were more or less successfully warded off in adulthood and are reactivated *only* within the analytic setting during treatment.

he replied, ragefully, that I might be correct, but that he could not collaborate with such a stickler for rules. He literally walked out of the session on the spot, never to return. My intervention may well have been ill-timed technically, but the patient's transparent reaction revealed his imperative insistence on being allowed to alter the rules to his own advantage; hence, his decision to discontinue treatment was probably sound.

Another patient, who started his treatment by proposing to defraud his insurance company to our mutual profit, responded to my statement that I could not be of benefit to him if I condoned his delinquencies by confessing (sic!) his lifelong wish to become an honest person. An idealizing transference subsequently emerged, based on the precedent of one of his important relationships of early childhood. In this case, however, as in so many others (see case 3 in Gedo, 1979b), the principal intrapsychic conflict turned out to involve the clash of competing value systems acquired in differing childhood contexts. Although the outcome of this conflict was in doubt for about two years, the patient was ultimately unable to reject and condemn the behavior of his father, a man who had never bothered to hide his criminal activities from his son.

I think it is of great interest that the childhood conflict between the world of this man's charismatic and delinquent father and that of his loving, self-sacrificing, and humble maternal grandparents was recreated in the course of the analysis via the formation of a complex constellation of *transferences*. If the analytic relationship revived, for the most part, the exploitative but lifesaving bond to his Sicilian grandmother, the patient also managed to repeat the circumstances of his childhood attachment to his father by submitting—with exceptions of Machiavellian subtlety and provocativeness!—to a tyrannical and unscrupulous mistress. He was quite able to despise his father for "not living like a white man," as he delicately put it, but was unable to oppose or even criticize his paramour's cruelty toward his children in the present.

In the end, the analysis suffered the same fate as the grandparents' moral code had undergone in later childhood—it was dismissed as both impractical and excessively puritanical. No doubt the patient would have preferred to enjoy his power and pleasures without having to sacrifice his integrity, but his dreams repeatedly portrayed this bigoted person scoring the winning touchdown in the Superbowl and then performing a savage victory dance as a black man—that is, a criminal.

I have organized this case vignette around the issue of the analysand's inability to repudiate his own corruption; it would be just as cogent, for other purposes, to formulate the material in terms of very different facets of his psychopathology. The patient's decision to sacrifice the analysis in order to appease his mistress, for example, could only have been based on the assumption that their relationship would preserve the relative peace that had supervened in his life as a result of the analytic work. Such a view constituted a repudiation of the cumulative evidence we had collected in the course of our collaboration, not to mention the interpretations I had offered during the same period. This man's pathology, in other words, included some defect in the capacity to process information. Although the treatment did not unequivocally reveal the presence of delusional thinking, the case does not constitute an exception to my previous categorizations of analytic failures caused by subtle thought disorders. In this instance, I did indeed witness several transient episodes of pseudologia fantastica—that is, periods during which the patient actually believed his own lies.

Another way to put this same point is to recall that the relatively primitive mode of organization characteristic of delinquent individuals implies a whole array of adaptive deficits, involving multiple lines of development (cf. Gedo & Goldberg, 1973). If we choose to pay closer attention to the issue of object relations, for example, we could approach the same patient's psychopathology from the vantage point of his simultaneous symbiotic enmeshment with a number of individuals and with the periods of acute stress that ensued when certain of these indispensable people pulled him in varying directions. From this perspective, we might describe the limits of effective psychoanalytic treatment in terms of the extent to which the analysand's symbiotic needs become focused within the analytic relationship. If a significant propensity to form symbiotic attachments continues to find outlets in extra-analytic contexts, we probably face a poor prognosis.

Let us pursue a bit further the object relations perspective on delinquent behavior. For the past generation, it has been a commonplace of the child analytic literature that the treatment of delinquent youngsters is unlikely to be successful unless one or both parents, whose attitudes codetermine the nature of the child's behavior, participate in the therapeutic process. General consensus about such findings probably led to the emergence of "family therapy" as a rational modality of treatment for individuals whose personality organization is characterized by those symbiotic attachments we might well term "syncytial." These attachments call to mind a mass of cytoplasm that has discernible nuclei, but has not undergone actual division into separate cells. We may recall, in this connection, that August Aichhorn's (1925) successes with delinquent adolescents were achieved in a residential setting where he had plenipotentiary powers—that is, where the patients did not have to contend with the undertow of symbiotic ties to family members who had a vested interest in perpetuating their maladaptive behaviors. I believe that the applicability of the same principles to certain adult patients has not been sufficiently emphasized.

This symbiotic constellation is often more blatant than in the case of the Pinocchio-like character I have just described. One instance of the more obvious kind concerns a young woman who was able to profit from almost two years of steady and accurate analytic feedback about the nature of her delinquent performances to reassess the actualities of her desperate situation. She was at first maximally uncooperative as an analytic patient, but the history of her exploitative and fraudulent behavior toward most persons gradually emerged nonetheless. The exception to this pattern was her relationship to her mother, a narcissistic woman who had been unable to cope with a child (i.e., the patient) whose infancy had been a nightmare of feeding problems. This apparent paradox in the patient's behavior was all the more puzzling because she was filled with hatred for a father who had always been kind and solicitous toward his beautiful little girl.

I encountered very little difficulty in reaching consensus with this woman about her vanity and selfishness, her ruthless sadism, and her hypocrisy and fraudulence. The analyst's reality-tested valuation of the patient's delinquent enactments is integral to the process of dealing with persistent childhood illusions; it imparts credibility to his role as the patient's optimal disillusioner. In this particular case, the cogency of the portrait that confronted this patient in my analytic looking-glass quite rapidly addicted her to the treatment, so that the worsening bulimia that initially prompted her to seek assistance disappeared in about a year. She was pleased and relieved to be able to confide in someone who recognized that, if it were not for her father's practically limitless subsidies, she would have tried to manipulate and defraud men by becoming a high-class hooker. In fact, her propensities in this direction occasionally spilled over into the enactment of a sadistic perversion.

As it was, the patient tried to guarantee her welcome in my office by taking steady, albeit menial employment for the first time. With this development, her father began a barrage of "encouragement" to induce her to undertake training for one of the major professions. It was at this point that her genuine humiliation at her lack of skills and accomplishments came into focus. It emerged that one source of her hatred for her father was his blind disregard of her lack of interest in, or suitability for, the type of difficult endeavors he wanted her to tackle. Clearly, he wanted to exploit her to satisfy his own narcissistic needs. The patient's initial inability to cooperate with the requirements of analysis echoed her despairing sense that she could never succeed in ways that would impress her father. Yet, she was simultaneously unable to trust my assessment that, far from being an underachiever, she had done well to graduate from college. The issue was finally settled when, on her own initiative, she underwent psychological testing which confirmed that her intelligence was barely above average.

Although the patient was more severely mortified at her competitive disadvantages than she had been at being identified as a psychopathic character, none of her encounters with unpalatable truths about herself caused her to regress in any way. Above all, she needed *not* to be confused by the unrealistic fantasies that other people were prone to spin around her, largely because she could act to perfection the part of a well-bred lady. As part of arriving at a reliable self-assessment, it was essential that she prove to herself that she could be self-supporting, despite the fact that she had to borrow to pay the fee for her continuing analysis. At my insistence, she formalized the latter arrangement through a written contract whereby the money for analysis was advanced to her out of her share of her parents' estate.

Even this concrete reminder of her actual autonomy proved to be insufficient, however, when further developments alerted her parents to the possibility that the patient might proceed to structure her future in a way that would make her independent of their influence. At first she was interested in the compromise solution of making a marriage acceptable to the family. But she soon came to terms with the fact that her characterological hatred of men made the prospect of any marriage—much less one meeting her parents' social requirements!—exceedingly implausible. Convinced she would have to forge a different type of future through her own exertions, she arranged to return to school to acquire skills commensurate with her aptitude. This decision, of course, made her dependent once more on family assistance.

It came as a complete surprise that it was the patient's *mother*, until then the sole family member to have disapproved of her irresponsibility and lack of "realism," who now began to question the necessity of this difficult new enterprise, rapidly undermining the patient's tenuous resolution to persevere in a program to achieve self-sufficiency—including her commitment to the analysis. The mother strongly recommended switching to some form of once-a-week group therapy. Too late, I realized that this girl's persistent fantasies that she would not only inherit much of her father's wealth, but also his prerogatives as the mother's primary companion, were not merely reflections of an unresolved negative oedipal constellation. They also constituted responses to her mother's unspoken promises and expectations! Faced, after decades of frustrated longings, with the imminent consummation of this quasi-incestuous pact, the patient inevitably came to see the analysis as an obstacle and an inconvenience, soon discarded, albeit with some shame.

I suspect that covert symbiotic attachments in adult life are more frequently formed in relation to a spouse (as in the case of the man who sacrificed his analysis to appease his mistress) and less often persist in their original version vis-à-vis one or both parents (as in the last example I have offered). The outcome of analytic efforts does not seem to depend on the mere presence of symbiotic needs. Many patients with such requirements rapidly form stable, if archaic, transference bonds to the analyst that gradually supplant their primitive attachments to others, and, in fact, give the analyst added therapeutic leverage. This circumstance has accounted for many transient "transference cures" in psychotherapy or in analyses that fail to heed adequately these archaic aspects of the treatment relationship. Thus, the destructive persistence of archaic transferences that are extra-analytic and thereby threaten to overwhelm the influence of the working relationship with the analyst must be accounted for on some other grounds.

One possible reason for the occurrence of such a "split" transference may be historical—that is, this condition may constitute a repetition of the very circumstances in childhood that led to the structuralization of this form of psychopathology in the first place. The delinquent girl whose mother seduced her to abandon the analysis was probably prevented in childhood from making full use of the relationship her father offered her in much the same way. I have already alluded to the childhood precedents for the moral conflict of the male patient who yielded to the pressure of his mistress to give up the quest to become "an honest man." In other instances, however, this explanation does not seem applicable; in fact, the siren call of delinquency frequently does not seem to emanate from a symbiotic matrix *per se*.

I may be able to illustrate such a circumstance through the example of a man who entered analysis because of stormy marital conflicts that turned out to be caused, for the most part, by his delinquent behavior. During several years of this lengthy but ultimately unproductive treatment, the patient used the influence of his wife as a resistance in the analysis in a way that suggested the persistence of a split transference of the kind found in the two cases I have just discussed. As a consequence of her own treatment, however, the patient's wife gradually learned to extricate herself from this symbiotic enmeshment, so that *her* behavior and expectations could no longer be blamed for *his*. Probably as a result of his wife's progressive refusal to preserve the status quo ante, the patient lost interest in the marriage and eventually initiated divorce proceedings, albeit with obsessional indecisiveness. This sequence of events finally clarified the fact that the analytic transference had been characterized for some time by the same negativism that formerly caused his marital problems. Now that his "resistance" could no longer be attributed to the influence of his spouse (with whom he had less and less contact now that she was liberated), we were able to discern its actual *raison d'être*: Negativism protected him from a loss of the sense of selfhood. This regressive collapse now began to be enacted within the analysis in the form of various failures to live up to the expectable performance of patients seeking psychological assistance.

These disruptive episodes, or (from another vantage point) these unexpected bouts of irresponsibility, always presented difficult technical problems; the specific variant I found most trying was the patient's tendency to lapse into a noncommunicative use of speech. Most often, this activity led to the production of associative chains that did not seem to have any consensual meaning. Lest I be misunderstood in turn, let me stress that these utterances were not merely difficult to "understand" from a psychoanalytic viewpoint; they made no coherent sense of any kind, even though the patient remained unaware of the fact that he had failed to communicate any meaning. To me, it seemed that, on these occasions, he was vomiting words. At the same time, the vomitus obviously consisted of phrases or even sentences that sounded like everyday speech. If I asked him to explain what he meant by such an utterance, the patient was often bewildered, but the question generally restored his capacity to communicate with me in an appropriate manner. Without prodding of this kind, he could not consistently stay in touch with his own thoughts, occasionally covering over his confusion by parroting the statements of others (or things he had formerly thought) as if they were his current associations.

Needless to say, these brief confusional states were highly disturbing to the patient, and his delinquency, negativism, argumentativeness, and provocative behavior were unconsciously designed to protect him from regressing into them. If I temporarily succeeded in overcoming all such obstacles and a brief period of untroubled collaboration ensued, he was generally overtaken by panicky paranoid fantasies about me. Such fantasies probably served to rationalize his sense of impending loss of self-cohesion in terms of an external threat from my direction. Nor did I ever succeed in altering this vicious circle through my attempts to put the sequence into words, for his capacity to grasp the intended meaning of my explanatory efforts would also be lost at crucial junctures. In this archaic maternal transference, he was unable to learn from me, but felt utterly bewildered without external assistance. He eventually extricated himself from our therapeutic impasse by withdrawing in a rageful huff.

I believe this material suggests that delinquent enactments in the analytic setting are just as likely to signify the analysand's inability to tolerate a symbiotic bond as the analysand's propensity to develop extra-analytic transference attachments of an archaic nature. It further shows that, in these primitive syndromes, we are usually confronted with a sea of troubles, including the thought disorders and threats of adaptive disorganization I previously designated the practical boundaries of the scope of psychoanalysis as therapy.

II

Am I conceding, after all, that the traditional policy of viewing delinquent enactments as contraindications for psychoanalytic treatment continues to be justified?[2] It is certainly clear that we can only undertake analyses with such patients if we are prepared to tolerate complications and even ultimate failure, that is, disappointments of the kind I have described in this chapter. Nonetheless, I do not believe that we should follow Shakespeare's injunction to leave these troublesome people "to Heaven"; in an encouraging number of cases, the kinds of problems that defeated my efforts in the foregoing examples proved to be analytically manageable through the special techniques I have advocated in my recent work (Gedo, 1979b, 1981a, 1981b). I have attempted to give a reasonably detailed account of such a treatment in Chapter 4; here, it will suffice to consider some of the technical lessons to be derived from the case material I have already presented.

2. This policy is aptly encapsulated in the anecdote, already alluded to in Chapter 6, concerning Sigmund Freud's response to the potential referral of a patient with perverse and delinquent propensities. He wrote one of his students:

> [A.] will always strive to mislead the analyst, to trick him and push him aside. . . .
> [N]othing would be gained by having him come into treatment with me or anyone
> else. . . . In the most unfavorable cases one ships such people . . . across the ocean,
> with some money, let's say to South America, and lets them there seek and find their
> destiny. (Weiss, 1970, pp. 27–28)

The therapist's expectable response to the task of undertaking a psychoanalysis with a person organized in archaic modes could not be articulated more clearly or forthrightly. Of course, Freud's statement must be understood in historical context as well. It was written in 1920 as a concession to the powerlessness of psychological methods when confronted with the effects of the repetition compulsion, as opposed to the efficacy of such methods in the treatment of transference neuroses, that is, conditions under the sway of the pleasure principle.

First of all, I must emphasize that, from an adaptive viewpoint, these treatments were extremely beneficial for all three patients. Their interrupted analyses failed to resolve their archaic needs to live in a symbiotic union, but they did succeed in bringing these needs to the patients' attention so that they could rearrange their lives to compensate better for these personality deficits. I suspect that these outcomes were rather similar to those which Kohut, in *The Restoration of the Self* (1977), claimed as the expectable results obtained through *his* methods with patients suffering from "narcissistic personality disturbances"; in his view—which I do not share—the acquisition of "compensatory structures" signals the readiness to terminate such analyses.

In my sample, a whole variety of dangerous behaviors (such as the woman patient's bulimia and forced vomiting as well as her incitement of strange men to sadomasochistic enactments; the fraudulent character's resort to dangerous driving, financial extravagance, and alcohol abuse; the third patient's actionable professional malfeasances) was replaced by the frankly symbiotic transference bonds established in the analytic setting. I have no information about the subsequent fate of two of these particular individuals, but I believe that all three patients learned enough in the course of our work to enable them to seek further assistance should they fail to extract the necessary symbiotic sustenance from their human milieu.[3]

Secondly, I should call attention to the extraordinary importance of the analyst's continuous monitoring of his own affectivity in response to the *actualities* of the patient's enactments in these cases. I suspect that my inability to overcome the technical difficulties in these specific instances may have been related to insufficient appreciation of the true extent of my aversion for the conduct of these individuals at the climactic phase of each of the analyses. I do not mean that my disapproval of certain aspects of their behavior was unknown to me (or to them!), but only that I was still surprised in all

---

3. I do have follow-up information about one patient, the man who left analysis at the insistence of his mistress. More than a year later, he requested my assistance to obtain optimal psychoanalytic care for one of his children. He expressed gratitude for the satisfactory results of our collaboration. After terminating treatment, he succeeded in concluding an equitable divorce, resumed relations with his children without involving his mistress in this painful enterprise, and brought his other affairs into reasonable order. He was making excellent professional progress, and even life with his mistress had become more peaceful. He emphasized that he was trying hard to live up to the ideals he had begun to profess in the analysis, however difficult he found it to adhere to them all the time. We agreed that he could resume work with me if he ran into major problems in this effort.

three instances by the *relief* I experienced when these clinical responsibilities came to an end.

I had not allowed myself to be drawn into malfeasances of my own, to be sure, but it was still difficult to avoid feeling like an accessory to many of the patients' delinquencies. Thus, the woman patient consciously rejoiced in the thought of wasting her siblings' inheritance by staying in analysis indefinitely (at the highest fee she could encourage me to charge!) by refusing to adhere to any of the ground rules of Freud's procedure. This was not simply a fantasy: Weeks and months would go by that could only be characterized as the enactment in the analysis of this scheme of malice and destructiveness—and my failure to put a stop to this "crime" was always construed by the patient as complicity in her designs, motivated by my wish for financial gain. The fraudulent man's virtual abandonment of his brood of young children—while he externalized responsibility for all moral judgments onto me in the grandmother transference— also put me in a position I found extremely distasteful. (My reactions were fortified by accusatory letters from the children's mother, calling on me to do something about the outrage!) Perhaps in an effort to curb my disapproval, I probably adhered too scrupulously to a position of "analytic neutrality" with respect to these enactments, thereby leaving others to fill the patients' symbiotic needs. I suspect this circumstance may have formed the main reason behind my lack of therapeutic leverage when the patients' other symbiotic partners went into opposition to the analyses.

In contrast, I may have swung too far in the opposite direction vis-à-vis the third patient's abuse of his naive and somewhat pathetic spouse. Specifically, I ended his previously interminable obsessions about the desirability of dissolving their failed marriage by stressing that his sole remaining motive for maintaining the status quo was an angry wish to exploit and punish her. Although the patient thereupon released his victim (and thus relieved me of the potential burden of sharing in the responsibility for her torture) without disputing my interpretation, he was probably justified in his later reproaches that I had been excessively committed to one particular mode of resolving his conflict—the one that presented no conflict for me! In other words, the wish to abuse his wife may not have been the *only* motive left for staying with her; it was merely the motive about which I was knowledgeable. In retrospect, I should have explored other possibilities: Perhaps the availability of a masochistic partner was a prerequisite for maintaining the therapeutic relationship without unmanageable anxiety about loss of his sense of autonomy.

The technical problems that defeated me in these specific analytic efforts may not remain unmanageable in the future, if, hopefully, they can serve as object lessons to expand our therapeutic armamentarium. They may help us to stay on the razor's edge that separates the Scylla of leaving regressed patients to wallow in their perplexity from the Charybdis of intruding on their autonomy in decision making. We must be guided in our approach by the realization that, in these cases, the delinquent behaviors represent a primitive channel of communication, the dramatic enactment of crucial archaic transactions for which these patients usually have no other vocabulary. The implications of this conclusion for various aspects of therapeutic communication will be considered in Chapters 8 and 9. Here, it is sufficient to observe that as a consequence of increased clinical experience with "acting out" patients who carry out these activities within the treatment setting—patients who have therefore also been referred to as "acting in"—the analyst's attitude toward the basic rule of free association has had to undergo a gradual shift. We no longer expect all of our analysands to be able to express their thoughts exclusively through verbal language, and we have more or less abandoned the view that departures from the verbal interaction we command are simply "resistances" to be overcome. There is much to be learned from these primitive enactments, if only we can successfully decode their meanings in a reliable manner (cf. Segal & Britton, 1981).

In recent years, a consensus has been developing about the significance of the analyst's own affective responses within the analytic transaction as one of the relevant guides to these meanings (see Gedo, 1981b, Chapter 11). Traditionally, these reactions on the part of the analyst have been classified under the rubric of "countertransference" (Tower, 1956). The evidential value of continuously monitoring the countertransference, however, has largely removed the onus that was originally attached to this term (see Gardner, 1983). If we have reason to believe that, other things being equal, our ordinary therapeutic stance is benevolently neutral, then subjective propensities to depart from this stance may be pregnant with clinical meaning. When we find ourselves reacting to an analysand as if he or she were a scoundrel who should actually be exiled to the Amazon, it is probably safe to conclude that this primitive fantasy points to our perception of an archaic transference that involves attitudes of ruthlessness and unconditional entitlement.

Needless to say, as the targets of such impossible expectations, analysts are quite likely to respond in idiosyncratic ways, that is, with "countertransference" attitudes in the narrower, pejorative sense of that term. The potential variety of such reactions precludes discussion *in extenso* here, but we may briefly consider two patterns I have frequently encountered in case discussions and in the course of my own clinical work. The more commonplace of these inappropriate responses is some type of refusal to acknowledge the reality or, still more commonly, the significance of an analysand's delinquent behavior, generally by invoking a reductionist formulation of the behavior in terms of putative structural conflicts. A somewhat less frequent but more interesting pattern is that of correctly perceiving the analysand's irresponsible enactments, but regarding their perpetrator as a fragile and pitiful being in need of "empathic" support.[4] Both patterns of countertransference proceed from the analyst's failure to acknowledge the need to make value judgments about patients' delinquent behaviors both in and out of the analytic setting (see Chapter 6).

Far from being fragile beings in danger of disintegration if insufficiently appreciated, many patients organized in archaic modes tend to be tough, resilient, and quite used to hearing unfavorable judgments about their behavior. It is true that they are also likely to be obnoxious and spiteful when they are frustrated, but, in my clinical experience, they seldom if ever experience the truth about themselves as a shattering blow. Kohut (1971) has rightly called attention

4. I encountered an example of the defensive disavowal of an analysand's fraudulent manipulations in the course of supervising the work of a woman colleague whose initial response to her aggressive male patient was fury about his ability to bully her into starting treatment in accord with his preferred conditions. As soon as the analyst had mastered the explicit fantasy of having been raped by her patient, she began to minimize the mounting evidence that his conditions for the analysis included a fee much lower than he could afford; he had concealed his actual resources at the time they had discussed these matters. Instead of addressing herself to this issue with consistency, as a matter *actually* to be remedied, the analyst insisted on attempting to decipher it as if it were a neurotic symptom. This sadomasochistic impasse was eventually brought to its natural conclusion when the patient casually left town, allegedly to pursue a favorable career opportunity. Even then, the analyst denied that this confidence-man had ever hurt anyone, presumably because her own pain did not find a place in her emotional accounts. He came, he saw, he conquered, and he departed for the Amazon! To put the matter differently, the analyst's failure to "own" up to her value judgments about the patient's behavior did not constitute empathic acceptance of him; on the contrary, her silence only led him into anxiety and confusion.

I can also draw on my supervisory experience to illustrate the second pattern I have chosen to discuss. The patient in question seemed pitiful indeed, a woman past her prime who neglected to inform those who screened her application to the low-fee clinic about her excessive drinking or the major congenital anomaly that deformed her thorax. I can briefly sum up her "acting in" with her female analyst in terms of an erratic refusal to take seriously the agreement to communicate her experience in the treatment setting. The analyst was keenly aware of the manipulative intentions behind these grim games of hide-and-seek, and she tried earnestly to maintain an analytic attitude in what seemed to be a most discouraging clinical dilemma. In the course of several years, it became more and more apparent that a policy of empathic concern and tolerance for the patient's limitations would not suffice to overcome a therapeutic stalemate.

THERAPEUTIC LIMITS OF PSYCHOANALYSIS

to the danger of bearing false witness to our patients by depreciating them: his demonstration of the specific pathogenic effects of overt and covert depreciation in childhood is one of his important clinical contributions. It does not follow from these facts, however, that patients need the corrective experience of being appreciated by their analysts—as some of the more cavalier "self psychologists" would have us believe (cf. Goldberg, 1978). On the contrary, they respond with the same anxiety and confusion to fatuous overestimation that they experience when their actual worth is denied or overlooked.

The *content* of archaic enactments can generally be interpreted in the same way that we deal with structured unconscious fantasies that are communicated verbally. Quite often, these enactments turn out to have perverse sexual connotations, generally connected with the oedipal phase of development. Although the interpretation of the varied meanings of such material is one of the crucial tasks of these analyses, I believe that insight into these meanings will be maximized if the analyst postpones interpretation until these issues emerge in the context of the transference.

In my experience with archaic personalities, it has not been terribly useful to stress the defensive displacement that leads to acting out, instead of reliving, within the analytic situation. I have found it much more productive to delay interpretation of the unconscious meanings of the enactments on behalf of consideration of the form in which these messages are encoded. To be sure, the *liaisons dangereuses* of these patients are generally replete with sadomasochistic

---

I had, from the beginning, advocated a focus on the predictably dire consequences of the patient's insensate bouts of irresponsibility, but the analyst found herself unable to issue these warnings with firmness or conviction. Although she realized that she was dealing with a trickster, she seemed to be afraid of the disruptive potential of putting a stop to the enactments—and even of labeling them with the designations they are generally given in the adult world.

In this instance, the impasse was broken after the analyst convinced herself that a change of tack was imperative. She was able to modify her approach, I believe, because she came to realize that she had projected an aspect of her own childhood self onto the patient. One of the more painful of her early experiences had involved depreciating comparisons of her physical appearance with that of a sibling. But the analyst had erred in assuming that her patient's primary problem involved self-esteem; the latter did not even experience humiliation when she was challenged about her misbehavior. The presenting psychopathology, it turned out, was derived from a more archaic phase of development; this patient was lost in a haze of depersonalization and reacted to any valid statement about herself with the shock of recognition and relief. It followed, then, that the analyst's expression of realistic concern about the disruptive consequences of her irresponsibility about her own treatment reverberated with her mother's efforts in later childhood to make contact despite the patient's aloofness and withdrawal; it did not resonate with the mother's initial disappointment with her defective child. This analysis, it should be noted, was carried to a successful termination.

and homosexual implications. Nonetheless, the most urgent technical task in such analyses is inquiry into the meaning of the patients' insensate flirtation with danger, not enlightenment as to the obvious implications of such matters as bisexuality. When, as a result of a consistent policy of challenging their disregard of the serious risks incurred through their enactments, these patients come to grips with their magical expectations that analysts can repair or undo whatever damage they might cause, they then begin—often, so it seems, for the first time—to develop conflicts about their impulses. Frequently, such conflicts are first manifested in growing fears that they will be dismissed from treatment if they fail to heed the voice of reason. As usual, Freud had it right: The voice of the intellect does ultimately gain a hearing—provided it is backed by credible sanctions!

Much later in the analysis, the patient's specific oedipal configuration, inevitably impregnated with an archaic sense of entitlement and grandiose illusions of sexual adequacy, usually emerges within the transference. The crux of the therapeutic task at this juncture goes beyond the interpretation of impulses and/or defenses, which often practically speak for themselves. It consists, instead, of lengthy efforts to eliminate the residues of childhood illusions. In the case of the young woman I have discussed in this chapter, for example, the illusory beliefs turned out to include convictions that her parents were literally immortal and that her own pregnancy fantasies had a reality basis through parthenogenesis or immaculate conception.

Let me, at this point, try to draw the threads of my argument together. Faced with the daunting task of dealing with those phenomena of the repetition compulsion that create irresponsible actions on the part of analysands within the analytic situation, analysts may be tempted to master their own sense of helplessness by responding to these contingencies in a manner that disavows their actual significance as primitive communications. Among the various avenues of denial, two are of special importance: (1) the tactic of regarding the patient's delinquency as a neurotic compromise formation, and (2) that of misidentifying the patient as unable to face the truth about these transactions without being severely traumatized. Yet, the usual response of persons organized in archaic modes to the description of their consequences, preferably conveyed with appropriate gravity and urgency, is one of gratitude, relief, and increased commitment to the task of self-inquiry.

If we look back to Chapter 6, we see that the management of delinquent enactments clearly depends on the capacity of individual patients to accept the values inherent in psychoanalysis. If analysis is to succeed, patients must, sooner or later, espouse truthfulness, probity, reliability, and fairness to others. In my clinical illustrations,

I have tried to demonstrate concretely how values and value judgments enter into the analytic enterprise at various levels. I have argued (1) that the analyst's status as a valuing creature is central to the analytic process with delinquent patients insofar as the analyst's ability and willingness to communicate his own value judgments in the course of the therapeutic work are essential to his indispensable role as provider of optimal disillusionment; (2) that the concordance between the patient's values and the values intrinsic to psychoanalysis is central to considerations of analyzability; and (3) that the values of a particular analyst are central to the range of patients he or she can effectively attempt to analyze.

8

Treatment as the Development of a Shared Language

INTRODUCTION

We have just passed the centenary of the invention of the "talking cure" by that pair of excellent Viennese wordsmiths, Josef Breuer and Bertha Pappenheim. The theme of this chapter is already implicit in Breuer's reluctant account of their encounter, the case history of "Anna O.," the joint publication of which Freud prodded him into writing more than a dozen years later (Breuer & Freud, 1895). It will be recalled that one of the symptoms of Fräulein Pappenheim's acute illness was mutism, and that Breuer succeeded in circumventing her inability to communicate in a most ingenious manner: He adapted the hypnotic techniques of contemporary psychiatry for the novel purpose of psychological investigation. For her part, Fräulein Pappenheim complied with these coercive measures with an exquisitely subtle rebelliousness: She engaged Breuer in conversation, but, for some time, she avoided the use of German in favor of *English*! Indeed, this prototypical psychological encounter already exemplified the need for the participants to develop a private language with which to communicate!

Perhaps, after all, this cautionary tale from the prehistory of psychoanalysis better serves to illustrate the fact that our language may conceal as much—or even more!—than it reveals. As Freud subsequently disclosed in a letter to Stefan Zweig (E. Freud, 1960, pp. 412–413; cf. Jones, 1953, pp. 224–226), Fräulein Pappenheim's English proved to be insufficient for the communication of some of the most vital concerns that preoccupied her during the treatment, including her awareness of the pregnancy of Breuer's wife, to cite one example (see Pollock, 1968). These matters emerged into the open when the weary Breuer prematurely terminated the treatment and was emergently summoned to his patient's bedside because Fräulein Pappenheim, in a dissociated state, was in the throes of enacting the imaginary delivery of a baby. The meaning of her behavior was encoded in the universal language of gesture, although Bertha made sure she was properly understood by articulating in words that it was indeed *Breuer's* child she was bringing into the world. We are not told whether this pronouncement was made in English or in German—a fascinating puzzle which, regretfully, I cannot confront at this time.

In her wonderfully hysteroid way, Bertha Pappenheim gave her "talking cure" still another designation: She termed it "chimney sweeping." For my purposes here, it is not the seductive and menacing reference to dammed up loves and hates implicit in her metaphor that is most significant; I wish to stress, instead, Fräulein Pappenheim's conception of treatment in terms of a wordless struggle to repair a defective machine. On one level, we may accept the term "talking cure" as an accurate portrayal of the therapist's hopes and intentions for any psychological treatment effort; to put the matter in the conceptual terminology of psychoanalysis, it is Bertha Pappenheim's conception of her therapy formulated in the language of secondary process.

At this same level of discourse, the "chimney sweeping" metaphor employs the primary process to convey a different—dare I say more profound?—perception on the part of this brilliant woman. Implicit in this communication is a view of treatment as passively endured, as devoid of responsibility on the part of the patient, who has never been granted the basic human prerogative of freely choosing her destiny. Bertha Pappenheim was letting Breuer know that hypnosis is equivalent to rape—and anal rape at that. Here, I am offering one interpretation of the latent meaning of Bertha Pappenheim's phraseology, fully aware that many equally plausible interpretations come to mind; I do so only to illustrate the familiar thesis that the transactions between patients and therapists are communicated through a multiplicity of codes and channels. Even if we do think of treatment primarily as a "talking cure," we must always simultaneously heed the primary process elements woven into the fabric of verbal discourse ostensibly encoded in the secondary process.

In the foregoing, of course, I have already betrayed my dissatisfaction with a concept of treatment based on the model of exchanging written messages. How could such a conception accommodate either a pseudocyesis or an unconscious fantasy of parturition? The shared language that must evolve between patient and therapist must go beyond words; it must include the paraverbal aspects of ordinary speech as well as the transmission of messages without verbalization. In addition to complex, dramatic enactments (like the one that marked the end of the case of "Anna O."), meaningful information is often communicated through facial expressions, gestures (cf. Deutsch, 1947), or the autonomic activities of various physiological subsystems. Another way of stating these familiar facts is to remind ourselves that the actual matrix of human communication is, in common with that of other mammalians, the repertory of basic affects (see Tomkins, 1970). These affects continue to be conveyed through body language throughout life, but with the acquisition of the capacity for speech, it is the music of vocalization that becomes the most obvious indicator of the individual's affective state.

It is hardly necessary to point out that in the presence of unequivocal cues about the affective realm we tend to discount verbally encoded messages that seem incongruous in the light of those cues. A patient may, *in all sincerity*, agree with a whole series of the therapist's interpretations in a tone of voice so laden with doubt, irony, or sarcasm that his assent is taken to constitute weighty evidence of the inaccuracy or the irrelevance of these statements. These matters, which are well-known to every clinician, are beautifully epitomized in Blaise Pascal's lovely line: "The heart has its reasons that reason knows not." It is the language of the heart that therapists must speak and also learn to understand.

A CLASSIFICATION OF THERAPEUTIC MODALITIES

If the common matrix of the therapeutic methods we call "psychological" is the establishment of a therapist–patient relationship mediated through a variety of communicative channels, how can we conceptualize the various modes of action of the vast range of differing treatments available in the contemporary market place? Obviously, there are many different approaches to this problem that might prove illuminating; I will confine myself here to a brief review of one particular proposal that I have espoused over the past decade since I developed it in collaboration with Arnold Goldberg (Gedo & Goldberg, 1973). It is my view that psychological treatment consists of a variety of (largely verbal) interventions—with the crucial proviso that the paraverbal aspects of speech and the occurrence of nonvocal messages that pertain to the communications of patients are, of course, equally relevant to the communications of the therapist.

If these varied interventions of a specific therapy are classified in terms of the psychological changes they are designed to effect, we can devise a list of treatment modalities that cuts across the usual criteria of treatment technique. Thus, regardless of the type of therapy that is ostensibly being employed, if the aim of an intervention is to bring to the level of explicit awareness some aspect of the patient's mental life that was hitherto unconscious, that therapeutic transaction can be classified as an interpretation. Alternatively, whenever the therapist merely lends himself as an empathic witness to the organized efforts of the patient to achieve self-understanding, the therapeutic modality operative during that interval of treatment, whatever else may occur at other times in the therapy, is the introspective activity itself.

In addition to these completely familiar modalities, I have elsewhere emphasized therapeutic realms which, for the sake of brevity, can be grouped together under a single rubric: They collectively lie "beyond interpretation" (see Gedo, 1979b). Arnold Modell (1976), borrowing a term introduced by D. W. Winnicott (1960), has characterized the same set of noninterpretive measures as providing a "holding environment" for the patient. Still other concepts that presumably focus on the same issues, although in a more global manner, include the "therapeutic alliance" and the establishment of an ambience of empathy.

Although most discussions of therapeutic technique stress the cognitive content of the dialogue, I believe a fair degree of consensus presently obtains about the findings, cogently stressed by Heinz Kohut (1971, 1978), that insight can seldom be imparted in an unempathic setting. The therapist's interpretations, that is, have to transcend mere validity and relevance; they must be presented in a manner that facilitates their accurate processing on the part of the patient. Beyond the choice of language, this requirement implies that an effective holding environment has been established and is being maintained.

What are some of the principal prerequisites for the maintenance of an unimpaired therapeutic alliance? In my experience, the provision of an empathic environment may require that the therapist refrain from interfering with a system of illusions that is, at least for the time being, essential to the patient's self-esteem. Such illusory beliefs may focus on the patient's own personal qualities, on those of the therapist (or, occasionally, of an equivalent figure who has been idealized), or on both. This is the realm of the "narcissistic" transferences that Kohut described in detail in *The Analysis of the Self* (1971). For the successful therapeutic management of such contingencies, Goldberg and I (1973) coined the term "optimal disillusionment." Whenever the self-organization has actually been disrupted, so that a patient is unable to sort out his priorities among a multiplicity of conflicting personal aims, urgent external assistance is needed to overcome the confusion. We have characterized the treatment modality appropriate to such states as "unification" of the self-organization. Finally, whenever even tension regulation is beyond the integrative capacity of an overstimulated patient, it is incumbent on the therapist to patch over this deficit by assisting the patient via measures aiming at "pacification." Only treatment that successfully provides these essential functions for patients unable to perform them for themselves will eventuate in that firm symbiotic bond which can form the basis for whatever further therapeutic measures may be indicated.

CLINICAL ILLUSTRATIONS

No conceptual schema of the therapeutic modalities that may be required to establish a "holding environment" can prescribe the precise interventions that will succeed in achieving these crucial prerequisites for the maintenance of a workable treatment situation. Clearly, the therapist's messages have to be encoded in one or more of the systems of communication also available to the patient. It follows that an optimal therapeutic relationship will be forged by means of increasing refinement in the communicative transaction between the participants. It is now commonplace in discussions of treatment outcome that a prospective patient's verbal skills are one of the most important factors that promise a good prognosis in any type of psychological treatment. Conversely, wide cultural differences between patient and therapist pose great handicaps for a successful outcome because they increase the difficulties of precise communication. Even in the absence of obvious disparities in sociocultural background, the danger of misunderstandings, particularly by way of reaching a false consensus, can never be overlooked. One of the most obvious sources of such semantic problems is the use of a professional jargon, frequently one that has passed into the public domain at the cost of losing any precise meaning. How often do patient and therapist truly understand each other when the latter talks about psychological traits such as passivity, narcissism, identity, or fragmentation? And how certain can the therapist be that a given patient uses such words as shame or guilt or depression or emptiness in precisely the same way as the therapist himself?

Beyond the need for each participant in treatment to help the other as much as possible to grasp the intended meaning of his statements (or, conversely, to listen to the other with maximal empathy for the probable meanings the latter wishes to convey through them), it is also crucially important to facilitate communication through the alternative channels I have mentioned: the latent meanings encoded in the primary process, the paraverbal aspects of speech, and the various modes of body language. This latter requirement becomes particularly essential if the treatment proceeds successfully, so that increasingly archaic levels of the patient's mental life gradually affect the therapeutic relationship in the form of transferences. The more remote the origins of these mental dispositions, the less likely it is that they can be expressed in the form of secondary process messages.

Perhaps a brief illustration of this principle is in order here. I once worked with an angry and rebellious young man of superior intellect who spent much of his time in the analysis trying to substantiate his suspicion that, as both a person and an analyst, I would eventually betray that I stank. After several years of systematic analytic effort, the therapeutic regression reached a stratum of his inner life that echoed the transactions with his caretakers late in the second year of his childhood. In order to grasp the significance of subsequent developments in the therapeutic situation, it must be noted that this man had been extraordinarily slow, for a person of his superior capacities, in acquiring language. According to his parents (who were decidedly not given to minimizing the accomplishments of their children), he had only mastered the words "mamma" and "out" by his second birthday.

The incident I wish to report involved a crescendo of mistrust and disappointment in the transference, probably correlated with events in his daily life that awakened fears of humiliation on his part. As the patient's distress mounted, his concerns about the manner in which I might fail him were replaced by olfactory hallucinations involving fecal odors. He was convinced that I was responsible for producing this stench, and for a short period during the treatment it was difficult to correct his misperception in this regard. Fortunately, by this time, we had a record of successful collaboration solid enough to weather the crisis: The patient continued to associate, and soon certain childhood memories emerged that threw light on this transference experience as a primitive communication.

To be precise, the patient recalled his crying mother trying in vain to feed him bananas which he refused to eat; the image of this scene might well be condensed into the phrase, "Mamma out!" This memory was the first clue to emerge about the fact that, for at least several weeks during the second year of life, he had suffered from a syndrome of foul smelling diarrhea that overwhelmed his mother with disgust and frustration. Tempting as it is to pursue the fascinating ramifications of the transference reenactment of such an early childhood event—one that constituted a major narcissistic trauma

133

and led to the erection of projective defenses against it—I must confine myself here to the issue of therapeutic communication.

Let us note that the central aspect of the childhood experience was reenacted in an affectively charged manner which the patient found himself unable to conceptualize as a recollection. At the climax of the repetition, his reluctance to accept my version of the actualities unfolding between us echoed his negativism when his mother had to combat his childhood disorder through her intrusive interventions. To be sure, the patient did not regress to a vocabulary consisting of two words, and his ability to persevere in the analytic task permitted him to use ordinary language to describe the crucial hallucinatory experience that actually formed the most important part of the early memory he was about to recover.

The transaction could well be summarized as, "You stink; I cry in rage; we struggle." Of course, the patient had been putting it that way all along, but his message was encoded in a language much too sophisticated to accommodate the archaic origins of his story. As a toddler, it will be recalled, he had had no language of words. Only when the stink was concretized as a foul smell and the patient's irrationality had me as worried as his mother had been when she thought he had sprue—only then were we communicating in a manner that reproduced the affective messages of his early childhood. Once these issues were understood both within the transference and in their childhood guise, translating them into the language of secondary process served to dispel the system of grandiose illusions through which this person had tried to disavow the intolerable burden of his sense of inadequacy. But I offer this clinical vignette not only to illustrate what I mean by "optimal disillusionment" as a therapeutic modality different from the customary effort to make the unconscious conscious; more to the point here, this incident from the middle of a complex and lengthy analysis shows how the development of the private language of one particular patient-therapist dyad can be facilitated.

Following the transaction I have summarized, my patient and I understood at all times that, whenever the patient began to be preoccupied with those of my rank offenses that might stink to high heaven, he was letting me know that his chronic humiliation about his manifold limitations was, once again, causing him more distress than he could tolerate. Consequently, I was able to address myself directly to his need to blunt this pain by focusing on his actual or imminent disappointments in others. (Previously, any such intervention on my part only led to deeper suspicions about my putative need to disclaim responsibility for my own imperfections.) Perhaps more important than the content of my message—by then quite familiar to the patient in any case—was the progressive change in the tone of our dialogue. The agonizing flavor of his earlier accusations and the strained sobriety of my responses were both gradually relinquished. On the patient's part, the accusatory tone was gradually supplanted by matter-of-fact reports about his quasi-paranoid ideation or even by detached curiosity about the reasons for its occurrence. On my side, pessimistic concern about these seemingly untoward developments gradually dissipated; in its stead, I was generally able to tinge my remarks with a bit of humor about the inevitable discomforts of our respective roles.

THE ESTABLISHMENT OF A SHARED LANGUAGE

I trust that the foregoing clinical illustration was not too condensed to demonstrate that the paraverbal aspects of communication in treatment lead, if only we can grasp their significance, to the elucidation of vital aspects of early transactions between the patient and his childhood caretakers. One advantage of psychoanalysis proper over other types of psychotherapy is the opportunity provided by the daily use of free association to make detailed observations about these formal parameters of the analysand's communicative style. In my experience, even two or three treatment sessions per week will not generally allow the clinical material to shift away from a topical organization in terms of the ongoing vicissitudes of everyday life.

Be that as it may, whenever the process of free association does in fact lead to the production of material that is primarily organized in terms of the vicissitudes of the transference, it is minor derailments in the usual course of the patient–therapist dialogue that constitute the most crucial source of information about the nature of early mother–child transactions for the particular analysand in question. Insofar as these departures from routine modes of communication involve paraverbal or mimetic channels, these therapeutic incidents lead us directly to certain aspects of the preverbal period of the patient's infancy—although, to be sure, subsequent developmental phases will have altered such behavioral patterns in numerous ways, so that we can never assume that the transference reenactments provide us with actual homologues of the patient's early childhood.

As I have tried to highlight through my clinical example, every time we succeed in identifying a source of miscommunication within the treatment situation, each participant subsequently has a better chance of avoiding the same source of misunderstanding. An accumulation of such incidents can, in the course of time, lead to the evolution of a unique set of communicative tools, a shared language characteristic to that particular therapeutic dyad. Obviously, perfection in this regard is unattainable; except perhaps for identical twins, some core of each person's subjectivity is destined to remain incommunicable. As the French say, *il faut vivre sa vie dans sa peau*: One must live one's life inside one's own skin. Nonetheless, a successful analytic experience may achieve a degree of mutual understanding probably unattainable in any other situation of adult discourse. In this context, I never tire of quoting one of my patients, who compared this experience to the singing of an *a cappella* choir, "blending the sweet voices of women."

The achievement of such a state of harmony is an extremely gratifying experience. From the analyst's vantage point, it is probably the most precious among the legitimate satisfactions his work may provide. And from that of the analysand, it may well turn out to be both unprecedented and never to be duplicated as a "holding environment." Franz Alexander (1946, 1956), it will be recalled, founded a psychotherapeutic school on the assumption that such benign therapeutic occurrences had the power to undo the damaging results of childhood deprivations and traumata, and many other voices within the field have seconded such views. Recently, Alexander's concept of the "corrective emotional experience" has been echoed in more sophisticated form by therapists who believe in the healing power of empathy (cf. Wolf, 1976).

Although I do not dispute the fact that the provision of an empathic ambience within a therapeutic setting has beneficial effects of a nonspecific sort, I cannot agree with the foregoing viewpoints. I do not see the achievement of a shared language by patient and therapist as a therapeutic measure that will produce desirable effects in and of itself. To be sure, the establishment of a holding environment may indeed produce real improvements in the patient's capacity to cope with the adaptive problems of everyday life—as long as the source of external assistance is available! Even a temporary period of peace and prosperity attained in this way may have further desirable consequences with long-term implications. The point, however, is that external results of this kind are not to be confused with genuine personality change.

Rather than conceptualizing the attainment of communicative harmony as a therapeutic agent in its own right, I believe it makes better sense to view it as an indicator that a change has taken place in the patient's capacity to make constructive use of a human relationship for whatever else the therapist may be able to offer. In psychoanalysis proper, the analyst is generally in a position to offer interpretations of the unconscious along with other explanations about the analysand's psychobiological functioning (including the rationales for the measures of pacification, unification, and optimal disillusionment required by the patient). I believe, in other words, that the establishment of a holding environment paves the way for the more specifically "curative" aspects of the analytic task. We must never forget, however, that the course of true love never does run smoothly, to wit, that people in need of psychological help are seldom able to form lasting collaborative relationships. More often, they are compelled to repeat in the treatment the difficulties that have generally characterized their human interactions throughout life. It follows that the therapist's earnest efforts to listen with empathy and to respond with clarity and tact are at first more likely to arouse resistances and negative therapeutic reactions than to produce enlightenment and concord. In order to arrive at that stage of *entente cordiale* we term a "therapeutic alliance," a great deal of preliminary work must in fact be done.

PSYCHOLOGICAL OBSTACLES
TO HARMONIOUS DIALOGUE

Can we spell out the nature of the preliminary therapeutic work required to assist patients to overcome their inability to tolerate being so well understood that the voice of the therapist may actually articulate what the patients themselves think and feel? When we pose the question in this way, it becomes evident at once that we are seeking to outline a methodology for achieving the optimal conditions in which interpretive work may be performed. One global way to answer the question is to state that, in order successfully to tackle intrapsychic conflicts that originate in relatively later phases of childhood, the archaic problems that cause miscommunication must be overcome, regardless of the resistances that interfere with this effort. In practice, this problem may defeat us, for our attempts to handle these resistances, that is, to overcome miscommunication, may themselves run into formidable barriers of miscommunication. Many psychotherapies disintegrate into an infinite regress of just such misunderstandings.

It goes without saying that a comprehensive discussion of these problems would have to examine the therapist's contribution to the failure of communication as carefully as it pinpoints the failure of the patient. Problems of countertransference and counteridentification, after all, are more or less ubiquitous, certainly expectable at the very least; perhaps more is to be gained from the discovery and modification of these problems than from periods of untroubled work. In disorders of communication, these difficulties on the part of the therapist are likely to manifest themselves as instances of miscommunication echoing or complementing those of the patient. Here, however, I shall confine myself to a brief survey of the main issues that render *patients* incapable of tolerating the longed for intimacy of communicative harmony with their therapists.

The acquisition of spoken language, usually beginning in the latter half of the second year of life, expands the toddler's capacity to process information exponentially. This expansion may be particularly dramatic for children whose caretakers have had unusual difficulties in comprehending the nonverbal signals of infancy. Whatever the specific quality of this childhood experience, the novel understanding of a patient's communications achieved in the course of psychotherapeutic treatment that gets off to a good start will inevitably echo that early experience. Unfortunately, the establishment of spoken communication or, to put this achievement into the framework of cognitive development, the underlying maturation of symbolic thought, also produces a revolutionary shift in the organization of behavior. Like every nodal point in development, that is, it constitutes a period of maximal vulnerability.

Newly aware of his separate individuality, the toddler may have greater or lesser difficulties in maintaining his sense of autonomy. The outward manifestations of difficulties in this sphere have been described by Margaret Mahler and her associates (cf. Mahler *et al.*, 1975) as the "crisis of rapprochement." In the midst of this crisis, numerous occasions may arise when the child's uppermost need is to keep "mamma out," to allude once again to the earliest words of my negativistic patient. But this may not always be possible. As Shakespeare reminds us, the Devil can assume a pleasing shape; most of all, like the poet himself, he can seduce us through his language. Caretakers who invade the child's private space through the use of words, rather than through force-feeding, for example, will create conflicts for that individual that center around the very process of communication, especially as it relates to spoken dialogue.

Hence, it is precisely those patients who are most uneasy about the consequences of intimacy for their sense of separateness and autonomy—who have if you will, the greatest anxiety about symbiotic experiences—who will prove the most resistant to the establishment of harmonious and untroubled communication with their therapists. On the other side of the same therapeutic dilemma, many patients are not particularly uneasy about harmonious intimacy; instead they find it strange and emotionally flat. These are the individuals who have learned to define meaningful relationships in terms of pain, tension, and discord. Insofar as verbal communication plays its role in producing such conditions, these patients use it to promote misunderstanding. Upon investigation, one usually discovers that their caretakers often misused language for the purpose of obfuscation. Such patients, in other words, do not actually *resist* mutual understanding through the therapeutic dialogue; more precisely they are addicted to creating false consensus with its predictably painful consequences.

When we are confronted with negativism, we can be reasonably certain that the patient's behavior represents some derivative of early childhood transactions from the phase of "separation-individuation." as Mahler (Mahler *et al.*, 1975) calls it. In contrast, the reenactment of painful episodes of miscommunication cannot be referred back with the same kind of specificity to any particular phase of early development. Traumatic vicissitudes at various age levels may draw verbal communication into the area of conflict in a manner that will lead to compulsive repetition in later life; this is particularly likely to be true in cases where the original caretaker is lost and the painful misuse of language takes place in the relationship with those who replace her. Nonetheless, most cases in which the patient is addicted to miscommunication ultimately point to a pattern of relatedness that even antedates primary reliance on spoken language: It constitutes regression to preverbal uses of speech.

My discussion thus far has focused only on those circumstances in early childhood that lead to patterns of clinging to disharmony largely as a result of behaviors of caretakers that prove to have deleterious consequences. Although my personal clinical experience has included a majority of cases of this kind, it should never be assumed on an a priori basis that psychopathology invariably derives from a failure on the part of the caretakers: The rights of infants, after all, do not include parental perfection! Even in the case I have reviewed in this chapter, it may well have been the child's atypical language development, rather than the mother's limitations, that contributed most heavily to the derailment of their dialogue. We might note in this connection that this patient's mother was reasonably successful in raising a number of other children, despite her characterological intrusiveness. The ease with which a coherent self-organization is established, or, conversely, its vulnerability to disruption in the event of unfortunate interventions by the caretakers, may well be maturational givens largely under the influence of constitutional variables. At any rate, in the present state of our knowledge about such archaic psychological dispositions, we must avoid dogmatism at all cost.

CONCLUSION

To recapitulate: If we acknowledge that psychological treatment must of necessity consist of an exchange of messages encoded in a variety of "languages," it follows that its success is absolutely dependent on the ability of the participants to communicate in a "shared language." The therapist's capacity to adjust his communication in accord with the patient's assets and limitations in information processing along with his aptitude for learning the latter's various languages may well constitute two of the most essential aspects of native endowment for successful psychotherapeutic work.

I have tried to show that the achievement of a shared language is a prerequisite for therapeutically mutative interventions; in and of itself, however this precondition for further therapeutic work can have only nonspecific beneficial effects at best. Nonetheless, the establishment of untroubled communication may encounter serious resistances in patients whose sense of self is buttressed by the experience of derailments of dialogue (cf. Spitz, 1964). Conversely, when treatment has overcome the initial difficulties standing in the way of harmonious communication, this achievement heralds the fact that it is providing a "holding environment" as well.

In terms of childhood precedents, the achievement of a shared language echoes the achievement of the toddler who has mastered the "mother tongue"—except that in treatment it is mostly up to the therapist to master the language of the patient. Close scrutiny of the difficulties in communication within a particular therapeutic dyad provides unparalleled opportunities for the reconstruction of crucial infant-caretaker transactions occurring as early as the second year of life; these transactions often include certain vicissitudes that preceded the child's acquisition of spoken language. Psychoanalysis provides matchless conditions for detailed study of these matters; this fact renders it the optimal arena for understanding and treating archaic personality disorders.

9

Psychoanalysis and Rhetoric

I

However important the nonverbal aspects of therapeutic communication may be in any kind of psychological treatment, psychoanalysis as a distinct form of therapy is characterized by the goal of articulating as many aspects of the analysand's "inner world" as possible in words that possess the same meaning to both participants. In the previous chapter, I tried to describe the difficult process of forging a shared language between patient and analyst, simultaneously bridging the gap between the individuality of each (see also Gardner, 1983) and overcoming the unavoidable negative reactions occasioned by the intimacy of such empathic contact.

Here, I wish to consider a different aspect of therapeutic communication, namely, the psychological impact of certain choices the analyst makes, on a continuing basis, about expressing his meaning through verbalization. Despite the pioneering studies of Victor Rosen (1977) and an earlier paper by Rudolph Loewenstein (1956), the vital topic of psychoanalytic rhetoric has been generally neglected, and I cannot hope to make more than a modest start in considering some of the basic alternatives available to the analyst in encoding his thoughts. Although choice of vocabulary is generally dictated by the need to communicate within the linguistic universe of the analysand, this constraint, we shall see, still leaves the analyst enormous latitude in determining how to phrase his interventions.

In this regard, one of the very few guidelines to be found in the literature is Levin's (1980) recommendation that we employ metaphors in the service of the interpretive task. Levin believes that interpretations cast in that mold are more potent than the same interpretations couched in a purely discursive style, that is, a style

141

that restricts itself to an articulation of the same propositions as a series of precise abstractions. Levin argues that metaphors exercise greater emotional power by virtue of the fact that they simultaneously exist in two realms of discourse—the realms that Freud termed primary process and secondary process, respectively. Levin points out that the very task of interpretation is to overcome the disjunction in the patient's psychological world between these complementary modes of thinking, a view of interpretation congruent with my own definition of this therapeutic modality (Gedo, 1979b, Chapter 2). At the same time, as Leavy (1980, pp. 72–74) has astutely noted, metaphor serves to introduce the element of the unexpected into the analyst's discourse—and the patient's discourse as well—thus promoting new lines of inquiry about issues previously understood in simpler terms.

Elsewhere (Gedo, 1981b, Chapter 11), I have proposed that certain patients require the analyst to employ linguistic tools even more powerfully emotive than metaphors. To wit, many individuals suffering from developmental disturbances or lags are poorly equipped to grasp the meaning of communications that rely primarily on verbal content. Such patients are best able to process analytic interventions on the basis of affective coloring. Although the latter is generally conveyed through rhythm, tone of voice, and other paraverbal means, the analyst's choice of words may also regulate the emotional impact of his message. To illustrate: A patient may be entirely unaffected if we tell him that his behavior might be construed as hard and selfish; the same person may pause to take notice if we tell him that he reminds us of Mack the Knife from *The Three Penny Opera*; but he may really be shaken to the core if we greet an account of his ruthlessness by whistling, in counterpoint to his associations, Weill's sinister setting of Mackie's identification with the shark and its big teeth![1] (For a clinical instance within an analytic context, see Chapter 5, pp. 79–80 and pp. 85–87.)

In fact, this technical principle was already well-known to Freud and his early coworkers at the turn of the century; they tended to stress the importance of interfering with analysands' evasive recourse to circumlocutions when wrestling with the obscene thoughts that cropped up in the process of free association. When he treated the Rat Man, for example, Freud (1909) professed not to have the authority to grant the patient leave to omit mention of his scatological

---

1. This example naturally presupposes that *The Three Penny Opera* is itself part of the patient's cultural universe. It is incumbent on the analyst, in this connection, gradually to learn the dramatic symbols available to a given patient. As this aspect of a "shared language" develops, the power of the analyst's interventions should correspondingly increase as a result of his freedom to use such devices.

associations. In another context, he wrote of the uncanny power of "primal words" (Freud, 1910b).

To return to my schematic example: Can we specify some of the reasons for the great differences in impact to be expected from encoding an analytic intervention in the three distinct ways I have suggested?[2] Clearly, Levin (1980) puts his finger on one of the relevant issues: The three statements range from an evaluation in the guise of generalized categories, through an analogy to a publicly accepted symbol for a person judged to belong to a particular category, to a complex metaphorical allusion to such a judgment, expressed in an affectively charged manner. In each instance, then, the message differs with regard to the extent of the speaker's personal agency or avowed involvement with its content (see also Chapter 6). The first statement is mere description; although the choice of adjectives implies that the speaker is not necessarily objectively neutral about the matters he is describing, the conclusion that these matters touch upon his personal values does not inevitably follow. The second formulation, in which the person is analogized to an unequivocal stage villain, betrays the speaker's value system but not the degree to which the actual situation has aroused him. In its third form, the intervention openly places the analyst's subjective response in front of the patient—for better or for worse, depending on the therapeutic requirements of the specific situation. In other words, metaphor possesses unusual emotional power not only because it reaches into the depths of the patient's subjectivity, but—perhaps even more crucially—because it emanates from the analyst's subjective depths as well.

We must note, of course, that the extent to which the analyst's subjectivity is exposed to the patient is not regulated only through the use of such rhetorical devices. To mention only two additional major avenues of its expression, such exposure also depends on the music of the relevant vocalization[3] and on the very syntax employed

2. For our purposes here, it is not to the point to go into the question of the precise intent of such an intervention. Obviously, it may constitute an interpretation in the narrow sense of the term (i.e., the translation of hitherto unconscious mental content into everyday language), but it may also serve as one of the therapeutic modalities "beyond interpretation" (see Gedo, 1979b; Gedo & Goldberg, 1973).

3. Because of the enormous importance of this factor, I have selected an illustration in which most readers will immediately identify the nature of that music, that is, an example in which the message is literally conveyed through a tune. (For a similar example, see Gedo, 1981b, case 16, especially pp. 301–302.) As all consumers of music well know, however, mere identification of a given piece of music is not in itself sufficient to decode its emotional message, for that meaning is largely a function of interpretive variations from one performance to the next that simply cannot be predicted.

to convey a given thought. With regard to the affective significance of the paraverbal aspects of the analyst's speech, there is no need to belabor the obvious: Even the strongest statements, judged on the basis of their verbal content, may be negated if they are conveyed in tones of ambivalence, doubt, irony, or other contrary undertones. We may call our patients "crocodiles" (cf. Chapter 5), but if we unconsciously admire or envy their capacity to behave with guiltless ruthlessness, our communication will be heard as "affectionate abuse" endorsing this conduct. (I drew on my supervisory experience to provide an example of an outwardly paradoxical response of this very kind in Chapter 7.)

As far as syntactical possibilities are concerned, Schafer (1976a, 1976b) has already made some pertinent observations. Most important among them is his demonstration that the passive voice is generally used—as in this sentence!—to disclaim responsibility. Thus the analyst may, through passive constructions, soften statements ostensibly intended to confront the patient with the active choices he has made; in similar fashion, he may use such constructions to hide his own active role in the treatment transaction. To state that one has judged the analysand's behavior as delinquent and/or destructive has connotations markedly different from saying that what one has just heard makes one think of Mack the Knife.[4] Schafer has also pointed out that interventions couched in technical jargon serve an analogous function by interposing an array of fictive "agents" (i.e., the constructs of psychoanalytic psychology misused in a reified manner) between the patient's subjectivity and his overt behavior.

One aspect of the analyst's syntax that has decisive rhetorical importance in evoking specific types of patient responses involves the issue of direct versus indirect address. The same variable might be described in terms of the conventions of private dialogue versus the conventions governing a statement made to an audience, even an audience of one. Everyone knows individuals with whom conversation invariably becomes painful because they are excessively didactic in their pronouncements. A psychoanalyst who confines his interventions to interpretive activity in the narrow "classical" sense structures the analytic situation in the same way. Hence our traditional technique in pure culture—a hypothetical situation probably seldom encountered in actual practice—does not lend itself to the type of object relationship expectable in adult social intercourse but, rather,

---

4. I have deliberately applied the passive construction in this pair of hypothetical examples to the formulation that uses a metaphor to make its point; I want to show that an intervention encoded in direct, prosaic terms may exceed a metaphorical intervention in impact, provided one manipulates the syntactical variable to favor the former.

typifies the kind of transaction we customarily experience with a lecturer. Whenever the analyst intervenes in this quasiobjective mode, the primary response will probably be directed to the cognitive content of his message. In the vast majority of instances, analysands are able to process this information at the level of their optimally organized adult intellects, and they generally try to respond, in their turn, with thoughts organized at this same advanced level.

By contrast, direct address involves language that encodes the same information in a form suited to private discourse. This distinction is not reducible to different degrees of formality, such as the use of colloquialisms or slang, although the choice of vocabulary usually *is* affected by this issue. The crux of the matter lies elsewhere—in such things, for example, as the deletion of personal pronouns and verbs in making a descriptive statement about the person being addressed. Thus the direct metonymic appellation "ballbuster" is infinitely more powerful than the declarative sentence "You wish to crush my balls." It is more likely to evoke a personal response that is organized concretely and charged with affect. Dialogue at this level produces an intimate relationship, however briefly, even if the analysand clearly understands that the analyst's decision to participate in this manner is a deliberate one, that the analyst is, in a way, like an actor reading his lines for a role on stage.[5]

II

Perhaps I have now sufficiently stressed the endless variety of communicative modes available to the analyst in making his interventions to switch to the opposite tack without being misunderstood. To counterbalance the emphasis I have laid on the varied uses of rhetoric in analytic work, it is necessary to pay equal heed to certain invariable features of therapeutic discourse that unavoidably produce important psychological consequences. In this regard, I wish to call attention to some implications of the so-called "basic rule" of free association—that is, the analyst's routine instruction to the patient to describe his experience in the analytic situation in words that spontaneously occur to him—and the traditional view that the analyst's complementary role is verbally to interpret the meaning of these communications in a rational manner.

5. Loewald (1975) has used the metaphor of mounting a drama on stage to characterize psychoanalysis. In his terms, the analysand is the "playwright" and the analyst is the "director," although both implicitly take on the various acting parts when the play is being performed.

One recent restatement of this consensus is found in Leavy's (1980, p. 77) characterization of the analytic dialogue as "asymmetrical." Leavy uses this term to underscore the fact that the ostensible subject matter of the dialogue is the analysand's psychic experience. From his varied responses to the stream of associations, the analyst selects for verbalized commentary only that segment of the analysand's productions which, in his judgment, will promote the elucidation of the analysand's inner world (see also Loewenstein, 1963). This asymmetry has been utilized to counteract the anti-regressive influence of the collaborative aspects of psychoanalytic treatment; the relative paucity of analytic interventions prescribed by traditional technique is designed to prevent the crystallization of the analytic transaction as rational discourse.

Without this asymmetry, the dialogue produced by adhering to analytic conventions would create an interpersonal transaction echoing those of the participants' previous social experiences in which the principal focus was the performance of a responsible collaborative task. In other words, therapeutic communication in psychoanalysis would necessarily become associated, for patient and analyst alike, with memories of private conversations that were largely encoded in secondary process. As a result, in its psychological effects, our verbal technique would run counter to the generally regressive pressure exerted by other aspects of the psychoanalytic situation, such as the analysand's recumbent posture and the analyst's position outside of the analysand's visual field.

The skepticism of analysts within the "classical" tradition, such as Anna Freud (1962), about the possibility of valid reconstructions of patients' preverbal experience is probably based on reasoned appreciation of these built-in limitations of analytic technique. Perhaps Freud decided that dreams constitute the royal road to the "unconscious"—or, more precisely stated, to the repressed and disavowed psychological world of the prelatency child—because these mental productions also constitute (both qualitatively and quantitatively) the most significant body of material available for analytic scrutiny that arises in a truly private context, in contrast to the dyadic intimacy of the psychoanalytic setting.

Still another way to approach the same disjunction between verbal technique and the regressive pressure of the psychoanalytic situation is to recall the commonplace observation that one of the most effective ways to counteract regressive episodes with patients who are prone to undergo such disorganizing experiences is to establish verbal contact with them. Correspondingly, the resistance of certain "silent" patients to analytic verbalization may represent a desperate effort to live up to the *spirit* of the basic rule, insofar as words are sometimes available to people only about matters that lack importance. The tendency of certain patients to chatter about triviali- ties—sometimes with a sense of despair about the compulsion to do so—is probably a less favorable variant of this syndrome, one that presents the analyst with a "false self."[6]

At any rate, the various clinical contingencies to which I have alluded all illustrate the role of the therapeutic dialogue itself in centering the analytic transaction on issues capable of verbalization. Moreover, it seems very likely that the specific developmental phase whose derivatives are most readily evoked by a particular segment of treatment can be correlated with the specific nature of the analyst's conversational style. In my judgment, the analyst who is relatively inactive unless (or until) he is in a position to make an interpretation about unconscious meanings is, by the very nature of his own activity, pushing the patient into a mode of organization characteristic of latency, or later. By contrast, the analyst who participates actively and in an affectively charged manner is more likely to evoke the psychological world of earlier childhood. Until recently, nuances of this kind were not conceptualized as genuine technical choices to be made on the basis of the patient's specific needs; they tended to be discussed as manifestations of countertransference. I do not dispute the fact that we often err in our technical choices on the basis of countertransferential or counteridentificatory pressures; by the same token, however, I believe we are entitled to take credit for effective technical decisions in this area that proceed from our informed aware- ness of the alternatives available to us.

Let me offer an example from clinical practice in which my initial manner of talking to the patient *did* reflect a poor choice that resulted from a (temporary) countertransference problem. This *contretemps* came to light because the analysand found herself incapable of think- ing about the contents of my communications, even though the subsequent course of the analysis bore out the validity and relevance of my interventions at the time. Instead of facilitating self-inquiry about these important issues, my communications shocked the patient into states of silent despair, sometimes lasting through several ses- sions. When, at length, I succeeded in restoring our dialogue—usually by asking how I had managed inadvertently to derail it—I generally received the reply that the pseudoscientific objectivity of my initial

6. I have presented such a case (Gedo, 1981b, case 9) as an illustration of the failure of an analysis. The patient, a highly intelligent and articulate person, complained bitterly about the fact that he had no language at his command that could convey his inner experience. His efforts to describe these states invariably falsified them, imparting a spurious adultomorphic distinctness to inner experiences that were inherently fuzzy and lacking in "distinction."

communication made her feel like a laboratory specimen being examined under a microscope. If the patient's bitterness was brimming over, she might add that my efforts were additionally doomed to failure because my optical instrument was no microscope; I was accused of looking into the wrong end of a telescope.

On one level, such a therapeutic crisis merely constitutes an intense transference reaction and thus forms grist for the analytic mill. But while such a formulation is undoubtedly correct, interpretations to this effect drove the patient in question into chronic states of impotent outrage: She was unable at the time to explore the causes of her specific vulnerability to this type of injury to her self-esteem. Instead, she insisted on her right to be guaranteed that I would mitigate these complications as fully as possible by examining my own motives for being so aloof.[7]

The repetition of such a sequence of events on several occasions within a limited time span eventually convinced me that I had to take the patient's observation very seriously. It seemed that, without conscious monitoring, I had altered my customary analytic stance in the direction of increased emotional distance—a shift betrayed by a corresponding change in my language that struck the patient as if I had rudely pushed her away. When I asked myself in what way this inoffensive, even promising, person had begun to threaten me, I gradually realized that the volcanic affectivity of her transference reactions, which often reproduced the loves and hates of a three-year-old abandoned by her primary caretaker, was sometimes on the verge of evoking subjective counterresponses in me that exceeded the appropriate intensity experienced when an analyst carries out his therapeutic task in the mode we generally call "neutral." It seemed that, on such occasions, I sought refuge by distancing myself through the use of academically correct analytic interventions.[8]

Following this acknowledgment of my countertransference dilemma, I decided to confront the problem by sharing my concern about experiencing untoward affective storms in identification with

---

7. A transaction of this kind highlights the value of Schwaber's (1981) emphasis on the analyst's obligation to listen to the therapeutic dialogue from the *patient's* vantage point. It is probably true, as Schwaber believes, that this is in fact the technical requirement Kohut (1959, 1975a) had in mind in his repeated call for an "empathic" response to whatever the analysand might do. In Kohut's work, however, this unobjectionable proviso is inextricably connected with a number of other highly controversial propositions (e.g., that the provision of an unfailingly empathic therapeutic milieu has curative powers in itself) that should not find general acceptance among psychoanalysts.

8. As the reader may well have inferred by now, this clinical excerpt is drawn from the same analysis that provided the illustrations in Chapter 3.

her own. Needless to say, such a communication could only be made in the most personal manner I could command. I am not certain that I can quote my exact words, but I said something like, "You know, I experience your expressions of emotion like an assault. I think I have pushed you away by acting formal because I am afraid your feverish manner is contagious." In making such an admission, I simultaneously confirmed the patient's interpretation of the reasons for our analytic impasse and tried to transcend the countertransference dilemma in action. In other words, both in verbal content and in the formal characteristics of the language employed, my intervention constituted an abandonment of the model technique of psychoanalysis that permits the analyst to avoid the spotlight which the procedure shines upon the patient.

I believe that the foregoing clinical illustration is not only significant as an example of the distorting effect of countertransference on the analyst's customary mode of expression. In my judgment, the vignette further demonstrates that certain profound issues which determine the climate of an individual's subjective world can only arise to the surface of the analytic transaction in the context of a particular kind of dialogue. Obviously, such issues cannot gain expression in the analysand's communications if all dialogue is disrupted, as it periodically was in this particular case whenever my "objective" style of interpretation traumatized the patient. It is imperative to note, however, that we could be no more successful in getting to the heart of the matter as long as the analysis was cast in the mold of the detached analyst processing (and commenting on) the associations of an individual in possession of the verbal resources of adulthood. For the crux of the analytic work at this stage in the treatment was precisely the production of an affective storm in a passive victim who was exposed to the poorly controlled behavior of irresponsible intimates. To put this differently, the transference interpretation which proved to be mutative about the problem of emotional assaultiveness was the interpretation which highlighted the fact that the patient was repeating not her own childhood behavior, but the behavior of one of her early caretakers. As the recipient of transference projections, the analyst's role was actually to reenact the *patient's* situation in the remote past. In this sense, the childhood situation was first encoded in language at the time I articulated my very good reasons for needing to get away from the patient's affective barrage.[9]

9. Although the need to avoid the patient's assault was legitimate, my method of doing so, that of a resort to increased formality, was a countertransference error. The most appropriate response would have been to explain directly the function of the patient's assaultive behavior.

In other words, the psychopathology in this instance consisted of the analysand's continuing inability to put into consensually meaningful language *her* excellent reasons for protecting her self-organization through various behaviors that kept her at a safe distance from potential aggressors. She was constrained to choose between an attitude of invulnerable aloofness (enacted through silence in her analytic sessions) and an attitude in which she became assaultive toward *others* in order to convice them that only aloofness can protect people from emotional assault. To be sure, some of these issues did make an appearance in the patient's dreams, as I have already recounted in Chapter 3 (see especially pp. 38–39 and pp. 41–42). But the dream material never led us directly into the era of the patient's earliest childhood in the manner of the transference reenactments I am describing here.

The foregoing example also shows that the need to view the material from the subjective vantage point of the patient, as advocated by Schwaber (1981)—to accept the assigned role of "selfobject," as some of Kohut's followers would have us do—desirable as it is in itself, is an insufficient posture for analytic purposes. Insofar as archaic reenactments may call on the analyst to accept the role of the patient-as-childhood-victim, it is equally important to focus on the subjective vantage point of the analyst in order to arrive at a comprehensive understanding of the original emotional complexities. It is in this latter sense that the analyst's countertransference reactions may function as essential indicators about the patient's dilemmas.

We see, finally, that the kind of dialogue we must establish in the psychoanalytic situation in order to enable patients to communicate about archaic aspects of their childhood experience is the therapeutic counterpart of the ways in which a small child conveys his experience to his caretakers. I believe this view is congruent with Stone's (1961) description of the emotional meaning of the psychoanalytic situation, including his emphasis on the fact that, for most analysands, such a transference of infantile expectations to the analysis is mediated by way of the authoritarian aspects of traditional physician–patient relationships. Because analytic patients are enjoined to communicate verbally, their messages about archaic issues generally maintain the form of an adult dialogue. Nonetheless, these transactions are radically discontinuous with those aspects of treatment I have characterized as a "responsible collaborative task," and they are necessarily encoded in language closer to the expressive modes of early childhood.

Depending on the particular phase of early childhood implicated and on the specific maturational timetable of a given individual's language skills, the analytic dialogue may be conducted to a greater or lesser extent in words. Insofar as the analysand at the relevant stage of childhood did not possess the linguistic capacity to articulate his message verbally, the analyst must understand the patient's nonverbal enactments within the transference as meaningful communications. Moreover, in order to facilitate conversations of this kind, the language through which the analyst himself participates in such transactions must be penetrating, concrete, simple, affect-laden, and dramatic.

III

If we accept the proposition that the psychoanalytic process unavoidably limits the nature of the psychological universe to be scrutinized by virtue of its defining dialogic character, we might well go on to consider whether the sequelae of experiences that did not take place in an interpersonal context are at all likely to enter the associative field in the analytic setting. My question here refers not only to infantile vicissitudes experienced either in the absence of caretakers or in circumstances that correspond to such absence from the infant's point of view, that is, whenever the child loses his capacity to recognize a familiar person as an agent in the interpersonal field. It also concerns problematic experiences in later childhood that do not involve any other person in a primary way—matters including the child's reactions to the inanimate milieu, to his own body, or to intellectual and aesthetic stimuli.

Obviously, analytic patients often speak about vicissitudes of such aspects of past history, from recollections going back to their early years to the sensations experienced in solitude when taking the elevator to the analyst's office just prior to the present session. As soon as such an event is shared with the analyst, however, the focus tends to shift from its primary significance to the secondary issue of what current or past caretakers were willing or able to do to mitigate the undesirable consequences of the occurrence. Aside from lending ourselves as empathic witnesses to the analysand's efforts at self-inquiry, is there anything we can do analytically to facilitate the reliving and mastery of past vicissitudes that did not involve the object world?

The answer to this question depends on the extent of our previous success in forging a shared language with the patient, as well as the degree to which the expectable resistances to the use of analysis as a symbiotic experience have been overcome. I have discussed these issues in detail in Chapter 8. Once an analysis has reached the stage at which the patient can, without undue anxiety, permit the analyst to become one voice in a process which the analysand experiences as an *internal* dialogue, we may be able to assist in these matters of solitary trauma or deficit in ways that go beyond the services of a silent witness. It should be clear that our opportunity to be heard in the guise of one of the patient's inner voices transcends the issue of empathic good will; it requires, in addition, faultless adherence to the use of the "shared language" previously developed by the participants.

It is perhaps the performance of this task that puts the greatest burden on the analyst with regard to the subtlety involved in accepting such constraints without abandoning the effort to carry the analysis forward. Kohut (1971, pp. 285–286) once described such clinical difficulties by citing a patient who responded with fury whenever his interventions went beyond whatever the analysand herself could have stated. Consequently, Kohut classified this state of affairs as an aspect of "mirror transference," specifically, one in which the patient with a "narcissistic disturbance" requires "echoing." Needless to say, I do not agree that such clinical contingencies necessarily betoken narcissistic problems; in fact, I do not believe that the therapeutic difficulty Kohut encountered was a function of the patient's specific pathology. On the contrary, as the foregoing discussion implies, I would understand the patient's anger when her analyst intruded opinions of his own into her psychic space as the natural outrage of a person who had first been given implicit assurances that her need for emotional solitude would be respected and was then disappointed in this expectation.

Kohut's example is not given in sufficient detail to permit an independent judgment as to whether the patient's anger in response to his interventions was caused by their intellectual content, as Kohut believed, or simply by the manner in which they were made. I can, however, provide an illustration of a similar transaction from my own practice in which the problem clearly resulted from the *manner* in which I made an interpretation and not from the content of the interpretation. The patient was a professional woman who was switched from one primary caretaker to another in the middle of the second year of life. She had never been able to adjust to this change, and her early childhood was characterized by emptiness and solitude. Following an interruption of our work to which she reacted as if a revolution had taken place in her life, she reported a hopeful dream, described in vivid detail, that could only have been based on a great painting she had seen in the Louvre during a previous solitary vacation. In the dream, the patient, bare-breasted, was leading a troop of insurgents onto a barricade. "Liberty leading the people?" I asked. But my patient did not know the title of Delacroix's great canvas, nor did she consciously recall having seen it at the head of the main staircase at the Louvre.

The dream probably did express the patient's wish to become free of the tyranny of her past, but the image, though cast in the form of a great public symbol, was the creation of a deprived preverbal child. In drawing on a percept she encountered in an art museum, she was almost certainly alluding to the promising start she had made in my office, a space filled with pictures, in overcoming the legacy of her past. At the same time, she was reaching toward mutuality in the use of symbols for communication, forging the kind of bond with a surrogate caretaker she had never been able to form with those available to her after she lost her original one. When I responded to the symbol she proffered at the level of its conceptual meaning (i.e., by alluding to the patient's fantastic ambitions when she felt abandoned) rather than grasping the significance of her imagery within the psychic universe of a preverbal child (e.g., the implicit identification with a lactating mother), I ruptured the illusion that my contribution to the analytic dialogue represented one voice within the analysand's inner world. She responded with the outrage Kohut believed to be characteristic of patients who, requiring an "alter ego," experience the analyst as failing to echo them. And the patient's sense that I could not be trusted to adhere to a language she would be able to master persisted for a number of years.

Perhaps the most significant aspect of this clinical vignette is the fact that my unempathic (albeit valid and relevant!) intervention did not lead to any cessation of analytic progress; it merely deflected the focus of our attention from archaic material related to the patient's unbearable solitude (material maximally difficult for both of us) to issues of self-esteem conceptualized in phallic terms. My acquaintance with the subject matter of Delacroix's masterpiece aroused the patient's competitiveness and led to fruitful exploration of her sense of inferiority vis-à-vis males, especially a patronizing older brother. In other words, my personal response to her dream led to the resumption of analytic work in the context of an ambivalent dyad.

In order to permit continuing exploration of an analysand's crucial experiences of childhood solitude, the analyst has to learn to keep himself from intruding his individuality into the transaction in this manner. Obviously, the most common tactic for achieving this end is the temporary renunciation of words—a posture of active listening that is, incidentally, by no means devoid of vocalization. Sooner or later, however, the analyst must intervene verbally, either to complement the patient's understanding of his or her experience or to forestall the potentially traumatic consequences that may ensue if the patient feels abandoned during the period of the analyst's "inactivity." If the next intervention is not to abort the patient's sense of solitude, it must be phrased, as I have indicated, as if it were one of the patient's own thoughts. Because the development of a shared language in analysis is a difficult accomplishment, frequently requiring lengthy efforts, the capacity to speak in the analysand's voice may supervene only in the later stages of treatment. Hence full exploration of those solitary experiences that are of crucial genetic significance for character formation is usually possible only when the analyst has made the patient's rhetorical style his own.

THE ANALYTIC COMMUNITY

10

On Some Dynamics of Dissidence within Psychoanalysis*

*Credo in un Dio crudel che m'ha creato. . . .
E credo l'uom gioco d'iniqua sorte. . . .
—Verdi/Boito, Otello (Act II, Sc. 2)*

The sources of dissidence within psychoanalysis probably transcend the arena of political and transference issues to which they have commonly been ascribed. At the outset, let me illustrate this claim by means of a personal example. One of my books was recently reviewed by a number of distinguished colleagues, including Hanna Segal, the *doyenne* of the Kleinian school (Segal & Britton, 1981). In her characteristically perceptive manner, Segal commented at some length on the fact that my proposals possess an unusual degree of coherence and internal consistency. Needless to say, I was initially delighted by such a tribute from unexpected quarters, but my joy was destined to be short-lived! Segal, it turned out, did not look with favor on such a tightly constructed conceptual edifice: *In principle*, she preferred a more intuitive—dare I say a more romantic?—approach to the theoretical task. Apparently, it was Melanie Klein's cavalier attitude toward theoretical coherence that actually attracted Segal to her work. Where are we to find an epistemological referee to blow his whistle on such unscientific conduct? And how many yards should the Kleinians be penalized? Of course, personally, I believe they have forfeited the game!

But I must turn from this subjective viewpoint to a broader perspective. Some years ago, Ernest van den Haag (1965) called attention to the similar outlook about the human condition of Freud

157

and St. Augustine. We may be initially startled by this comparison, for we are accustomed to emphasize the difference between psychoanalysis and our religious traditions.[1] In my view, however, it is indeed reasonable to classify both religious orthodoxy and psychoanalytic orthodoxy as doctrines occupying middle-of-the-road positions between the extremes of philosophical pessimism and utopian optimism. The theological controversies to which van den Haag alluded do find their echoes in contemporary psychoanalytic discourse. It is true that Freud simultaneously rejected views paralleling the Pelagian heresy, with its concept of man's limitless perfectibility, and Manichaeanism, with its notion of irremediable human wickedness. And it should come as no surprise that similar divergences in outlook have splintered the Moslem world (see Hodgson, 1974). Such fundamental differences in the view of human nature, I suspect, may be destined to polarize every intellectual community.

At the level of competing theoretical and clinical proposals, then, psychoanalysts have collectively been guilty of dismissing all too readily the ideas of rival schools. Rothstein (1980) has attributed this irrational propensity to the fact that analysts are narcissistically invested in their theories (i.e., in the psychoanalytic "paradigms" that guide their activities, to use the terminology of Kuhn, 1962). Rothstein is doubtless correct in pointing out that the theory which reduces a practitioner's helpless uncertainty in the clinical arena can easily assume the aura of perfection. But I do not share his hope that it may be possible to divest analytic theories of such irrational incrustations, for we choose our preferred schemata on the basis of underlying philosophical judgments about human nature which are, themselves, nonrational. It follows that sectarian disputes about theory invariably reflect underlying value judgments, a point I have already made in Chapter 6.

In terms of clinical performance, our customary parochialism has not been justified by demonstrably superior results within our home parishes (cf. Gedo, 1981b, Chapter 5), so that we tend simultaneously to castigate ourselves for the unseemliness of the general dogmatism in our midst. How embarrassing it is! We turn out to be believers, like Thomas Aquinas—except that we cannot match his insight that one is forced to have *faith* precisely because what one believes is absurd!

---

1. In an illuminating article on the sociology of new scientific schools (such as psychoanalysis in its early stages), Weisz (1975) convincingly demonstrates that "the early pioneers of psychoanalysis often behaved more like followers of a religious sect than like scientists" (p. 350). But even Weisz stops short of van den Haag's radical viewpoint: He explains the unseemliness of such unscientifc conduct in terms of certain "institutional imperatives of scientific life" (p. 350) without applying the designation of a belief system, analogous to a religious one, to the psychoanalytic view of man.

Moreover, whatever we find unfamiliar can be permanently disowned by pronouncing it anathema: It is simply *"not* psychoanalysis." But I have found the ideal rejoinder to such facile dismissiveness: With Louis XIV, one simply declares, *"La psychanalyse, c'est moi!"*

At those moments when a more ecumenical spirit prevails, most psychoanalysts will concede the value of a wide gamut of clinical theories that have guided various groups of analytic practitioners in the bewildering task of processing their observational data. Each of these conceptual schemata encodes one or another of the primary meanings implicit in human existence—unfortunately, often to the exclusion of all other meanings. Thus, the view of man embodied in the libido theory, especially in the form it took prior to 1920, attributed primary significance to the satisfaction of the appetites. By contrast, Melanie Klein's psychoanalytic system teaches the need to make reparation for man's constitutional wickedness—in other words, it is a species of psychoanalytic Manichaeanism! In the 1970s Heinz Kohut promulgated views that give comparable emphasis to the unique healing power of empathy while acknowledging man's entitlement to an affectively gratifying milieu—a position that comes close to the optimism of the Pelagian heresy. Let me hasten to add that I am emphatically in agreement with the need to satisfy appetites, to curb human destructiveness, and to provide an affectively gratifying environment for our children. And I am for other desiderata to boot! Isn't everyone?

Well, of course, we know that everyone does agree on these matters, public statements to the contrary notwithstanding. The passionate declarations of commitment to reductionist formulations do not involve the real world of human transactions—the "green of experience," as Goethe called it—but only the arcane realm of psychological theory. How can we account for the fact that the psychoanalytic community seems to regard the theoretical scaffolding around our collective enterprise as the crux of psychoanalysis, despite Freud's injunctions to the contrary? I would hazard the conjecture that this attitude harks back to the origins of the discipline within the matrix of 19th-century biology (cf. Sulloway, 1980). Freud's attempts at theory construction continued the tradition he first imbibed from Brücke, the eminent physiologist in whose laboratory he began his scientific career. This tradition was anchored in the epistemology formulated by Descartes in the 17th century. It delimited the material world (*res extensa*) from the world of the spirit (*res cogitans*) in order to make possible the study of "matter" through the methods of physical science: consensually validated observation and reason.

Within this epistemological context, simultaneously empiricist and rationalist, Freud undertook the seemingly impossible task of applying scientific methods to the study of the *res cogitans*. He developed a "metapsychology" to serve as the explanatory theory bridging the two realms of discourse; in accord with the positivistic standards that informed the philosophy of science at the turn of the century, Freud felt obliged to commit himself to explanations at a neurobiological level (see Freud, 1895). The psychoanalytic *psychology* he began to articulate in 1900 did not abandon the aim to develop scientifically valid propositions. The fact that, by the current criteria of empirical science, Freud's metapsychology lacks *explanatory* value has introduced a Babel of confusion into our discourse—but most of us have persevered (or perseverated?) in searching for a theory that embodies biological Truth.

One of the most prominent ideological fissures among psychoanalysts has opened along this fault line in our conceptual terrain. On the one hand, we have scientific Jeremiahs—I confess to being among them myself. The idols of our energeticist past must be overthrown, we cry! We cringe to hear respected colleagues render homage to false doctrines such as narcissism or the ego—sometimes even to that chief abomination, psychic energy! We feel that our sanity is being assaulted when traditionalists continue to adhere to these outworn rituals at the same time as they acknowledge that the latter have no scientific standing. The traditionalists tell us that, in using such terms they are speaking mataphorically; yet we cannot help but suspect them of continuing to lay claim to biological Truth. Their attitude strikes us as scientific Dadaism—or delinquency. On the other hand—but no, I will not presume to guess how they might characterize *us*; I am reasonably certain, however, that their indictment could sound just as devastating and, alas, would be just as persuasive.

From a historical perspective, the fate of Freudian metapsychology is a curious paradox, for its principal rationale was the need to anchor psychoanalysis within natural science. Since components of this system have long since lost their connections with neurobiology, Freud's metapsychology can no longer lay claim to materialist foundations. To the contrary, its continuing currency amounts to a return to pure rationalism—to be precise, to a revival of the doctrines of vitalism that Freud had been intent on opposing through his energeticist theories in the first place. One recalls C. G. Jung's reminiscence (1963, pp. 150–151) that Freud enjoined him to cleave to the libido theory because it protected psychoanalysis from engulfment by a "black tide of occultism." I submit that contemporary analysts who would make do with a theory composed of metaphors are reverting to a prescientific, idealist doctrine, very much in the footsteps of Jung! Like him, they tend to clothe such quasi-mystical attitudes in the noncontroversial outer garb of empiricism (cf. Stepansky, 1976). The most unequivocal example of this "heresy" on the current clinical scene is the mythology promulgated by the students of Melanie Klein, for example, their insistence on the presence of primal envy in infants shortly after birth.

Needless to say, I regard the work of such biological visionaries as antithetical to true empiricism. As I have observed, their position is actually much closer to the philosophical viewpoint antithetical to empiricism, that of rationalism. Rationalists espouse deduction from ideal schemata; empiricists, for their part, eschew presuppositions about the nature of things in favor of making and ordering observations. It follows that true empiricists tend to view the mind as a *tabula rasa* that becomes filled as a consequence of external stimulation. Hence, this viewpoint underlies a wide variety of nurture psychologies, including behaviorism. Although Freud's emphasis on the inborn patterns of behavioral disposition he termed "drives" has probably deterred most of his followers from embracing such empirical views without reservations, the pragmatic bent and philosophical optimism of American intellectual life have pushed a substantial segment of the analytic community in this direction. If the election were held today, Pelagius might well defeat St. Augustine by a comfortable margin. The most common form of nurture psychology within psychoanalysis at this time is a heterogeneous group of clinical theories centered on object relations. By and large, these hypotheses tend to pay a bit of lip service to the importance of some constitutional ground plan for personality development, but they clearly regard the nature of early transactions with the caretakers as the most crucial variable in this regard.

The decision to place object relations at the center of man's motivational system appears to elevate to a position of primacy in theory construction an issue that does not seem to be a matter of major import for pathogenesis in the majority of people. Can anyone have forgotten that it is possible to create beautiful neuroses while being raised optimally by the best of parents? Or that acts of God are just as likely to ruin a person's character as the peculiarities of a caretaker? To be sure, such lessons have not been permanently forgotten—they are overlooked only at the moment of truth, when confronted by the brave bulls of choice in the conceptual arena! What leads certain theoreticians to choose so unlikely a focus as object relations for articulating the universal crux of human psychology?

Before I hazard an answer to this question, let me note that the majority of those analysts who advocate nurture psychologies actually disavow the fact that they are proposing an *alternative* to Freud's system. They wish to eat their conceptual cake and have it too—and they manage this feat by claiming the privilege of using several uncoordinated theoretical perspectives simultaneously, even if they happen to be mutually contradictory. Such incoherence is routinely justified by appealing to the precedent of the coexistence of two valid theories of light. Needless to say, I regard this argument as a gross misuse of the concept of complementarity, for the physicists resorted to this desperate expedient only because a single explanation was unavailable—a situation that has not arisen in psychoanalysis. I *have* long espoused the principle that we need a number of subsidiary hypotheses, each applicable to a different mode of the organization of behavior in the developmental sequence (see Gedo & Goldberg, 1973). Nonetheless, we very much need a consistent and unitary meta-psychological framework into which we can fit each of the subsidiary hypotheses we wish to employ.

To return to the main thread of my discussion: If it is granted that theorists of object relations do indeed give human relatedness primacy of place in their psychological systems, what induces them to do so? Perhaps we may be able to discern their motivation by review-ing the intellectual history of the most influential recent convert to a nurture psychology, Heinz Kohut. Kohut himself termed his version of clinical psychoanalytic theory "self psychology," but the designa-tion is in reality something of a misnomer. I would characterize his theory as a clinical orientation centered on object relations, because his hypothesis about the formation of the structure he calls the "self" involves only the activities of the caretakers.

By the mid-1970s, Kohut had begun to deemphasize the accurate interpretation of structural conflicts involving primitive grandiosity and/or idealization (see Kohut, 1975a, 1975b). The rationale for this change seems to have revolved around the issue of empathy; Kohut apparently decided that the truth value of analytic interventions was much less important than their effect on the therapeutic relationship. In this context, he began to stress the healing power of the analyst's "empathic" behavior. In practice, this was tantamount to a thera-peutic stance stressing the legitimacy of the patient's claims on the caretakers. With this step, Kohut's analytic system effectively crossed the continental divide into the realm of the nurture psychologies. Kohut, it should be noted, was admirably clear about the fact that his basic point of difference with analytic traditionalists concerned values (cf. Kohut, 1982)—he decried the exclusive commitment of the disci-pline in the past to the attainment of valid knowledge.

Most analytic theorists who anchor their work in the issue of object relations have failed to think through the logic of their posi-tion with Kohut's intellectual rigor. By and large, therefore, their

proposals have been less threatening to the cohesion of the psychoanalytic community than the essentially similar ideas that Kohut
propounded, with complete justification, as a new dispensation within
our field. In underscoring the discontinuity of his views with traditional psychoanalysis, he really meant to say that one cannot be a
Buddhist and a Shintoist at the same time, whatever the Japanese
practice may be; his work forced all analysts to make a choice. Many
responded with the shock and horror that the Ayatollah Khomeini
aroused in our secular culture with his indifference to oil revenues.
What a fanatic, we cry; he really *believes!* To be sure, Shiite mysticism
and self psychology are by no means the only belief systems extant
on the current scene; Pelagian nurture psychologies are hardly alone
in being based on absolutist value systems. Indeed, as Michael Polanyi
(1974; Polanyi & Prosch, 1975) has shown, *every* scientific theory is an
expression of such beliefs. *Even our own.*

In recent years, it has become fashionable to disavow the need
for psychoanalysts to make a priori commitments to one or another
of these rival conceptions of human nature. This evasion generally
takes the form of rigidly circumscribing the range of subject matter
that is implicated in our therapeutic activities from the standpoint of
the basic rule of free association. If we frame our work in this way, it
follows logically that our psychoanalytic interventions can only consist in deciphering the latent meanings of the analysand's messages,
so that we do not have to concern ourselves with very much that is
beyond language *per se.* Probably the most prominent contemporary
exponent of such views is Jacques Lacan, but a number of American
analysts also exemplify this tendency to repudiate the need for a
metapsychology.[2] Such an a priori epistemological position places
these theorists in the rationalist camp.

Of course, the refusal of these advocates of a purely hermeneutic,
structuralist approach to specify their a priori biological assumptions
does not actually mean that they have no such assumptions. Like M.
Jourdain, the psychoanalytic hermeneuticists are unaware of the fact
that they speak in prose—or, I should say, that they speak psycho-
biologically. They systematically ignore those aspects of the psychoanalytic transaction that do not conform to the model of an *explication
de texte;*[3] in so doing, they reduce the scope of psychoanalytic psychology to one delimited area of mental life. Specifically, they focus

2. Gill and Holzman (1976) have edited an indispensable volume to which the principal
proponents of this viewpoint contributed chapters. See especially the chapters by Gill
(1976) and Schafer (1976a); for a thoughtful rebuttal of their position see Rubinstein's
(1976) contribution to the same volume.

3. In my judgment, Paul Ricoeur's influential book, *Freud and Philosophy: An Essay on
Interpretation* (1970), introduced this fashion to the American psychoanalytic community.

on derivatives of those phases of childhood development that follow the acquisition of language or equivalent symbolic systems. Preverbal issues, if they are considered at all—and it is my impression that they are rarely taken seriously—are viewed as prehistoric *anlagen*. In a purely hermeneutic approach, the existence of these archaic dispositions as vectors that contribute to the specific configuration of later mental properties must be inferred through deductive reasoning. Direct observations of nonverbal behavior (i.e., the "ethological" mode), performed in the manner of a natural scientist, are allegedly never attempted. Of course, many analysts, among whom I count myself, remain skeptical of such claims and continue to insist that there is always more to effective psychoanalytic treatment than meets the ear—especially in instances where the communicative use of language is impaired (see Chapter 8).

In attempting to understand the presuppositions about human existence implicit in the hermeneuticists' restrictive viewpoint, it may be easiest to note what exactly is left out of their account: the area of experience Freud believed to be under the sway of the repetition compulsion and thus "beyond the pleasure principle," as he put it in the title of what is perhaps his most profound monograph (Freud, 1920). In Freud's sober view, the area of man's mastery over his inner experience is severely limited. By contrast, the hermeneutic approach seemingly implies that, instead of being lived by the daemonic forces that Freud called "Thanatos," humanity regularly triumphs over them through the magic agency of words. Would it were so! In fact, the most fundamental discovery of psychoanalysis about mankind may well be that the Word is not our Beginning.

In terms of the polarity between philosophical pessimism and utopian optimism, the analytic hermeneuticists take their place with the object relations theorists at the optimistic end of the scale. How ironic! Visionary biologists, visionary culturalists, and visionary structuralists share only their utopian assumptions—or, if you will, their disclaimer of Freud's therapeutic modesty. Can the Centre hold, contrary to the predictions of W. B Yeats? Need I say that I look upon my own conceptual work as a last ditch effort to save the Freudian acropolis from the assaults of the Persians? Of course, this is the claim of each and every competitor in the current free-for-all of psychoanalytic discourse: We declare one and all that our views have captured the viable essence of Freud's thought (cf. Gedo, 1972).

What, then, is my own version of this essence? Without recapitulating the lengthy expositions I have provided elsewhere (Gedo, 1979b, 1981b), let me say this much. I share Freud's conviction that psychoanalysis must ultimately be construed as a biological discipline, so that our basic theories must be congruent with contemporary knowledge in cognate fields such as neurophysiology and developmental psychology. I believe that the most essential of our therapeutic activities pertain to preverbal and even presymbolic issues, including optimal tension regulation and the establishment of a stable hierarchy of biological aims and patterns, especially in the affective realm. I assume that this hierarchy, which I have termed the "self-organization," is established on the basis of infantile experiences that are codetermined by constitutional factors and the nature of the early milieu. The archaic dispositions that collectively constitute the self-organization are almost always assimilated within networks of subjective wishes of later origin, wishes encoded in verbal symbols that mask their primitive beginnings. In postulating the assimilation of a set of biological dispositions into the hierarchy of the individual's personal aims, I believe I have provided one solution to the problem of bridging the gap between the separate levels of organization we term "physiological" and "psychological," that is, Descartes's *res extensa* and *res cogitans*. At any rate, whenever the archaic constituents of the self-organization find no acceptable pathway to expression in later adaptation, their effects are destined to be experienced as alien forces that overwhelm the individual in terms of his subjective sense of being an autonomous agent. As sentient beings, we are indeed passive victims of the daemonic within us; this, I believe, is what Freud meant in reiterating that the Unconscious is truly unknowable (1900, p. 615; 1915, p. 187; 1938, p. 158).

It has fallen to David Rapaport (1974) to show that Freud's insistence on giving equal weight to nature and nurture in his developmental propositions constitutes an attempt to reconcile the antithetical approaches of empiricists and rationalists. These simpler alternatives to his complex position represent polar opposites along the continuum of philosophical possibilities, whereas Freud occupied a complex middle ground.[4] But we might just as well encapsulate these different viewpoints in the terms proposed by van den Haag, as the alternatives proffered by theological anthropology 1500 years ago—the alternatives of Augustine, Pelagius, and Mani.

4. As Rapaport (1974) has shown in convincing detail, Freud followed in the footsteps of Leibniz and Kant. The empirical tradition established by Bacon and Hobbes, on the other hand, has dominated the intellectual life of English-speaking communities over several centuries; its greatest exponents were Locke, Berkeley, and Hume. Freud's youthful labors as the German translator of several works of John Stuart Mill (see Jones, 1953, pp. 55–56) provided him with significant exposure to empiricism's characteristic reliance on inductive methods. Rationalism derives from Descartes; hence, the French analytic community continues to be heavily influenced by this viewpoint. We should recall that in Kant's own estimation, his philosophy was attempting to reintroduce a necessary measure of rationalism into contemporary epistemology following the triumph of the British empiricists. See also Gedo (1973).

Claude Bernard succeeded in ejecting vitalism from the biological study of mankind only one generation before Freud began his investigative work. We may reasonably postulate that this achievement was contingent on the exclusion of the psychological vantage point from the study of the organism—it depended, if you will, on the continued relegation of the soul or human spirit to the realm of religion and the arts. Viewed from the perspective of general intellectual history, Freud's accomplishment was the reintegration of psychology into natural science in spite of the continued sway of Cartesian dualism in Western epistemology. It should therefore cause little surprise that, adhering to the traditions Freud brought to the discipline, many psychoanalysts through the years have clung to the concept of mind-body dualism. This position, in turn, permits an integration of their clinical data about mental functions on the basis of a variety of vitalist notions: Jungian archetypes, psychic energy active in a nonmaterial matrix, and the Unconscious as a "language." I see no hope of reconciling these dualist theories with psychoanalytic hypotheses built on monistic, non-Cartesian foundations.

If we construe the Right Wing of psychoanalysis as an assemblage of reactionaries who wish, consciously or unconsciously, to revert to prescientific conceptions, such as that of the soul, how can we characterize the psychoanalytic Left? Insofar as these opponents of metapsychology are neither dualists nor monists, it is scarcely a pun to call them "nihilists," Turgenev's term for subversives in Tsarist Russia; many of them, after all, explicitly deny the need for any philosophical framework at all. From an epistemological standpoint, they are probably "naive realists," observers who believe that their perceptions capture the essence of things without further thought-processing. What do they care about the soul or the brain? Their psychoanalysis concerns itself only with the behavioral output of the black box, "the psyche." This position is not merely prescientific; it takes us back two-and-a-half millennia to undo the genesis of Western thought.

Shall we acknowledge them as psychoanalysts, these strange bedfellows of ours? Well, as the French say, *"Faute de mieux, il faut coucher avec sa femme,"* which may be roughly paraphrased as, "If there is no one better behind the couch, why not?"

11

Essay on Psychoanalytic Education

I

Discussion of the problems of psychoanalytic education has generally been directed at two of the fundamental components of the form it has assumed since the psychoanalytic community established special training institutes over half a century ago. Perhaps most frequently, questions have been raised about the "training analysis" as a prerequisite for matriculation (e.g., McLaughlin, 1973; Calef & Weinshel, 1973), with much thoughtful attention given to the antitherapeutic effect of any procedure undertaken as a step in advancing a professional career. The second major aspect of psychoanalytic education to have received adequate study pertains to the candidate's supervision in the performance of his initial clinical endeavors (e.g., Ekstein & Wallerstein, 1958; Fleming & Benedek, 1966; Wallerstein, 1981). In contrast, the third and final component of our educational tripod has been given scant notice; I am referring, of course, to the didactic process itself, to the instruction carried out within the institute setting (but see Kohut, 1962; A. Freud, 1966).

I have little doubt that the emphasis in our publications accurately reflects the relative importance hitherto given to these various aspects of analytic training. I substitute the word "training" for the term "education" advisedly, because the primary function of the psychoanalytic institutes has been the production of competent clinicians. This assumption has sometimes been made explicit; more often, it has remained unstated. It accounts for the overriding importance of

An earlier version of this chapter appeared in *The Annual of Psychoanalysis*, 7:315–325, 1977.

the candidate's success with his supervised cases for his progress through our institutes; this factor carries much more weight than the personal vicissitudes of the candidate's training analysis—an issue which, in many training centers, tends to be regarded as a private matter. In any case, certification by one of the institutes affiliated with the American Psychoanalytic Association and thereby meeting its minimal training standards is the analytic credential that comes closest to professional licensure in other fields.[1]

Within the bounds they have set for themselves, the analytic training provided by the approved institutes can probably be regarded as a success; it represents an achievement analogous to that of other professional schools which turn out large bodies of practitioners prepared to perform essential public services. In this context, we need not consider the fact that professional training based on this model has come under increasing attack in a wide variety of disciplines, so much so that its earliest prototype, the medical school, may not survive in its age-old form for very much longer. Cogent as many of the critiques of professional schools have been, it would not be realistic to expect that any method of professional preparation could avoid qualifying a significant proportion of marginally adequate graduates whose skills can only be expected to diminish as they lose contact with the stimulation and implicit control of their training matrix, and as they fail to keep pace with advances in their discipline after graduation. What needs to be stressed here is the fact that psychoanalytic education, like the education provided by its models, the schools of major professions such as medicine, law, and theology, has always intended to do more than turn out the equivalent of "general practitioners" of psychoanalysis.[2]

To be sure, the responsibility for the acquisition of specialized skills or knowledge has been left to the initiative of the individual analyst; there has been no provision, that is, for imparting scholarly competence or specialized research skills within the institutes themselves. On the contrary, psychoanalysis has sought to enrich itself by recruiting established scholars and investigators in other disciplines to go through routine analytic training in order to accomplish these latter goals. Both curricula and methods of instruction, in other

1. Analogously, certification by the Board on Professional Standards of the American Psychoanalytic Association is comparable to board certification in the various medical specialties.

2. Historically, it is true that the original model for the Berlin and Vienna Institutes (which served as prototypes for their American successors) was the German academic research institute (Pollock, 1977, pp. 7–8). One may speculate that the American popularization of psychoanalysis following World War II resulted in the lowering of institute standards.

words, have been designed, with negligible exceptions, to implement the training of the average clinician. The body of knowledge the candidate is expected to master consists of a corpus of psychoanalytic classics, centered on the writings of Freud and, depending on the current theoretical orientation of a particular institute, on writings of a selected group of his students and successors. These readings cover the psychoanalytic theories of the development and nature of mental functioning, of the treatment process, and of psychoanalytic technique. These areas may be covered via a consideration of the historical unfolding of analytic ideas or, alternatively, on a topical basis; in either case, much the same ground is invariably covered.

From the student's point of view, the heart of the curriculum is usually the series of clinical conferences and case discussions that focus on the practical management of the process of psychoanalytic therapy. The customary method of instruction is that of the classroom lecture, with obligatory resolutions to encourage student participation in the discussion. Except for case presentations, in the course of which one person's interpretation of significant trends is almost as likely to receive a respectful hearing as another's, candidates are seldom willing to engage in such discussions freely, generally limiting their participation to requests for clarification from the instructor. Occasional attempts to organize instruction in a seminar format may be vitiated by enrolling too many participants in the course.

Although some dissatisfaction has arisen with respect to the so-called "trade school" atmosphere implicit in the arrangements I have described, those rare appeals for reform, such as A. Freud's (1966) call for an "ideal institute," have quite properly highlighted the necessity of eliminating the single most objectionable feature of the system, at least as it operates in many training centers. The authors of these appeals have demanded that the didactic work in analytic institutes be given during the working day, instead of being offered as part of a "night school." In fact, there have been calls for changing the institute curriculum into a full-time activity, on the model of other professional and graduate schools. With regard to this latter proposal, it should be noted that no serious arguments have been advanced for the need to expand the usual program of didactic instruction, so that the switch to a full-time institute would presumably involve no real change in the content of the course work; it would merely permit schedules that might enable students and faculty to perform at their potential best.

The spread of psychoanalytic institutes organized on the model established in Berlin and Vienna in the 1920s has produced a large body of analytic practitioners; in most metropolitan areas of North

America, there is no longer a shortage of competent clinicians to fulfill the demand for analytic treatment. To the contrary, there have been notes of alarm about a potential oversupply of analysts in the near future, faced as we are with growing public disfavor, competition from antiintrospective treatment methods, and increasing exclusion from public schemes of health insurance. On the other hand, there has also been a concomitant diminution in the number of well-endowed medical applicants for training, and it might seem that the forces of supply and demand would suffice to establish a rough balance in this regard. But such a hope is almost certainly doomed to disappointment: The demand for analytic training by candidates with nonmedical backgrounds is increasing and, insofar as it cannot be met by the institutes affiliated with organized psychoanalysis, it *will* be met by the rapidly expanding number of training centers lacking such official sponsorship.

It is no doubt quite tempting to dismiss the graduates of these "bootleg" programs as less than proper analysts, but, proper or not, they are undoubtedly quite real and legitimate competitors in the therapeutic marketplace. Individually, many of them are of more than average competence, both as clinicians and as contributors to the literature. Even if our natural assumption is presently correct that, on the average, institutes affiliated with the American Psychoanalytic Association train better qualified analysts than institutes which are not so affiliated, it is clearly only a matter of time before some of these unapproved training institutions become fully competitive. Sponsorship by universities and the collaboration of well-trained teaching and supervising analysts from the organized psychoanalytic community are predictable developments. Consequently, we may indeed anticipate an oversupply of analytic practitioners, and the continuing production of more and more marginally needed clinicians cannot be regarded as a rational program for our existing educational establishment. We need to turn away from our past commitment to professional training in favor of a new orientation.

II

It might be appropriate to continue this essay by asking "What is to be done?," the classic question posed by revolutionaries when social forms have reached the limits of their usefulness. Aware of the history of revolutions, our answer must be that whatever is done must be done on the basis of local options and in the light of specific local circumstances; what must be avoided above all is any bureaucratic solution imposed from above. We are most likely to emerge from our time of troubles if a hundred flowers are indeed allowed to bloom and if the most viable alternatives are given an opportunity to prove themselves in action. Many institutes may opt to continue to adhere to a formula that they regard as successful and congenial; others, perhaps inevitably the largest ones, may diversify their programs, simultaneously pursuing several options. The particular vision of psychoanlytic education that I wish to describe here is only one among many possible courses of action. It also happens to be a maximally ambitious program that could not be envisaged as long as the primary mission of our institutes was the recruitment and training of a requisite number of clinicians. In a future in which we should be able to substitute a concern with quality for our past preoccupation with numbers, it will no longer be appropriate to dismiss proposals for strengthening our didactic programs on the ground that we must not have unrealistic expectations for our candidates.

In other words, my proposal begins with the assumption that if we offer a truly outstanding education in psychoanalysis as a unique intellectual discipline, we shall attract students of outstanding gifts. This is another way of saying that the vicious circle of routine student bodies and watered-down standards must be broken by uncompromising adherence to the highest expectations. In principle, this rigor should suffice, by itself, to make it very unlikely that unsuitable individuals will seek to enter such a program. If we are truly convinced that we would rather have no students at all than mediocre ones, public knowledge of this policy will drastically simplify the process of candidate selection.[3] Per contra, it may bring us an elite corps of applicants from the entire country, perhaps even outside it. There is no reason that outstanding psychoanalytic institutes cannot achieve the reputation and quality of the best graduate institutions in technology, business, law, and the health sciences. To be sure, we must be ready to welcome serious students—be they humanists such as Ernst Kris, natural scientists such as Robert Waelder, social scientists such as David Rapaport, or creative individuals without academic backgrounds such as Erik Erikson. On the other hand, candidates with a primary interest in rendering public

3. Since I initially drafted this essay almost a decade ago, I have served for six years on the Committee on Institutes of the American Psychoanalytic Association. This work has given me the opportunity to learn in detail about the specific operation of each of our institutes. With respect to the question at issue here, recent experience has confirmed my prediction: In metropolitan areas served by more than one institute, prospective students tend to apply to the one with the most liberal admissions criteria, that is, to the institute that graduates the highest proportion of its matriculated candidates. Correspondingly, students within a given institute tend to avoid supervisors who have a reputation for "toughness."

service may well prefer to affiliate with one of the traditional psycho-analytic training programs.

Am I implying that candidates committed to clinical work to the exclusion of other intellectual pursuits do not *deserve* to be exposed to the maximally enriching educational model being proffered here? Certainly not. Any candidate who prefers the more rigorous and challenging atmosphere of the more innovative program deserves the opportunity to try it. In the contemporary world of psycho-analysis, however, it is unrealistic for faculty to expect students even to read *Freud* in a thorough manner; the requirements I believe to be appropriate for the institution I am describing are literally unthink-able for the majority of current students. If the advantages of my proposed training institute seem self-evident, it is only because I have propounded them with conviction and fervor; an equally persuasive case could be made for training psychoanalytic practitioners willing to come down from my ivory towers.

At any rate, if we succeed in attracting candidates of the highest caliber from a variety of backgrounds, the traditional didactic cur-riculum of the past will prove unserviceable on two separate grounds. First, students of the kind I have in mind would not need to be prodded into learning the basic fabric of psychoanalysis; they could be counted on to cover the subject matter of the traditional cur-riculum independently and as a matter of course. Secondly, both the individual preparation and the specific interests and goals of each candidate would presumably be so different from that of most other candidates as to require a curriculum specifically tailored to the student's personal needs. Consequently, I would envisage a psycho-analytic education without scheduled course work. Within institutes which would opt to offer several parallel educational programs, stu-dents pursuing the independent track I have in mind would naturally be free to audit whatever courses they wish among those being offered at the time. I would insist, however, that such attendance be regarded as a strictly private decision, on a par with the candidate's undertaking other, extra-analytic course work on his own initiative.

I believe that, for the dedicated and scholarly students for whom the best psychoanalytic education should be designed, nothing short of fully individualized instruction will be adequate. In other words, the curriculum for these candidates should be oriented around a tutorial system. Because, in all probability, no single tutor will have expertise in every aspect of psychoanalysis and allied disciplines that a particular candidate might need to explore in depth, each student should in fact have experience with a number of tutors. As we know from 50 years of struggle with the supervisory system, exposure to a series of instructors is essential in any case to minimize the risks of irrational student–teacher alliances and antipathies, with the resulting tendency to form cliques. It would seem to be a logical extrapolation from the existing apprenticeship method of clinical instruction to have each tutor supervise one of the candidate's initial clinical efforts, so that didactic instruction would flow directly from the psychoanalytic situation. Needless to say, such tutorial–supervisory meetings would have to be longer or to take place more frequently—or optimally both—than the customary process of supervision now permits. I would therefore envisage that both candidates and those members of the faculty engaged in the tutorial program would devote more time than is now customary to their joint work, rather than opting for this innovative training procedure in order to reduce their commitments.

With such a system, success will naturally be entirely dependent on the quality of the tutors, and few existing institutes can be expected to have a sufficient number of faculty members with the requisite knowledge, enthusiasm, and time to invest in this type of educational effort. In the beginning, then, the program might have to be set up on a very limited basis, for just a very few students who would therefore need just a very few instructors. The long-term viability of the program would be determined by the success of various institutes in raising funds for endowing faculty positions—in the manner long practiced by major universities—in order to be able to recruit the best possible teachers for the program on a national, and even international, basis. I am quite aware, of course, that major administrative initiatives of this kind are unthinkable without some prior demonstration of feasibility and some proven results through the use of largely volunteer personnel.

Although I am just as reluctant to prescribe the exact number of supervised cases each candidate would be expected to start (or to finish) in order to "complete" his education as I am to dictate the content of what he should learn, I will assume, for illustrative purposes, that each student will on the average utilize four tutor-supervisors. If this were the case, a program could be started with a commitment from as few as four faculty members. If one of these students were to require additional instruction, most institutes could meet this need on an ad hoc basis. A team of four tutors would presumably be able to service as many as four candidates as an autonomous unit. It would be highly desirable if the members of such a unit could bring to their task a varied range of skills, that is, if they complemented one another's areas of expertise. Once again, I must stress that I am taking for granted that every faculty member concerned would have superior clinical skill and mastery of the psychoanalytic literature; additional expertise would have to be in areas such as research methodology, the philosophy of science, the social sciences, the humanities, psychophysiology, or cognitive psychology.

III

A cardinal feature of the plan I have in mind would be a shift in responsibility for most educational decisions from the faculty to the individual candidate. To be more precise, the faculty would have to concentrate on shouldering a burden which, in the past, psychoanalytic educators have tended to shirk: It would have to devise reasonably objective and consensually validated measures by which to judge the candidates' performance in the fields of specialization they have chosen as well as the fundamentals everyone should master. Thus, mastery of the basic core of psychoanalytic knowledge might well be tested by a rigorous qualifying examination; clinical competence could be similarly evaluated on the basis of the presentation of the narrative of a completed analysis the candidate has conducted, either under supervision or independently, in a manner that highlights the unfolding of the analytic process; investigative expertise would be documented in the usual manner, that is, through the submission of a thesis. The first two of these three requirements could be discharged either orally or in written form, or both. It is not necessary at this point to discuss the details of the preferred methodology; what is crucial for the plan is acceptance of the assumption, by students and faculty alike, that completion of the program should signify the attainment of real mastery. Given such a consensus, there should never be any question of avoiding public demonstrations of what each candidate knows and what he is able to do. The other side of this coin is that the faculty cannot avoid the unpleasant task of barring those who have failed to achieve the required levels of competence from advancement, no matter how worthy, likable, and well analyzed the individuals in question may be.[4]

In propounding this precept as the sole *administrative* responsibility of the faculty, I am reiterating the claim with which I began this

4. In my experience, most candidates unable to complete psychoanalytic training in existing institutes (as well as the overwhelming majority of those candidates graduated "compassionately," more or less on condition that they refrain from doing clinical work in psychoanalysis) are dedicated individuals of excellent character who have been successfully analyzed. If they are emotionally troubled, this is often the result of the continuing injury to self-esteem implicit in pursuing a career for which they are not qualified. Their handicaps in doing analytic work are most often of a cognitive nature.

discussion: that educational decisions need to be made by each candidate for himself. It is important for his personal development that each analytic scholar have the freedom to make his own mistakes, and the institutes, for their part, need not and should not assume the role of protective schoolmarms who would rescue their charges from the consequences of their rashness and inexperience. Thus, I am opposed to the drawing up of any rules or regulations about when, and in what sequence, a candidate would be expected to do what. Each student should decide for himself how he wishes to prepare for the various qualifying exercises and when he wishes to undertake them. In this manner, as in that of the initial selection of the candidates, public knowledge of what is required for success would very quickly eliminate the applications of poorly prepared individuals.

For the very same reasons, it should not even be necessary for the institutes to involve themselves in the question that has always been considered the most essential aspect of the candidates' preparation, that of the personal analysis. The educators need only evaluate the student's evolving *competence* and give him adequate, forthright, and continuing feedback about the results of their evaluation. If a personal analysis is likely to increase the candidate's success in performing his educational tasks—a proposition that cannot be seriously challenged more than a century after Josef Breuer's flight from Anna O.'s transferences and his own countertransference reactions to her—it should be up to the student to arrange for this advantageous experience on a private basis. Every serious candidate would undoubtedly do so in good time. But *when* a candidate decided to have a personal analysis would remain a private matter, not the business of the institute. In unfortunate instances where such privately arranged treatment failed to bring the benefits the candidate had anticipated, so that the shortcomings of his clinical work continued to make the need for analysis apparent, the candidate would once again draw the relevant conclusions for himself. Otherwise well-qualified candidates will doubtless take the same steps that psychoanalytic students have always taken: They will seek personal help, and they will do so mostly from the clinicians who have the greatest status within the community.

From the point of view of the educational process, we may expect substantial dividends to accrue from switching our focus from

---

It is surprising that we commonly fail to appreciate that the talent required to perform analyses effectively is just as rare as the analogous gifts required to become a musical virtuoso, a "living national treasure" in the arts (as the Japanese put it), or a major achiever in the sciences. When people of insufficient talent attempt to enter the psychoanalytic field, they are constrained to reduce the complexities of human psychology to a small repertory of formulae.

the mental health of our students to their skills and knowledge. The most obvious, but by no means the only dividend, would be the elimination of the numerous unsatisfactory candidates to whom I have already alluded, that is, those candidates who *have* been adequately analyzed but do not perform well because of inadequate talent or motivation. But there are two further benefits to be derived from this change of focus. I am referring to (1) the potential therapeutic advantages to be gained from the actual separation of the personal analysis of every prospective analyst from his education and (2) the corresponding benefit to members of the faculty of removing the status distinction among psychoanalytic educators introduced by the circumstance that the institutes, in assuming responsibility for their students' emotional well-being, are obliged to appoint "training analysts" to provide the necessary therapeutic assistance.

With respect to the separation of the personal analysis from the candidate's education there is now all but general consensus that this policy is an essential desideratum: The training analyst's participation in decisions about the candidate's professional advancement, however indirect it may be, places an impossible burden on the training analysis. In most institutes, this separation is effected through a policy discouraging (or, at the very least, of not requiring) reports about the training analysis to the educational authorities. But this compromise policy is unsatisfactory: It deprives the institute of information it could profitably use to make decisions about the candidate's educational needs without actually liberating the training analysis from the shadow of its nontherapeutic function as an instrument of career advancement. I believe the candidate's analysis could be relieved of this burden of corruptive "secondary gain" only if all the participants accepted in *principle* that the candidate's ability to do analytic work bears no necessary relationship to his prior experience as an analysand.

As to the matter of appointing certain members of the institute faculty "training analysts," it is widely known that this issue is the most frequent source of discord within institutes. Admittedly, analysts could just as easily struggle over various other teaching or administrative responsibilities, but the fact remains that the monopoly in performing the analyses of candidates granted to training analysts offers them enormous financial benefits. In the competitive marketplace of American society, it is very rare indeed to find a clinician with a significant number of analytic cases who is *not* a training analyst. The privilege of providing service to the institute is seldom sought with the same enthusiasm that analysts seek the prestigious and materially rewarding status of being "clinicians to the profession."

IV

Although individualized instruction, rigorous examinations, the broadening of scholarly and investigative skills, and candidate autonomy in determining the educational program are, separately and in combination, of great potential usefulness for improving the quality of psychoanalytic education, they must not be viewed as ends in themselves. In other words, I do not regard these measures, necessary though they are, as sufficient to effect a radical change in the results to be expected from psychoanalytic education. They might produce somewhat better clinicians and investigators than the traditional training programs have done, and they would certainly prevent the less satisfactory segment or, in terms of some overall rating scale, perhaps the lower half of the graduates of those programs from being certified. Such results, however, would by themselves fail to justify the effort involved in putting this proposal into practice, because psychoanalysis as a discipline requires much more than a desirable improvement in its educational standards if it is to survive as a vital force.

In stating this conviction, I am once again confronting the issue of the basic aims of our educational enterprise: Do we ask to produce ever new cadres to carry out the clinical, educational, and—in rare, fortunate circumstances—research tasks traditional to our discipline? If so, we might content ourselves with the "quantitative" improvements in our graduates which the steps I have thus far described might produce. On the other hand, we cannot rest content merely with raising our standards if the primary task of our elite educational institutions is *not* to be analogous to the task of schools of social work or nursing, or to the training of teachers. Analysts may find these comparisons to be offensive, but they are not out of place as characterizations of the traditional analytic training programs. Those of us who conceive of psychoanalysis as an intellectual system with a role in the humanities and the science of man comparable to the role of mathematics in the natural sciences (see Gedo, 1978a, 1978b) are enjoined to promote the establishment of the psychoanalytic universities Freud first called for in 1926.

One facet of the transformation of our existing institutes into universities is the requisite administrative work; I am referring both to negotiations with accrediting agencies that could yield the authority to grant appropriate degrees upon graduation from our programs and to complex dealings with more or less receptive institutions of higher learning that already sponsor psychoanalytic activities or might be willing to do so in the future in order to recast such activities on the broadest possible intellectual basis. Here I am addressing myself to the other aspect of that transformation, the shift from analytic training programs that are conducted by part-time teachers who are primarily involved in patient care to the creation of centers of intellectual activity where interested participants at all levels of experience, from matriculation as candidates until retirement, could join together for mutual stimulation and collective learning.

To put the matter in a different way, psychoanalytic education will have undergone a real revolution only when it ceases to concern itself with the training, or even the veritable instruction, of neophytes and becomes, as education has become in the better departments of our elite universities, the advancement of knowledge by the continuous intellectual growth of every participant. The change to a tutorial method of instruction should facilitate this goal even as it serves to rectify some of the shortcomings of the traditional curriculum. Every tutorial could potentially turn into a collaborative intellectual quest which, at later stages, could enlist additional participants as a workshop or a more formal research project. The thesis of every candidate would present a similar opportunity. Many theses would undoubtedly reflect the current preoccupations of the most creative members of the faculty. The candidate's participation in these manifold activities could naturally continue beyond graduation and lead, in the course of time, to greater responsibilities within the institute, that is, to joining the faculty. In the nature of such a program, only those candidates deemed qualified for such appointments should be permitted to graduate.

I shall refrain from a tedious enumeration of the various permutations of creative activity familiar to everyone acquainted with centers of learning. Perhaps it will be worthwhile to point out, however, that in successful centers of this kind, the opportunities for gratifying work capture significant numbers of creative people in a manner that renders meaningless any concern about "full-time" or "part-time" involvement. Such persons devote the most significant portion of their time and energy to their intellectual work, and it is both absurd and impertinent to ask them to account for the rest of their schedule. In the *literal* sense of the word, there can only be part-time scholars, since man cannot live by work alone. In a truly meaningful sense, however, a scholar is committed either fully or not at all. Freud must have been alluding to this fact of life when he observed that psychoanalysis will either grip its practitioners totally or leave them untouched.

12

A Winter of Discontent: Contemporary Psychoanalysis in America

For the moment, American social conditions do not favor the acceptance of psychoanalytic ideas. The current age of mass culture is inhospitable to most products of high civilization; the psychoanalyst, like other practitioners who belong to the cultural elite, tends to be ignored—unless he can be turned into a popular superstar. I have previously discussed the corrosive effects on true creativity of this pervasive pressure to conform to the demotic mainstream (Gedo, 1983, Epilogue). Here, I would like to focus on a different aspect of these circumstances: the manner in which they have undermined and even corrupted our psychoanalytic institutions.[1]

1. I believe that I am exceptionally informed about these matters as a result of extensive scientific and organizational contacts with the American psychoanalytic community. Over the years, I have had the opportunity to take an active part in the scientific programs of the American Psychoanalytic Association (hereafter "the American") and some 18 of its component local societies, of some branches of the Canadian Psychoanalytic Society, and of a number of psychoanalytic organizations not affiliated with the International Psycho-Analytic Association (hereafter "the International"). From an administrative vantage point, I have learned a great deal from six years of service on the Committee on Institutes of the American, where every training program is regularly reviewed in some detail. As part of this work, I participated in extensive site visits to six institutes. Six years with the Committee on Research and Special Training and significant periods with the Committee on Scientific Activities and the Editorial Board of the *Journal of the American Psychoanalytic Association* have also provided me with valuable lessons about the status quo within organized psychoanalysis. In a local context, I have observed the Chicago Psychoanalytic Society and The Institute for Psychoanalysis over three decades, participating in their affairs at multiple levels, and holding the office of Society President.

Sigmund Freud's persistent distaste for America has never been satisfactorily explained. Perhaps the fulfillment of his most pessimistic intuitions about the possibility of psychoanalysis taking root in American soil without becoming denatured should convince us that his aversion was not simply based on prejudice. On the contrary, Freud's view must have stemmed from his deep appreciation of the place of his own thought within the great tradition of European ideas from Plato to Nietzsche (see Gedo, 1983, Chapter 11)—a tradition essentially alien to the pragmatic optimism of the New World. For some decades following the 1930s, with the influx of refugees from Nazism to North America, the development of psychoanalysis on this side of the Atlantic took on a seemingly Central European flavor. The intellectual leadership of Hartmann, Jacobson, Kris, and Loewenstein (or, in a vein of dissidence, of Horney and Rado) in New York, the Bibrings and the Deutsches in Boston, Waelder in Philadelphia, Alexander and Benedek in Chicago, the Sterbas in Detroit, Rapaport in Topeka and Stockbridge, to name only a few of the most prominent émigrés, screened the actualities of the development of American psychoanalysis.[2]

But 45 years have now passed since the outbreak of hostilities in Europe stopped the flow of émigré intellectuals; even those who arrived as preadolescents, like me, are approaching the twilight of their analytic careers. Hence we no longer have a cadre of analytic leaders, trained abroad and possessing unchallengeable prestige, to counteract the impact of the autochthonous mass culture upon our discipline. At any rate, American psychoanalysis has become more and more therapeutic in its orientation; we have largely abandoned Freud's intellectual program of supplying the psychological core for a science of man (Rieff, 1959; Gedo, 1978a). This circumstance has allowed certain French authors, notably Lacan, to heap scorn upon the non-Freudian characteristics of recent American psychoanalysis. In a similar vein, Eissler (1965) has excoriated this reduction of our horizons as the "medical orthodoxy" of American psychoanalytic organizations. In the interval, a growing number of rival nonmedical analytic groups has produced graduates no less pragmatic in their orientation than North American analysts with a background in psychiatry. Thus the retreat from Freud's standards has not resulted simply from the policy of excluding nonmedical therapists from our establishment; rather, it seems to be an inevitable concomitant of

2. Even more recently, a large proportion of influential analytic authors has been of European origin—for example, Erikson, Kernberg, Kohut, Loewald, and Mahler.

training contemporary mental health professionals of whatever background.

To be sure, our recruitment policies over the past decade have proven to be disastrous even at the most practical level: As American psychiatry has increasingly espoused a biological orientation, it has attracted a shrinking proportion of physicians, and those who have recently chosen this specialty have tended to be among the less able students.[3] Consequently, the number of candidates accepted for psychoanalytic training has failed to expand; in fact, it has only remained constant as a result of the spread of analytic training to the few remaining major cities where it was previously unavailable. Elsewhere, institutes have only been able to maintain themselves by sacrificing our nominal standards of competence. In every institute, one finds many "problem candidates" who have no hope of mastering the skills required to perform adequate clinical work.

Many of these individuals should have been turned away as unqualified in the first place; certainly, almost all should have been advised to drop out early in their training as their deficiencies became apparent to the faculty. Nowadays, according to conventional wisdom, it is legally unsafe to fail these unsatisfactory students. Most of them are allowed to exist in the indefinite limbo of interminable candidacy, in the hope that, in discouragement, they will disappear of their own accord. Just as often, they are finally granted a "compassionate graduation," with the not-so-secret proviso that their failure to meet the certification standards of the American will serve as the needed caveat emptor to prevent them from practicing as analysts.

In principle, all institutes approved by the American have the same minimal criteria for graduation: In addition to the candidate's personal analysis (almost always performed by a designated "Training Analyst") and the satisfactory completion of didactic course work (a curriculum that can be covered in no less than four years), the candidate must conduct at least three analyses for a minimum of one year in each case. These analyses must be regularly supervised by a faculty-appointed "Supervising Analyst," and at least one of them must be brought to a satisfactory termination. These minimal criteria are now periodically breached by allowing the supervised analyses to be conducted at a less than reasonable frequency of visits, by providing less than the requisite supervision, or by graduating candi-

---

3. For a generation after World War II, about 10% of the graduates of American medical schools chose psychiatry as a specialty. For the last several years, this proportion has fallen to about 2%. Moreover, statistics regularly compiled and published in medical education periodicals indicate that, at the same time, the ranking of these students within their medical school classes has fallen, on the average, from the "top third" to the "bottom third."

dates who have not achieved a successful termination with any of their patients—presumably because the delay in reaching this goal is not attributable to any deficiency in the student.

The Committee on Certification of the American has chosen to do no more than check on the manner in which these minimal criteria have actually been met through written (and occasionally oral) narrative accounts of each supervised analysis, supplemented by briefer reports from the institutes and supervisors. Hand in hand with this official laxity, voices for egalitarianism and a larger membership now demand that we find places for technically "uncertifiable" individuals within the American: Are they not, after all, bona fide graduates of institutes whose training is approved by that organization? In the last several years, approximately half of the institute graduates who made application for certification were approved. Moreover, some candidates whose applications are initially declined eventually do obtain certification, often by addressing whatever deficiencies the committee has found in their training.

It is difficult to blame the beleaguered faculty of specific institutes for this general debasement of the currency of its graduation diploma. All educational institutions must adapt themselves to the needs of the students they are able to attract; the only alternative is to allow the institution to collapse. The individuals who staff psychoanalytic institutes, generally on a volunteer basis that entails considerable sacrifices in time and money, are for the most part persons in later middle age. They almost universally demonstrate an intense loyalty to their organization—a passionate commitment most likely to surface when an institute threatens to splinter into rival camps—so that they will go to great lengths to protect its institutional survival. At a more personal level, they have scarcely any other option, for it is typically too late in their professional careers to develop alternative academic/intellectual commitments.[4]

Of course, psychoanalytic educators can always follow Candide into cultivating their private gardens—or private practices. But academicians are understandably reluctant to fall back into the position of mere providers of services. Moreover, the very fact of being members of the faculty of a psychoanalytic institute gives analysts an opportunity to develop private practices of a particular type—practices

4. In this regard, part-time, so-called "clinical" professorships in medical school psychiatry departments once constituted a career line of almost equivalent prestige. Over the past decade, however, the increasingly biological orientation of most psychiatry departments has contracted such opportunities for psychoanalysts. At the same time, for many analysts who continue to serve in this capacity, the shift of administrative support in other directions, as well as the unexceptional caliber of many recent trainees, have considerably impaired the satisfactions to be derived from such activities.

more focused on the performance of analytic work proper, rather than on other forms of psychological therapy.[5]

All in all, then, we must expect psychoanalytic institutes to provide instruction to applicants willing to pay, in preference to persevering in self-defeating efforts to uphold the training standards of the American. To be sure, exceptions exist, particularly in certain of our smaller training centers which are dependent for applicants on only one or two psychiatry departments that have turned against psychoanalysis. In some of these institutes, a high-minded spirit of commitment to official standards has led to the virtual disappearance of regular candidates. Others have limped along by obtaining waivers for the training of nonmedical applicants from the American's Committee on Research and Special Training. Such waivers are ordinarily reserved for promising researchers, educators, or administrators; institutes on the verge of extinction request them for candidates who allegedly occupy a "strategic position" on the local psychoanalytic scene. Of course, when an institute has only one or two candidates a year, every application necessarily assumes a position of strategic importance!

Instead of lapsing into endless committee meetings devoted to the problem of creating old-style psychoanalytic candidates out of thin air, certain institutes have devoted more and more effort to educational activities beyond what is euphemistically called the "core program," that is, the shrinking enterprise of training "professional" psychoanalysts. These new activities generally fall within the rubric of an "Extension Division," and they are justified in terms of promoting an interest in psychoanalytic ideas in whatever segments of the public may be receptive: psychiatrists, social workers, teachers, cultivated laymen seeking to broaden their education, and so forth.[6]

To my knowledge, individuals who take courses in such extension divisions have thus far not presented themselves to the public as

5. Periodic surveys of the professional activities of the membership of the American have consistently shown that, among those who respond (presumably a sector of the membership more actively involved in psychoanalytic activities than the nonresponding membership), training analysts *on the average* have two more analytic patients at any one time than colleagues who do not have that title. In view of the fact that nontraining analysts in the latest sample reported doing fewer than three analyses at any one time (again, on the average), the two additional cases of the average training analyst can reasonably be attributed to the need of psychoanalytic candidates, actual or potential, to undertake their training analyses with these specially designated members of institute faculties. Indeed, in most institutes each training analyst treats an average of two to three candidates, so that achieving "training analyst" status means, in practice, a steady supply of analytic referrals.

6. I have the impression that clinical psychologists are relatively less likely to suffer the humiliations of such second-class status than members of other professional

full-fledged analysts, but this development is bound to occur shortly. Moreover, for all one knows, some of these individuals may be as competent as certain graduates of the weaker institutes, including institutes affiliated with the American. I make this assertion on the basis of the fact that courageous (or brash!) individuals have always been able to become capable analysts outside the establishment, most often through private consultation about their clinical efforts with respected senior colleagues. Such "bootleg" training has been prohibited by organized psychoanalysis, with expectably discouraging results. In France, private enterprise has triumphed in this regard, and it may do so in many other places in the near future.

At the same time, a number of centers, notably Anna Freud's Hampstead Clinic, have trained people of diverse vocational backgrounds to do child analysis.[7] Some of the extension divisions train people to do "psychoanalytic psychotherapy" with children, and it is difficult indeed to distinguish among this variety of more or less analytic professionals on the basis of formal credentials. Winners in the professional marketplace therefore tend to be those individuals who inspire confidence in their colleagues, creating a private referral network for themselves. Under these circumstances, how can psychoanalytic institutions resist the demand of would-be students of every sort to receive instruction at whatever level these students require?

It may seem somewhat odd to emphasize these "below stairs" developments within organized psychoanalysis at a time when our official debates concern the possibility of admitting a limited number of clinical psychologists for training as regular candidates. But the situation is similar to the one Jean Genêt depicted in his play *The*

---

groups. The recent formation of a separate psychoanalytic division ("39") of the American Psychological Association has proved to be the first step in the creation of an alternative group of analytic training institutes for psychologists. This recent development renders the complex situation I am trying to describe even more confusing, but I do not believe it will fundamentally alter the balance of forces. Psychologists have long been in a position to obtain analytic training, either through the waiver route that now provides a significant number of candidates to institutes affiliated with the American, or through the score of more or less satisfactory independent programs now available throughout the country. Until recently, most of these programs were located in the New York area; like other avant-garde cultural phenomena, they have quickly reached the provinces! At any rate, Division 39 has over 1700 members at this writing. It should be noted, however, that many of these psychologists do not claim to be practitioners of psychoanalysis as treatment.

7. These individuals are not eligible for membership in the International or the American, of course. They practice analysis, however, and no one can compel them to give up their patients when the latter attain the age of 18, or 21, or 30, or 65. Furthermore, they have a separate psychoanalytic professional organization and can hardly be prevented from multiplying their training centers.

Blacks: Ostensibly, the drama depicts the overthrow of white coloni-
alism, but the *real* action, difficult to discern until the denouement, is
the struggle for power after the approaching end of the old regime.
The admission of a few hundred psychologists to regular candidacy in
the next decade or so may ease the acute crisis of the institutes
within the American (especially by allowing some upgrading of the
enforceable standards without thereupon precipitating the collapse
of the "core programs"), but such an emergency transfusion of new
blood into our ranks will hardly alter the unfavorable prospects of
psychoanalysis as an intellectual discipline in America.

II

In contending that a reform of American psychoanalytic training that
would bring the latter into line with the procedures followed everywhere else in the world (or, for that matter, in such American
training centers as the William Alanson White Institute in New York,
to cite only the best known of those programs available to psychologists and psychiatrists alike) would do little beyond safeguarding the
continuity of the educational institutions sponsored by the American,
I wish to stress that the actual condition of psychoanalysis as a
"discipline" must not be confused with the fortunes of its various
schools. I can best illustrate this point by citing the fact that, to date,
none of the 26 institutes affiliated with the American has provoked
the parent organization to suspend its accreditation by violating the
medical admission requirements for regular candidacy, regardless of
how tenuous the continued existence of the local institute may have
appeared at the time. Faculties and the administrators of all institutes
are keenly aware of the national crisis in recruitment, but nowhere
has it been possible to create a local consensus different from that of
the American as a whole: The medical requirement has everywhere
embodied the wishes of the membership.[8] For the past decade, a
succession of committees of the American's Board of Professional
Standards, that is, the corpus of Fellows delegated by local institutes,

8. The Academy of Psychoanalysis, a rival organization not affiliated with the International, admits the medical graduates of a broad spectrum of institutes, in or out of
the orbit of the American; it is, however, even more exclusively medical than the
American. This seeming paradox reflects the fact that the Academy is strictly a
"membership" organization, unconcerned with training functions as such. If the proposed admission of psychologists to training institutes affiliated with the American
should fail, these schools could conceivably save themselves by seceding en bloc from
the American. The arrangements within organized psychoanalysis, whereby a single
body controls both the educational and the professional activities of a discipline, are, in
this country at any rate, without parallel in other fields of study.

has brought forth recommendations in favor of relaxing the medical requirement. Thus far, they have met without success. It is therefore clear that there is an ongoing conflict of interests between psychoanalytic educators and psychoanalytic practitioners.

This clash of interests can be understood in terms of the institutes' need for students in the context of an oversupply of analytic practitioners in most major American communities.[9] The surveys of private practice conducted by the American certainly substantiate this impression: Extrapolating from the raw data, it seems clear that the average analytic case load of nontraining analyst respondents represents no more than 25% of their respective practices (American Psychoanalytic Association, 1979, p. 23). Although most responding analysts seem to desire a mixed practice, including cases that do not call for analysis, they also profess a desire to do more analysis proper than they in fact do. If the sample incorporated graduates of institutes who are not members of the American, as well as analysts in the American who did not respond to the survey, these disappointing figures would probably have to be lowered considerably more.

These numbers, admittedly discouraging, may lead to unwarranted pessimism. In every community, be it noted, one finds colleagues—including some of the youngest!—able to build exclusively analytic practices. Whenever I have questioned such individuals about how they have managed this feat, I have invariably received similar answers. These colleagues attribute their success to the establishment of a reputation for clinical excellence along with a wholehearted commitment to the psychoanalytic method as the treatment of choice in a broad range of disorders. We might note that members of the American Committee on Certification, whose judgments I trust, report that only one applicant out of six or eight submits accounts of clinical work that convince *all* the committee members of his or her competence. It would be important to find out whether these applicants are the young analysts who subsequently succeed in establishing analytic practices, but data about this question are not available at this time.

Whenever I have asked colleagues—both successful analysts and analysts unable to build analytic practices—about the probable explanation for the saddening fact that perhaps only one analyst out of eight or ten appears to be able to establish a fully analytic practice

9. The Boston–Washington corridor and the cities of the West Coast seem to have reached the saturation point more than a decade ago; certain areas where psychoanalysis took root much later are still hostile territory, presenting the analytic "pioneer" with a difficult struggle. A few midcontinental cities—Chicago, Denver, Houston—seem for the moment to hover at the fortunate midpoint between these unhappy extremes.

(despite the fact that most colleagues give lip service to the ideal of doing so), I have, once again, received remarkably consistent answers. Patients ready to undertake psychoanalysis are very rare, except for members of the mental health professions; analysands are not born, they are created through careful preparation. In order to accomplish that task, the therapist who has been consulted must be genuinely convinced that he can do a better job for the patient if they jointly choose the method of psychoanalysis.[10] It follows, I believe, that students who finish their supervised experience with the conviction that they have gained clinical competence often seek to achieve true mastery by acquiring as much analytic experience as possible.[11] Those who fail to adopt this policy seldom blossom as analytic clinicians. In this manner, the psychoanalytic community tends to fracture into two groups, increasingly divergent in their characteristic career development: a minority of enthusiastic individuals who become increasingly involved with psychoanalysis proper (in the natural course of events, other things being equal, these individuals achieve faculty and ultimately training analyst status at the institutes), and a larger number of persons with analytic credentials whose involvement with psychoanalysis tends to become increasingly nominal.[12]

We find ourselves, then, confronted with a paradox: Opposition to broadened recruitment of potential analysts is probably strongest among that segment of the psychoanalytic community that feels threatened by more intense economic competition, that is, by those very individuals who are relatively less successful in maintaining an *analytic* practice. In my judgment, practitioners in this group are condemned to the loss (or impaired development) of their clinical

10. Contrary to the fears of some people, there is no financial advantage in recommending analysis in preference to other treatment methods: Analytic fees per unit time are invariably lower than a given therapist's fees for other services, unless the patient happens to have unlimited financial resources so that a maximum fee is feasible even if the annual expense is truly formidable.

11. In my judgment, very few practitioners do achieve mastery before completing 15 to 20 reasonably successful analyses, that is, after about a decade of full-time analytic work. There are exceptions, of course, and some of these unusually gifted people may not be satisfied with a career confined to clinical encounters. Nonetheless, I would never take a chance of referring someone for analysis to a practitioner of lesser experience, no matter how gifted, if a colleague ripened in the analytic trenches was available. It is equally true that a variety of circumstances, including aging as such, may impair analytic capabilities.

12. Not infrequently, the natural disappointment of these colleagues may turn them against psychoanalysis altogether. Just as often, they try to compensate for their injured self-esteem by idealizing their formal credentials, including both psychoanalytic and medical diplomas. Opposition to the admission of nonmedical candidates is often bitterest within this group.

skills in any case, caught as they are in the vicious circle of inexperience, lack of self-confidence as analysts, and—inevitably—increasing resort to nonanalytic methods with their clientele. Hence their tendency to opt for a status quo that has severely interfered with the expansion of the cadre of well-trained analysts is actually dictated more by considerations of nominal status than by rational calculations of self-interest. The presence of a significant number of effective analysts in a given community, that is, should actually increase the proportion of people in that locality who will seek analytic assistance: The most effective advertising for any method of treatment is the word-of-mouth recommendation of a satisfied patient. We may also put this matter conversely: If the pragmatically oriented American consumer has turned away from psychoanalysis as his preferred method of therapy for personality disorders, the most important reason for this disaffection may well be the fact that, as actually performed by its practitioners today, this form of therapy has not been sufficiently effective (see also Chapter 1).

III

The activities of graduate analysts cannot be monitored by anyone, but the unsatisfactory results of analyses performed by trainees, despite supervision, have been widely reported (e.g., Firestein, 1978; Erle, 1979; Erle & Goldberg, 1979; Schlessinger & Robbins, 1983). It is true that a considerable proportion of the less competent among these would-be analysts do get weeded out, either before graduation from an institute, through the certification procedure of the American, or through the kind of self-selection I have just attempted to describe.[13] In the present context, however, I raise this matter not to argue for more stringent criteria for candidate selection and progres-

---

13. Nonetheless, the damaging effects of the poor work of such trainees on the public reputation of psychoanalysis should not be underestimated. Ex-patients who are bitter and even outraged about their therapeutic experiences will often share their grievances with anyone willing to listen. Institutes are often more concerned with giving candidates every opportunity to "make it," whatever that may mean, than they are with protecting the patients whose analyses are botched by these marginal students. It is by no means unusual to encounter candidates in good standing who have provoked more than a half-dozen patients into flight shortly after starting analysis with them. My experience as a site visitor to various institutes where I have personally observed a score of ongoing supervisory sessions has led me to conclude that no more than 15 to 20% of the ongoing analyses about which I heard were conducted in a manner that promised any *chance* of success. The supervisors were almost always aware of the candidate's unsatisfactory performance, but seldom expressed genuine skepticism about his or her suitability for the profession.

sion, although such policy changes are certainly desirable (see Chapter 11). I do so in order to examine the implications of the all but universal lack of concern on the part of all participants for the lamentable outcome of most analyses conducted under institute auspices.[14] I should, in fact, put the issue more strongly, for lack of concern is a relatively benign form of official reaction to these failures: It is actually just as common to hear contemptuous statements about various qualities or behaviors of the patients who did not achieve a satisfactory analytic result—as if every analysand always gets his just deserts.

Both attitudes—bland complacency as well as self-exoneration through blaming the patient—imply a conception of psychoanalysis as a healing ritual rather than a scientific procedure.[15] It is characteristic of such belief systems that they are unaltered by the outcome of the performance of the prescribed ritual: The proportion of happy results attributable to chance alone suffices to confirm believers in their faith. Failures are invariably attributed either to insufficient attention to liturgical purity or to the unworthiness of the petitioner. Psychoanalyses carried out in this spirit are equivalent to medieval trials by ordeal: Poor results either mean that the analyst did not carry out his task with the requisite sacred fervor or that the patient was irredeemably wicked.

Unfortunately, this spirit of esoteric ritual is widely prevalent within psychoanalysis, and indifference about the outcome of analyses conducted by less than competent candidates (or graduates, for that matter) is by no means the only evidence pointing to this corruption of its scientific essence. To cite one further indication of the presence of such regression to magical ideation, witness the widespread tolerance of the use of ready-made interpretive schemata, a tolerance of inadmissible dogmatism which is thrown into bold relief by the contrasting attitude of moralistic outrage that even minor proposals for technical innovation, however well-reasoned they may be, are likely to evoke. In other words, the outward *forms* of psychoanalytic therapy are viewed as sacrosanct by many cultists; at the same time,

14. For the clearest expression of such complacency, see the comments of the supervisors of the analyses surveyed by Firestein (1978): Not one among them showed any trace of chagrin about the results of these analyses, despite the manifestly disappointing outcome of each and every case!

15. *A propos*, French psychoanalysts almost unanimously reject the idea that their discipline is a branch of science, an attitude that dominated the first Franco-American psychoanalytic encounter (Paris, March 1983). Although French characterizations of psychoanalysis are quite varied, most consign it to the status of a form of art in the realm of human transactions. In my judgment, such views parallel the quasi-religious cultism prevalent in North America, albeit in an avant-garde, secularized form.

these subverters of scientific methodology silently lay claim to the esoteric wisdom of the guru or Zen master.[16]

Psychoanalysis conducted in this spirit of disavowed omnipotence may well have great therapeutic influence, but its beneficial effects in the adaptive sphere necessarily remain contingent on the possibility of continued idealization of the analyst (or, at best, of psychoanalysis as a movement). The most familiar instance of this type of "cure" was Freud's original treatment of the Wolf Man (Freud, 1918); in this case, the therapeutic benefits disappeared about a decade after the analysis was terminated, when the patient learned about his analyst's fallibility.[17] Analytic patients who become professional psychoanalysts have the best opportunity to maintain therapeutic gains achieved on the basis of the magic of the discipline as a healing cult; they need only conceive of themselves as the inheritors of that magic. Kohut (in press) has rightly emphasized that training analysis as an institution serves the function of perpetuating such a priestly conception of the analytic role.

Under the circumstances, one hears repeated calls for restricting the application of the psychoanalytic treatment method to that narrow segment of the patient population consisting of individuals who can allegedly profit from the use of a "classical" technique, that is, from an exclusive resort to interpretations of intrapsychic conflicts that manifest themselves in analysis in the form of transference and resistance. Even if we granted the dubious claim that patients actually exist who require nothing more in the way of analytic intervention, the adoption of such a policy would amount to the reduction of psychoanalysis to a role of insignificance through the relegation of the vast majority of prospective patients to nonanalytic therapeutic methods. Such a program, advocated by sincere devotees of our discipline, can only mean that these proponents value psychoanalysis as a numinous phenomenon, all the more precious for its rarity. The adoption of more complex analytic techniques, such as those that I, among others, have advocated over the past decade, is perceived by

16. As I have tried to show elsewhere (Gedo, 1983, Chapters 12 and 13), psychoanalytic cultism was first institutionalized by C. G. Jung. As Weisz (1975) has emphasized, marginal disciplines generally tend to develop cultist tendencies; at the present stage of the development of psychoanalysis, however, one would surmise that only its marginal adherents *need* to resort to such desperate collective measures for buttressing professional self-esteem.

17. As Martin (1984) has demonstrated, the immediate precipitant of the patient's disillusionment was a letter from Freud casting doubt on the validity of his interpretation of the famous dream of the wolves. I have previously focused on the role of Freud's malignancy in setting in motion the Wolf Man's illness of 1923 (see Gedo & Goldberg, 1973).

these analyst-shamans as the vulgarization or defilement of a sacrament.[18]

For the moment, the political realities within American psychoanalysis have assured the dominance of these doctrinaire attitudes; moreover, the most important dissidence within the profession in recent years, the school of thought that Heinz Kohut chose to designate "self psychology," has also been characterized by a religious fervor, fully as intense as that of the defenders of the traditional dogma. In these circumstances, one can only fear that our Valhalla will founder; this is indeed the Twilight of our profession in the New World.

IV

In his last great novel about the dilemmas of contemporary man, Thomas Mann correctly predicted the fate of psychoanalysis in the late 20th century: "Psychology—God warrant us, do you still hold with it? That is bad, bourgeois nineteenth century. The epoch is heartily sick of it, it will soon be a red rag to her, and he will simply get a crack on the pate, who disturbs life by psychology. We are entering into times, my friend, which will not be hoodwinked by psychology . . ." (1947, p. 249).

Mann's Mephistopheles thus announced that the age of science has begun to show the signs that herald the fall of a civilization. In contrast, Freud (1927, 1930) dared to hope that psychoanalysis might play an essential role in the preservation of high culture by positing human values that would be acceptable to large populations. The passage of half a century has undermined the basis for Freud's optimism: Psychoanalysis has turned out to be unwelcome in every area of the world—excluded from the Communist empire, a precarious survivor in the Catholic sphere, and watered down or replaced by mythic variants in North America. Perhaps psychoanalysis demands too much of people; as Waelder (1960) observed, it "presents a

---

18. In this connection, let me call the reader's attention to the fact that in the issue of *Psychoanalytic Inquiry* devoted to a critical consideration of my work (Vol. 1, No. 2, 1981), none of the several commentators critical of my technical proposals deigned to comment on the implications of the successful results that I reported with cases which at least one reviewer acknowledged to have been exceedingly "difficult." To the contrary, the only critic who alluded to these results (Dewald, 1981) dismissed them with the cavalier claim that such happy outcomes can be obtained regardless of the type of therapy employed. Dewald failed to explain, however, why such ostensibly unexceptional clinical results are so seldom reported when the chosen form of treatment is the "classical" analytic method.

constant challenge to complacency and mental laziness and perpetually interferes with wishful thinking." But this doctrine, offering neither salvation nor faith, does not seem sufficiently inspiring to stem the tide of primitive religiosity. Plato's view that the masses need myths and slogans for their edification appears to apply even to the majority of psychoanalysts.

Rieff (1966) was the first to declare that psychoanalysis would be undermined by the inability of its adherents to preserve a scientific outlook: "The analytic movement . . . has been ruined by the popular (and commercial) pressure upon it to help produce a symbolic [sic] for the reorganization of personality, after the central experience of [religious] deconversion" (p. 21). As Rieff saw it, the mutation of psychotherapies into religion began with the defections of Adler and Jung from psychoanalysis. Freud alone continued to insist that psychoanalysis should be judged on the basis of its explanatory power, thus affirming his loyalty to the tradition of post-Baconian science. In contrast, the dissidents returned to the prescientific system: Their major aim was not to *know* but to *cure*. Their apostasy has now triumphed within psychoanalysis proper, with the devastating results I have tried to describe in this chapter.

Freud developed a psychology that views much of human behavior as a compromise between instinct and culture. His recognition of the relative intractability of human nature has always been intolerable to philosophical meliorists (see Chapter 10). Optimistic splinter groups have continually arisen within the field, adopting philosophies close to Dewey's operationalism, or, as Rieff (1959) earlier put it, to faith in social engineering. These purveyors of cheery platitudes have labeled Freud a philosophical pessimist. Rieff has effectively refuted this charge, pointing out that a view of personality that conceives of conscience as emerging from instinctual roots and trusts in the prudence and rationality of the ego is not a tragic one. As the critic of the passions and of the irrational conscience, psychoanalysis is mankind's tutor in prudence and compromise. Although the only explicit aim of the psychoanalytic procedure is self-cognition, it is implicitly understood that deepened self-knowledge will, in turn, lead to self-control.

Mann ended his *Doctor Faustus* with the despairing cry, "When, out of uttermost hopelessness . . . will the light of hope dawn?" Might psychoanalysis still contribute to the consolidation of modern culture through the propagation of the scientific value system? Three hundred fifty years ago, Francis Bacon (1620) observed that "by far the greatest obstacle to the progress of science and to the undertaking of new tasks and provinces therein, is found in this—that men despair and think things impossible." We must not despair. It may still be possible to fulfill the hope that psychoanalysis will enable mankind to achieve a new triumph of humanism.

In the silted up harbor of Aigues-Mortes, the abandoned 13th-century lighthouse became a prison for recalcitrant Huguenots after the revocation of the Edict of Nantes. Marie Durand was incarcerated there for 37 years. In the stone floor of her dungeon, one can still see her carved inscription: *Résistez!*

REFERENCES

Aichhorn, A. (1925). *Wayward Youth*. London: Imago, 1951.

Alexander, F. (1956). *Psychoanalysis and Psychotherapy*. New York: Norton.

Alexander, F., & French, T. (1946). *Psychoanalytic Therapy*. New York: Ronald.

American Psychoanalytic Association (1979). *Report of the Committee on Private Practice*. Mimeographed.

Appelbaum, A. (1981). *Beyond interpretation:* A response from beyond psychoanalysis. *Psychoanalytic Inquiry*, 1:167–185.

Arlow, J. (1981). The treatment of difficult character disorders. Discussion. R. A. Glick, reporter. *Bulletin of the Association for Psychoanalytic Medicine*, 21:10–12.

Bacon, F. (1620). Novum Organum. In *Modern Classical Philosophers*, 2nd ed. Cambridge, Mass.: Riverside, 1936.

Basch, M. (1975). Toward a theory that encompasses depression: A revision of existing causal hypotheses in psychoanalysis. In E. Anthony & T. Benedek, eds., *Depression and Human Existence*. Boston: Little, Brown, pp. 483–534.

Bergin, A. & Lambert, M. (1978). The evaluation of therapeutic outcome. In S. Garfield & A. Bergin, eds., *Handbook of Psychotherapy and Behavior Change*, 2nd ed. New York: Wiley, pp. 139–189.

Bergler, E. (1961). The six herculean labors of the psychic masochist. *Diseases of the Nervous System*, 22:218–222.

Berliner, B. (1958). The role of object relations in moral masochism. *Psychoanalytic Quarterly*, 27:38–56.

Breuer, J., & Freud, S. (1893). On the psychical mechanism of hysterical phenomena: Preliminary communication. *Standard Edition*, 2:3–17. London: Hogarth Press, 1955.

Breuer, J., & Freud, S. (1895). Studies on hysteria. *Standard Edition*, 2. London: Hogarth Press, 1955.

Calef, V., & Weinshel, E. (1973). Reporting, nonreporting, and assessment in the training analysis. *Journal of the American Psychoanalytic Association*, 21:714–726.

Calef, V., & Weinshel, E. (1982). Some clinical consequences of introjection: Gaslighting. *Psychoanalytic Quarterly*, 50:44–66.

REFERENCES

Deutsch, F. (1947). Analysis of postural behavior. *Psychoanalytic Quarterly*, 16:195–213.

Dewald, P. (1981). Revision: Yes. Improvement: No. *Psychoanalytic Inquiry*, 1:187–204.

Eissler, K. (1953). The effect of the structure of the ego on psychoanalytic technique. *Journal of the American Psychoanalytic Association*, 1:104–143.

Eissler, K. (1965). *Medical Orthodoxy and the Future of Psychoanalysis*. New York: International Universities Press.

Ekstein, R., & Wallerstein, R. (1958). *The Teaching and Learning of Psychotherapy*, rev. ed. New York: International Universities Press, 1972.

Erle, J. (1979). An approach to the study of analyzability and analyses: The course of forty consecutive cases selected for supervised analysis. *Psychoanalytic Quarterly*, 48:198–228.

Erle, J., & Goldberg, D. (1979). Problems in the assessment of analyzability. *Psychoanalytic Quarterly*, 48:48–84.

Firestein, S. (1978). *Termination in Psychoanalysis*. New York: International Universities Press.

Fleming, J., & Benedek, T. (1966). *Psychoanalytic Supervision*. New York: Grune & Stratton.

Freud, A. (1936). The ego and the mechanisms of defense. *Writings*, 2. New York: International Universities Press, 1966.

Freud, A. (1962). The theory of the parent–infant relationship. Contribution to the discussion. *Writings*, 6:187–193. New York: International Universities Press, 1971.

Freud, A. (1966). The ideal psychoanalytic institute. *Writings*, 7:73–93. New York: International Universities Press, 1971.

Freud, E., ed. (1960). *The Letters of Sigmund Freud, 1873–1939*. New York: Basic Books.

Freud, S. (1895). Project for a scientific psychology. *Standard Edition*, 1:175–397. London: Hogarth Press, 1966.

Freud, S. (1899). Screen memories. *Standard Edition*, 3:301–332. London: Hogarth Press, 1962.

Freud, S. (1900). The interpretation of dreams. *Standard Edition*, 4 & 5. London: Hogarth Press, 1953.

Freud, S. (1908). "Civilized" sexual morality and modern nervous illness. *Standard Edition*, 9:179–204. London: Hogarth Press, 1959.

Freud, S. (1909). Notes upon a case of obsessional neurosis. *Standard Edition*, 10:153–249. London: Hogarth Press, 1955.

Freud, S. (1910a). Leonardo da Vinci and a memory of his childhood. *Standard Edition*, 11:59–137. London: Hogarth Press, 1957.

Freud, S. (1910b). The antithetical meaning of primal words. *Standard Edition*, 11:155–161. London: Hogarth Press, 1957.

Freud, S. (1915). The unconscious. *Standard Edition*, 14:166–215. London: Hogarth Press, 1957.

Freud, S. (1918). From the history of an infantile neurosis. *Standard Edition*, 17:3–122. London: Hogarth Press, 1955.

Freud, S. (1920). Beyond the pleasure principle. *Standard Edition*, 18:3–64. London: Hogarth Press, 1955.

REFERENCES

Freud, S. (1923). The ego and the id. *Standard Edition*, 19:3–66. London: Hogarth Press, 1961.

Freud, S. (1924). The economic problem of masochism. *Standard Edition*, 19:157–170. London: Hogarth Press, 1961.

Freud, S. (1927). The future of an illusion. *Standard Edition*, 21:3–56. London: Hogarth Press, 1961.

Freud, S. (1930). Civilization and its discontents. *Standard Edition*, 21:59–148. London: Hogarth Press, 1961.

Freud, S. (1933). New introductory lectures on psycho-analysis. *Standard Edition*, 22:3–182. London: Hogarth Press, 1964.

Freud, S. (1937). Analysis terminable and interminable. *Standard Edition*, 23:216–253. London: Hogarth Press, 1964.

Freud, S. (1938). An outline of psycho-analysis. *Standard Edition*, 23:144–207. London: Hogarth Press, 1964.

Gardner, R. (1983). *Self Inquiry*. Boston: Atlantic Monthly Press.

Gedo, J. (1964). Concepts for a classification of the psychotherapies. *International Journal of Psycho-Analysis*, 45:530–539.

Gedo, J. (1972). The dream of reason produces monsters. *Journal of the American Psychoanalytic Association*, 20:199–223.

Gedo, J. (1973). Kant's way: The psychoanalytic contribution of David Rapaport. *Psychoanalytic Quarterly*, 42:409–434.

Gedo, J. (1975). Forms of idealization in the analytic transference. *Journal of the American Psychoanalytic Association*, 23:485–505.

Gedo, J. (1977). Notes on the psychoanalytic management of archaic transferences. *Journal of the American Psychoanalytic Association*, 25:787–803.

Gedo, J. (1978a). Some contributions of psychoanalysis to a science of man. *The Annual of Psychoanalysis*, 6:67–73. New York: International Universities Press.

Gedo, J. (1978b). A grammar for the humanities. *The Annual of Psychoanalysis*, 6:75–102. New York: International Universities Press.

Gedo, J. (1979a). A psychoanalyst reports at mid-career. *American Journal of Psychiatry*, 136:646–649.

Gedo, J. (1979b). *Beyond Interpretation*. New York: International Universities Press.

Gedo, J. (1979c). Theories of the object relations: A metapsychological assessment. *Journal of the American Psychoanalytic Association*, 27:361–374.

Gedo, J. (1981a). Measure for measure: A response. *Psychoanalytic Inquiry*, 1:289–316.

Gedo, J. (1981b). *Advances in Clinical Psychoanalysis*. New York: International Universities Press.

Gedo, J. (1983). *Portraits of the Artist: Psychoanalysis of Creativity and Its Vicissitudes*. New York: Guilford.

Gedo, J., & Goldberg, A. (1973). *Models of the Mind*. Chicago: University of Chicago Press.

Gedo, J., & Pollock, G., eds. (1976). *Freud: The Fusion of Science and Humanism* [*Psychological Issues*, Monograph 34/35]. New York: International Universities Press.

Gill M. (1976). Metapsychology is not psychology. In M. Gill & P. Holzman,

REFERENCES

eds., *Psychology versus Metapsychology: Psychoanalytic Essays in Memory of George S. Klein* [*Psychological Issues*, Monograph 36]. New York: International Universities Press, pp. 71–105.

Gill, M. (1981). The boundary of psychoanalytic data and technique: A critique of Gedo's *Beyond Interpretation*. *Psychoanalytic Inquiry*, 1:205–232.

Gill, M., & Holzman, P., eds. (1976). *Psychology versus Metapsychology: Psychoanalytic Essays in Memory of George S. Klein* [*Psychological Issues*, Monograph 36]. New York: International Universities Press.

Glover, E. (1931). The therapeutic effect of inexact interpretations. In *The Technique of Psychoanalysis*. New York: International Universities Press, 1955, pp. 353–366.

Goldberg, A., ed. (1978). *The Psychology of the Self: A Casebook*. New York: International Universities Press.

Grossman, W., & Simon, B. (1969). Anthropomorphism: motive, meaning, and causality in psychoanalytic theory. *The Psychoanalytic Study of the Child*, 24:78–114. New York: International Universities Press.

Grünbaum, A. (1979). Epistemological liabilities of the clinical appraisal of psychoanalytic theory. *Psychoanalysis and Contemporary Thought*, 4:451–526. New York: International Universities Press.

Handler, J. (1970). Report of meeting of the Chicago Psychoanalytic Society, March 25, 1969. *Bulletin of the Philadelphia Association of Psychoanalysis*, 20:74–79.

Hartmann, H. (1939). *Ego Psychology and the Problem of Adaptation*. New York: International Universities Press, 1958.

Hartmann, H. (1960). *Psychoanalysis and Moral Values*. New York: International Universities Press.

Hodgson, M. (1974). *The Venture of Islam*, vols. 1 & 2. Chicago: University of Chicago Press.

Jones, E. (1953). *The Life and Work of Sigmund Freud*, vol. 1. New York: Basic Books.

Joseph, E. (in press). Further comments on the therapeutic action of psychoanalysis. In J. Gedo & G. Pollock, eds.,*Psychoanalysis: The Vital Issues*, vol. 2. New York: International Universities Press.

Jung, C. (1963). *Memories, Dreams, Reflections*. New York: Vintage.

Kernberg, O. (1975). *Borderline Conditions and Pathological Narcissism*. New York: Aronson.

Kernberg, O. (1976). *Object Relations Theory and Clinical Psychoanalysis*. New York: Aronson.

Kohut, H. (1959). Introspection, empathy, and psychoanalysis. *Journal of the American Psychoanalytic Association*, 7:459–483. (Also in Kohut, 1978).

Kohut, H. (1962). The Psychoanalytic Curriculum. *Journal of the American Psychoanalytic Association*, 10:153–163. (Also in Kohut, 1978.)

Kohut, H. (1971). *The Analysis of the Self*. New York: International Universities Press.

Kohut, H. (1975a). The future of psychoanalysis. *The Annual of Psychoanalysis*, 3:325–340. New York: International Universities Press. (Also in Kohut, 1978.)

Kohut, H. (1975b). The psychoanalyst in the community of scholars. *The*

REFERENCES

Annual of Psychoanalysis, 3:341–370. New York: International Universities Press. (Also in Kohut, 1978.)

Kohut, H. (1977). *The Restoration of the Self*. New York: International Universities Press.

Kohut, H. (1978). *The Search for the Self*, vols. 1 & 2, ed. P. Ornstein. New York: International Universities Press.

Kohut, H. (1982). Introspection, empathy, and the semi-circle of mental health. *International Journal of Psycho-Analysis*, 63:395–407. (Also in J. Gedo & G. Pollock, eds., *Psychoanalysis: The Vital Issues*, vol. 2. New York: International Universities Press.

Kohut, H. (in press). *How Does Analysis Cure?* Chicago: University of Chicago Press.

Kuhn, T. (1962). *The Structure of Scientific Revolutions*. Chicago: University of Chicago Press.

Leavy, S. (1980). *The Psychoanalytic Dialogue*. New Haven: Yale University Press.

Levin, F. (1980). Metaphor, affect, and arousal: How interpretations might work. *The Annual of Psychoanalysis*, 9:231–249. New York: International Universities Press.

Loewald, H. (1975). Psychoanalysis as an art and the fantasy character of the psychoanalytic situation. *Journal of the American Psychoanalytic Association*, 23:277–299.

Loewenstein, R. (1956). Some remarks on the role of speech in psychoanalytic technique. *International Journal of Psycho-Analysis*, 37:460–468.

Loewenstein, R. (1957). A contribution to the psychoanalytic theory of masochism. *Journal of the American Psychoanalytic Association*, 5:197–234.

Loewenstein, R. (1963). Some considerations on free association. *Journal of the American Psychoanalytic Association*, 11:451–473.

Mahler, M., Pine, F., & Bergman, A. (1975). *The Psychological Birth of the Human Infant: Symbiosis and Individuation*. New York: Basic Books.

Malcolm, J. (1981). *The Impossible Profession*. New York: Knopf.

Mann, T. (1947). *Doctor Faustus*. New York: Modern Library, 1948.

Martin, J. (1984). The fictive personality. *The Annual of Psychoanalysis*, 12. New York: International Universities Press.

McLaughlin, J. (1973). The nonreporting training analyst, the analysis, and the institute. *Journal of the American Psychoanalytic Association*, 21:697–713.

Modell, A. (1976). "The holding environment" and the therapeutic action of psychoanalysis. *Journal of the American Psychoanalytic Association*, 24:285–308.

Modell, A. (in press). Self psychology as a psychology of conflict: Comments on the psychoanalysis of the narcissistic personality. In J. Gedo & G. Pollock, eds., *Psychoanalysis: The Vital Issues*, vol. 2. New York: International Universities Press.

Panel (1976). New horizons in metapsychology: View and review. W. Meissner, reporter. *Journal of the American Psychoanalytic Association*, 24:161–180.

Panel (1983). Interpretation: Toward a contemporary understanding of the term. A. Rothstein, reporter. *Journal of the American Psychoanalytic Association*, 31:237–245.

REFERENCES

Panel (1984). Value judgments in psychoanalytic theory and practice. S. Lytton, reporter. *Journal of the American Psychoanalytic Association*, 32:147-156.

Peterfreund, E. (1983). *The Process of Psychoanalytic Therapy*. Hillsdale, N.J.: The Analytic Press.

Polanyi, M. (1974). *Scientific Thought and Social Reality* [*Psychological Issues*, Monograph 32]. New York: International Universities Press.

Polanyi, M., & Prosch, H. (1975). *Meaning*. Chicago: University of Chicago Press.

Pollock, G. (1968). Josef Breuer. In J. Gedo & G. Pollock, eds., *Freud: The Fusion of Science and Humanism* [*Psychological Issues*, Monograph 34/35]. New York: International Universities Press, pp. 133-163.

Pollock, G. (1977). The Chicago Institute for Psychoanalysis: From 1932 to the present. *The Annual of Psychoanalysis*, 5:3-22. New York: International Universities Press.

Rangell, L. (1981). A view on John Gedo's revision of psychoanalytic theory. *Psychoanalytic Inquiry*, 1:249-265.

Rangell, L. (1982). The self in psychoanalytic theory. *Journal of the American Psychoanalytic Association*, 30:863-891.

Rapaport, D. (1974). *The History of the Concept of Association of Ideas*. New York: International Universities Press.

Rapaport, D., & Gill, M. (1959). The points of view and assumptions of metapsychology. In M. Gill, ed., *The Collected Papers of David Rapaport*. New York: Basic Books, pp. 795-811.

Rappaport, E. (1960). Preparation for analysis. *International Journal of Psycho-Analysis*, 41:626-632.

Reich, W. (1930). *Character Analysis*. New York: Orgone Institute Press, 1945.

Richards, A. (1982). The superordinate self in psychoanalytic theory and in the self psychologies. *Journal of the American Psychoanalytic Association*, 30:939-957.

Ricoeur, P. (1970). *Freud and Philosophy: An Essay on Interpretation*, trans. D. Savage. New Haven: Yale University Press.

Rieff, P. (1959). *Freud: The Mind of the Moralist*. New York: Viking.

Rieff, P. (1966). *The Triumph of the Therapeutic*. New York: Harper & Row.

Rosen, V. (1977). *Style, Character, and Language*, eds. S. Atkin & M. Jucovy. New York: Aronson.

Rothstein, A. (1980). Psychoanalytic paradigms and their narcissistic investment. *Journal of the American Psychoanalytic Association*, 28:385-395.

Rubinstein, B. (1976). On the possibility of a strictly clinical psychoanalytic theory: An essay in the philosophy of psychoanalysis. In M. Gill & P. Holzman, eds., *Psychology versus Metapsychology: Psychoanalytic Essays in Memory of George S. Klein* [*Psychological Issues*, Monograph 36]. New York: International Universities Press, pp. 229-264.

Schafer, R. (1976a). Emotion in the language of action. In M. Gill & P. Holzman, eds., *Psychology versus Metapsychology: Psychoanalytic Essays in Memory of George S. Klein* [*Psychological Issues*, Monograph 36]. New York: International Universities Press, pp. 106-133.

REFERENCES

Schafer, R. (1976b). *A New Language for Psychoanalysis*. New Haven: Yale University Press.

Schlessinger, N., & Robbins, F. (1983). *A Developmental View of the Psychoanalytic Process* [*Emotions and Behavior*, Monograph 1]. New York: International Universities Press.

Schwaber, E. (1981). Empathy: A mode of analytic listening. *Psychoanalytic Inquiry*, 1:357–392.

Segal, H., & Britton, R. (1981). Interpretation and primitive psychic processes: A Kleinian view. *Psychoanalytic Inquiry*, 1:267–277.

Spence, D. (1982). *Narrative Truth and Historical Truth*. New York: Norton.

Spitz, R. (1964). The derailment of dialogue. *Journal of the American Psychoanalytic Association*, 12:752–775.

Stepansky, P. (1976). The empiricist as rebel: Jung, Freud, and the burdens of discipleship. *Journal of the History of the Behavioral Sciences*, 12:215–239.

Stone, L. (1954). The widening scope of indications for psychoanalysis. *Journal of the American Psychoanalytic Association*, 2:567–594.

Stone, L. (1961). *The Psychoanalytic Situation*. New York: International Universities Press.

Stone, L. (1981). Notes on the noninterpretive elements in the psychoanalytic situation and process. *Journal of the American Psychoanalytic Association*, 29:89–118.

Sulloway, F. (1980). *Freud: Biologist of the Mind*. New York: Basic Books.

Tomkins, S. (1970). Affects as the primary motivational system. In M. Arnold, ed., *Feelings and Emotions*. New York: Academic Press, pp. 101–110.

Tower, E. (1956). Countertransference. *Journal of the American Psychoanalytic Association*, 4:224–255.

van den Haag, E. (1965). Psychoanalysis and utopia. *Bulletin of the Philadelphia Association of Psychoanalysis*, 15:61–78.

Waelder, R. (1960). *Basic Theory of Psychoanalysis*. New York: International Universities Press.

Waelder, R. (1962). Psychoanalysis, scientific method, and philosophy. *Journal of the American Psychoanalytic Association*, 10:617–637.

Wallerstein, R., ed. (1981). *Becoming a Psychoanalyst*. New York: International Universities Press.

Weiss, E. (1970). *Sigmund Freud as a Consultant*. New York: Intercontinental Medical Book Corp.

Weisz, G. (1975). Scientists and sectarians: The case of psychoanalysis. *Journal of the History of the Behavioral Sciences*, 11:350–364.

Winnicott, D. (1960). The theory of the parent–infant relationship. In *The Maturational Processes and the Facilitating Environment*. New York: International Universities Press, 1965, pp. 37–55.

Wolf, E. (1976). Ambience and abstinence. *The Annual of Psychoanalysis*, 4:101–115. New York: International Universities Press.

INDEX

INDEX

L

Lacan, J., 163
Lambert, M., 34, 195n.
Language, x, 128–154, 164
Leavy, S., 142, 146, 199n.
Length of treatment, 23, 24
Levin, F., 141–143, 199n.
Loewald, H., 145n., 199n.
Loewenstein, R., 11, 141, 146, 199n.

M

Mahler, M., 138, 139, 199n.
Malcolm, J., 20n., 199n.
Manichaeanism, 158, 159
Mann, T., 191, 192, 199n.
Marcuse, H., 104
Martin, J., 190n., 199n.
Masochism
    depression association, 9–15
    hierarchical model, 14
    interpretation technique, 16–18
Materialism, 160
McLaughlin, J., 167, 199n.
Medical requirement, training, 185, 186
Meissner, W., 9n., 104, 105
Metaphors, 141–145
Michels, R., 105n., 106, 110
Mill, J. S., 165n.
"Mirror transference," 152
Modell, A., 17, 47, 131, 199n.
Models, hierarchical, 14–16, 18, 19
Models of the Mind (Gedo), 15, 33, 63, 197n.
Moral masochism, 12
Moral values, analyst, 102–111, 124, 162, 163

N

"Narcissistic neuroses," 5, 6
Narcissistic personality disturbances, 7, 121
Narcissistic transferences, 131, 152

Nature/nurture controversy, 160–162, 165
Negativism, selfhood protection, 119
Neurobiology, 12, 13, 162, 164, 165
"New Horizons in Metapsychology" panel, 9n., 199n.
New Introductory Lectures (Freud), 102, 197n.
New York Psychoanalytic Institute, 25
New Yorker, The, 20n.
Nonverbal communication, 130, 133–135, 164
Nosology, history, 4, 5
Nurture psychology, 160–162, 165

O

Object relations
    and delinquent behavior, 115, 116
    as theory, evaluation, 6, 161, 162, 164
Objectivity, analyst, 101–111
Oedipal conflicts, 39, 40
"Optimal disillusionment," 40, 42, 49, 63, 65, 81, 86n., 134
    definition, 131, 132
    examples, 134
Outcome studies, criteria, 28, 34

P

"Pacification," 132
Panel (Journal of the American Psychoanalytic Association), 9n., 12, 104, 105, 105n., 106, 110, 113, 199n., 200n.
Pappenheim, B., 128, 129
Paradoxical effects, dream interpretation, 35–49
Paraverbal communication, 130, 133–135, 144
Pascal, B., 130
Passive voice, 144
Paternal transference, 79
Pelagian heresy, 158, 159, 161

INDEX

Symbiotic relationships
  case study, 53–73
  and delinquent behavior, 115–121
  separateness and autonomy
    relationship, 139
  with spouse, 118
Syncytial attachments, 115
Syntax, 144

T

Talking cure, 128, 129
Tempest, The (Shakespeare), 104, 107
Tension reduction, 43, 44
Termination
  and adaptative capacity, 27, 28
  success rates, 25, 26
"Therapeutic alliance," 131, 137
Therapeutic process, 28
Three Penny Opera, The (Weill), 142
Tomkins, S., 130, 201n.
Tower, E., 123, 201n.
Traditional psychoanalysis, 21, 160, 161
Training, 167–178, 181–186
"Training analysts," 176, 183n.
Transference, ix
  and intrapsychic value conflicts, 114
  nosology relationship, 5, 6
  value issues, 107
Transference neurosis, 70
"Transmuting internalization," 18n.
Traumatic neuroses, 36–40
Tutorial system, 172, 173, 178

U

Unconscious, 165, 166
"Unification," self-organization, 132

V

Values and psychoanalysis, 102–111, 124, 162, 163
van den Haag, E., 157, 158, 158n., 201n.
van Gogh, V., 17n.
Vitalism, 160, 166

W

Waelder, R., 3, 191, 201n.
Wallerstein, R., 167, 196n., 201n.
Weill, K., 142
Weinshel, E., 49, 167, 195n.
Weiss, E., 102, 103, 120n., 201n.
Weisz, G., 158, 190n., 201n.
Winnicott, D., 17, 43, 201n.
Wolf, E., 136, 201n.
Wolf Man, 29, 190, 196n.
Work, as outcome criterion, 26, 27

Z

Zweig, S., 128